Pelican Books
Escape Attempts

Stanley Cohen was born in South Africa, where he completed a degree in Sociology and Psychology at Witwatersrand University, Johannesburg, in 1962. He worked in London as a psychiatric social worker and then went to the London School of Economics where he completed his Ph.D. research on societal reactions to juvenile delinquency. He has taught at Enfield College, the University of Durham and the University of California. Since 1974 he has been Professor of Sociology at the University of Essex.

Professor Cohen has written various articles on the Teddy Boys, Mods and Rockers, vandalism, political violence, mass media, prisons and other topics in criminology and sociology. His books include *Images of Deviance* (Pelican, 1971), *Folk Devils and Moral Panics* (1972), *Psychological Survival* (with Laurie Taylor, Pelican, 1972) and *The Manufacture of News* (with Jock Young, 1973).

Laurie Taylor is Professor of Sociology at the University of York. He graduated in Psychology from Birkbeck College, University of London, and then completed his postgraduate studies at the University of Leicester. His books include *Psychological Survival* (with Stanley Cohen, Pelican, 1972), *Deviance and Society* (1973), *Crime, Deviance and Socio-Legal Control* (with R. Robertson, 1974). Laurie Taylor has also edited *Politics and Deviance* (with Ian Taylor, Pelican, 1973) and *Young People and Civil Conflict in Northern Ireland* (with Sarah Nelson, 1977).

ESCAPE ATTEMPTS

THE THEORY AND PRACTICE OF RESISTANCE TO EVERYDAY LIFE

by STANLEY COHEN
AND
LAURIE TAYLOR

PENGUIN BOOKS

Penguin Books Ltd, Harmondsworth, Middlesex, England
Penguin Books, 625 Madison Avenue, New York, New York 10022, U.S.A.
Penguin Books Australia Ltd, Ringwood, Victoria, Australia
Penguin Books Canada Ltd, 2801 John Street, Markham, Ontario, Canada L3R 1B4
Penguin Books (N.Z.) Ltd, 182–190 Wairau Road, Auckland 10, New Zealand

First published by Allen Lane 1976
Published in Pelican Books 1978
Copyright © Stanley Cohen and Laurie Taylor, 1976
All rights reserved

Made and printed in Great Britain by
Hazell Watson & Viney Ltd, Aylesbury, Bucks
Set in Monotype Plantin

Contents

For me the self-conscious ego is the seat of boredom. This increasing, swelling, domineering, painful self-consciousness is the only rival of the political and social powers that run my life (business, technological-bureaucratic powers, the state). You have a great organized movement of life, and you have the single self, independently conscious, proud of its detachment and its absolute immunity, its stability and its power to remain unaffected by anything whatsoever – by the sufferings of others or by society or by politics or by external chaos. In a way it doesn't give a damn. It is asked to give a damn, and we often urge it to give a damn but the curse of noncaring lies upon this painfully free consciousness. It is free from attachment to beliefs and to other souls. Cosmologies, ethical systems? It can run through them by the dozens. For to be fully conscious of oneself as an individual is also to be separated from all else. This is Hamlet's kingdom of infinite space in a nutshell, of 'words, words, words,' of 'Denmark's a prison'.

Humboldt's Gift, Saul Bellow

Preface

A preface is a place for genealogy, apology and the acknowledgement of debts.

First a genealogy. This book started life some seven years ago, as a text on the sociology of deviance called 'The Defiant and the Defeated'. At that time our present concern with everyday life – the banal, the trivial, the mundane – was far from our professional minds. Indeed, as sociologists of deviance, we were by definition at the opposite pole from this concern.

For many years we had written exclusively about deviants and criminals, doing research upon relatively specialized groups of people who by their behaviour set themselves apart from others – declared themselves to be different. It was not everyman's behaviour which concerned us then, but rather the exotic doings of industrial saboteurs, sex offenders, vandals, Mods and Rockers, and long-term prisoners. These were the people whom we believed to be making significant statements about reality and our relationship to it. They were specialized commentators upon man's predicament, individuals whose behaviour suggested a way of thinking about the world which was especially sensitive and insightful.

Our determined pursuit of the subjective views of these groups was reinforced by the contempt with which such aspects of their lives were treated by their observers and custodians. Unlike them, we were interested in the consciousness of the deviant and the criminal. We wanted to know the meaning behind his behaviour, the way in which *he* regarded it, the way in which he related his criminal experience to other elements within his mind. Nowadays this emphasis is hardly original. But a decade ago when we first began to talk about such matters we found ourselves in the most radical possible opposition to conventional criminologists.

These criminologists already appeared to 'know' the motives behind the behaviour: it was, they declared, irrational or mindless, it was not a meaningful response to any of the matters which might reasonably pre-occupy the consciousness of modern man. We set ourselves to change this state of affairs by demanding to know exactly what the deviant had in mind. We did not accept that he was the possessor of an inadequate or flawed or undeveloped consciousness, but rather believed that the matters to which he attended, and possibly the style in which he attended to them, were evidence of his existence within a different life-world.

Our method of establishing this proposition involved studying the deviant within his own setting, observing his behaviour, talking to him and his friends. In pursuit of this contextual view we travelled with football hooligans to away matches, wandered around the shop floor with industrial saboteurs, slept on the beaches of Clacton with Mods and Rockers and simultaneously took notes about our own 'normal' deviance: smoking dope with our students, organizing anti-Vietnam war demonstrations, watching porno movies.

We had some limited success in this task. In cooperation with the many friends and colleagues we met on these various trips, we managed to show the essential meaningfulness of much behaviour that had previously been regarded as irrational, as simply indicative of some pathological lesion, some psychic disorder.

But we wanted to do more than show that deviance and crime were meaningful, we also wanted to characterize the consciousness of the deviant, to show that there was, perhaps, some homogeneous view of the world which linked together the individual groups that we studied. Specifically, we hoped to establish that the deviant held a picture of the world as a repressive place. His actions were a way of fighting against that repression. He was a social critic, a rebel, even a revolutionary.

It wasn't easy to establish this proposition. Deviants themselves did not help very much. Apparently unimpressed by the new radical role which was held out to them, they continued to give accounts of the world and their actions which were difficult to press into our theoretical framework. We were undeterred. The silence of the criminals could be remedied by importing the intentional and meaningful statements made by others whose behaviour looked the same. So we tried to find some similarities between our pathetic and despised collection of 'deviants' (the 'defeated') and the glorious romantics, ideologues, radicals and outsiders to whom society accorded dignity and recognition, if not approval (the 'defiant'). If our deviant would not or could not speak then we would use the words of others who had done apparently similar things. We were anxious to detect similarities between groups, on the one hand, like vandals, industrial saboteurs, football hooligans and sex offenders, and on the other, groups endowed with full-blown ideological systems. This sometimes entailed attributing political significance to 'ordinary' deviance on the assumption that both the overtly political and the overtly non-political deviant were responding to similar features of contemporary capitalist societies.

There were good historical reasons for this emphasis but despite the ways in which deviant groups *were* becoming militant and politicized (to use the words that punctuated every conference paper), we gradually observed a certain blurring of our 'heroic' conception of deviant behaviour. Our early romantic wish to impress ideological, political and aesthetic meaning into a whole range of deviant behaviour began to diminish. Instead we found ourselves increasingly aware of the complexities of the behaviour and of the intentions which lay behind it.

Whereas we had originally believed, along with Durkheim and Freud, that we might use the abnormal, the extreme or the psychopathological as a way of throwing light upon the 'normal' features of the relationship between the individual and society, we now began to have doubts about the suitability of using our collection of deviants for this purpose. The meaning of their behaviour is still of obsessive interest to us but their struggles did not provide us with an adequate model for describing either the range or the nature of the ways in which all men might resist the demands of society. Their behaviour remained resolutely 'abnormal' despite our relative success in uncovering its meaning. And when at times we attempted to place it within a 'normal' context, to argue for example that their behaviour was explicable in terms of such everyday problems as boredom and dissatisfaction with routine, we found that our listeners simply countered by declaring that they had exactly similar problems. Why then did they not resort to deviant solutions? And if we said that they had developed other solutions they wondered why we weren't writing and talking about these.

It was about this time that we seriously began our research with a group of long-term prisoners. And unexpectedly it was from them – the most extreme group of deviants – that we found our steps leading to everyday life. This route we explain in Chapter 1.

Successive drafts of the book metamorphosed beyond recognition; gradually a whole book about deviants became parts of one chapter and a preface. We put on one side books about rape, murder and revolution and started reading holiday brochures, gardening magazines, do-it-yourself manuals. We examined in detail the simple ways in which those around us got through their days.

Whenever we started getting worried about the apparently trivial nature of such subject matter, we self-indulgently reflected upon the general insights obtained by other social scientists who had concentrated upon equally banal matters. We found in Freud's early obsession with slips of the tongue and lapses of memory, an equivalent to our interest in petty dissatisfactions and irritations. We reminded ourselves of the sophisticated theory of society which Erving Goffman formed from his observations of such apparently petty behaviour as table manners and greetings. Their interests – reflected respectively in the titles of two of their major books *The Psychopathology of Everyday Life* and *The Presentation of Self in Everyday Life* – gave us some licence for our own developing concerns.

The principal apology (or justification) we need to make about this book concerns the character of the evidence we provide for our descriptions of everyday life and the extent to which these descriptions apply to groups beyond those we know most intimately (or indeed beyond the two of us). In the absence of sociological literature, we have necessarily had to rely at times upon anecdotes, fictional accounts, and personal observation. We would have wished that it were otherwise and take some comfort from the way in which some of our students are now questioning in a more rigorous fashion some of the assumptions which are scattered throughout this work. But the autobiographical elements in the book are self-evident and others have been even more sensitive to these than we ourselves. Its historical location is that of advanced Western capitalism and many of its preoccupations are those of the middle-class intellectuals of this society and moreover male middle-class intellectuals. (Our persistent references to 'men' and 'everyman' are not just for stylistic reasons.) But when critics have pointed out that our escape attempts are pretty weird and idiosyncratic and that they have very different ones, we can only reply by demonstrating the ways in which their novel examples conform to our general model.

In many ways then, this book is profoundly self-indulgent (at least in terms of established sociological conventions). It has become a hobby, a property which we have kept to ourselves over all these years. The mental space we have cleared for it has constituted what we describe in Chapter 5 as a 'free area'. It is, as friends have pointed out, our own 'escape attempt'.

These genealogies and apologies recorded, we must now acknowledge our gratitude to those who have helped us create this free area. In intellectual terms, two figures stand out: Georg Simmel, that most neglected 'founding father' of sociology, and fifty years later, Erving Goffman, the most imaginative and original of contemporary sociologists. If we don't always cite their work at obvious places it is only because their continual presence is so close to our thoughts that it would be gratuitous to just list references abstracted from the whole body of their work. We can only hope to have done justice to their central intellectual concern: the tension between the individual and society.

Other influences should also be acknowledged here, for we have tried not to clutter the text with too many academic references and footnotes. This diverse list must include at least: William James, Gregory Bateson, Aldous Huxley, Saul Bellow, John Gagnon, Luke Rhinehart, Hunter Thompson, Norman O. Brown, Charles Bukowski and Anton Artaud.

We also wish to record our thanks to the following people who have read or heard drafts of the book and provided helpful comments: Andrew Tudor, Roland Robertson, Brian Stapleford, Ken Plummer, Basil Bernstein, Herbie Butterfield, and Howard Becker.

And, finally, as a poor acknowledgement of what they have meant to us – intellectually and personally – we dedicate the book to all those people who have helped us create free areas and who have accompanied us on our escape attempts; especially Ruth Cohen, Kate Leigh,

Preface

Mario Simondi, Harry Ree, Paul Corrigan, Vic Lockwood,
Cecile Toutant, Thérèse Encieu, Anna Coote, Jock Young,
Roy Bailey, Stuart Hall, Tom Baker . . . and others.

Stan Cohen
Laurie Taylor

Holiday Inn, Leicester
1975

1

Open
Prison

This is a book about everyday life, the precariousness of that life, and the tenuousness of the identities that we construct within it. It searches out, follows and accompanies people into their homes, work-places, holidays, hobbies, cinemas, pubs, football grounds, love affairs, books and daydreams.

God knows how many other sociologists have announced that everyday life is just what they are after. And yet rarely in the elegant theories, the careful research on the sociology of the family, industry, education, mass media, adolescence, mental illness, deviance, organization, social welfare, religion . . . does everyday life appear. There are few accounts of boredom, elation, despair, happiness or disappointment, no sense of the one obsessive problem which we always knew was ours (but sociologists never let on to us that other people shared): how to get through the day.

Like everybody we have ever known and everybody we have read about, we are forever assessing our degree of satisfaction or dissatisfaction with everyday life.

Few days go by in which we do not consider how much better or worse life was yesterday or last year. On some mornings we feel at home in the world, happy with its arrangements, and content about our relationship to them, only to find at midday that the world was less than we thought, that it presses uncomfortably against us, that we have to find some way in which we can follow or divert its demands. Our days are punctuated by expressions of content and discontent, riddled with feelings of fulfilment and frustration, satisfaction and resignation.

Every morning when we wake we confront a familiar world. Considering the day ahead we mark off that which might be pleasurable from that which will produce anxiety, irritation, boredom or depression. Every day's living constitutes a series of projects in which we either accept the arrangements that await us, or attempt to manipulate them, so that they will be more amenable, more compatible with the view that we hold of ourselves.

In this book we talk about how people make out in their world, the whimsical, pathetic, desperate, outrageous ways in which they manipulate its demands. The dilemmas they encounter and resolve in this process have been translated by philosophers, poets, and sociologists into the abstract language of alienation, anomy, estrangement, angst, dread, fear and trembling, and the sickness unto death. We wish to be more concrete, to heed Saul Bellow's advice:

> Novels are being published today which consist entirely of abstractions, meanings, and while our need for meanings is certainly great, our need for concreteness, for particulars is even greater. We need to see how human beings act after they have appropriated or assimilated the meanings. Meanings themselves are a dime a dozen.[1]

We will therefore try to see how men act in everyday life, to examine the working philosophies which accompany them from the breakfast table, to the office desk and back to the marital bed, the spontaneous wisdom which they bring to bear upon the concrete problem of living.

Closed Prison

The book's birthplace couldn't have been much further removed from this eventual concern with everyman's days and nights: hours spent talking with a group of long-term prisoners in a converted chapel of the maximum-security wing in Durham prison. There was little of everyman about them: murderers, serious sex offenders, bank robbers, protection-racket bosses. And when we first came into the wing in 1967 to run a series of sociology classes, we found it difficult not to be fascinated by the criminality, the uniqueness of the men who lived there.

After a class in the wing we met in the pub alongside the jail and tried to discuss such impersonal matters as the content of our lectures, and their general reception and the nature of imprisonment but in a very short time we would fall back into earnest chatter about the characteristics of the individual prisoners. Some of this talk rose little above the type of gossip about notorious criminals which fills the Sunday papers; we were as interested as anyone else in finding out what famous criminals really looked like, in comparing their 'underworld' stereotypes with their actual behaviour. Could that amiable individual who talked so learnedly of Plato really be the 'most dangerous man in Britain'? We justified the talk, however, by reference to our criminological interests. We were after all sociologists of deviance who had, over the years, developed a commitment to the understanding of abnormal behaviour, in particular to the attribution of intelligibility and rationality to actions which other criminologists regarded as irrational or psychopathic.

We were inclined at that stage to view our inmate students as primitive social critics. We entertained slightly romantic notions about the extent to which their outrageous crimes could be seen as an attack upon capitalist society. Of course, we could not pretend that the activities of the prisoners were explicitly political. On the surface, their crimes seemed more directly related to the satisfaction of selfish personal needs than to the promotion of any revolutionary ideology. But there seemed to be some affinities worth exploring, some motivations which were shared.

Gradually our pub talk began to infiltrate our lectures. The prisoners showed no great eagerness to confirm our tentative hypotheses. They listened politely to our discussions of anarchism, banditry, guerrilla warfare and sexual deviance but chose not to find any connection between their own activities and those of our romantic subjects. Several of them were prepared to make routine condemnations of capitalism and all its ways but these condemnations hardly lay at the heart of their own criminal careers. These they regarded more as ways of making out in the world than radical techniques for confronting it.

Our problem was that we were unable to shift away from a concentration upon their crimes. It was their outrageous deviance which distinguished the men from others that we knew; the first task was to make sense of that behaviour. We spent so much time talking about the world outside the prison – the anarchists in Spain, hippies in Haight Ashbury, Hemingway's Paris – that we paid little attention to the men's day-to-day prison predicament. The men didn't talk about it very much and in any case it had already been covered in the standard sociological literature on the 'pains of imprisonment' and the 'inmate subculture'.

Our complacency about the relatively unproblematic nature of their life in prison – our sense that it was much the same as that experienced by other prisoners, and already adequately comprehended by existing sociological descriptions – was finally undermined by the arrival of a research team who had come to study 'The Psychological Effects of Long-Term Imprisonment'. The men in the wing immediately objected to the limited range of effects which were to be studied – changes in reaction times, and in such personality attributes as extraversion and introversion. 'What about the real problems – the real effects?' they asked. We began to listen. We were in an odd position. The men regarded us as likely sympathizers in their campaign to make the research more comprehensive, but we had little idea about the nature of the 'real problems' which they felt deserved attention. So we turned the talk back to them, tried to suspend our voyeurish interest in them as criminals.

It started slowly. In the beginning nobody wanted to be first to speak. As we realized later, there was a sense in which publicizing the problems was difficult for the prisoners. It placed them again to the forefront of consciousness, made them matters which required renewed attention. But gradually we found a way of talking together, not about the evident physical problems of living in the wing, the locks, the landings, the guards on every corner, the oppressive heat, the lack of ventilation, but rather about the types of inner subjective life which developed in response to these oppressive circumstances. We began to realize that the whole business of actually getting through each day, let alone each month, or year, or decade of their sentence, was a far more precarious and problematic journey than we had ever taken it to be. The central question was about how to accommodate to prison life. In what ways should one resist or yield to its demands in order to make life bearable, in order to preserve some sense of identity?

And behind this question lay their greatest anxiety – the consequence, as it were, of failing to solve the accommodation problem – the sense of imminent deterioration. Outside prison this is hardly a problem. Most of us simply continue to live, relatively secure in the knowledge that we remain the same person, with the same interests, ideas, intelligence and self-consciousness. But inside the security wing consciousness had to be monitored and guarded against the insidious processes which attacked personal identity. If you did not constantly attend your own state of mind then you might drift into that condition which characterized some of those in the prison who already had served long sentences, men who now appeared to be more dead than alive, 'zombies', 'catatonics', 'vegetables'. The men we knew were determined to avoid this type of degeneration. Accordingly every key aspect of life had to be examined anew in order that it might be manipulated – either in thought or in action – so as to improve the chances of retaining self-identity in this new world. It was a fight in which all were involved, and none the less real because the evidence of its existence was to be found in the subtle manipulation of everyday life rather than in the dramatic or revolutionary gesture.

Fear of deterioration provided a general background to the men's conception of their world: it was far from being the only matter to which they attended. In our research we established some of the other concerns which dominated their minds. Many of these matters also might go unattended outside prison, but suddenly stepped out of the familiar run of everyday life once you found yourself inside for twenty years, such usually taken-for-granted matters as time, friendship and privacy. We found, for example, that the prisoners tried to avoid any timetabled discussion of the years that they had to spend in prison. This imperilled accommodation to the regime. Unlike short-termers who might make calendars or wall charts which indicated how long they had to serve, these men saw freedom as too distant to be a matter for constant reflection. Their internal timetables were not marked out in terms of the days or months of their sentence but were constructed around such matters as the change in seasons, the gap between visits or letters, the length of time that had been spent in a particular security wing.

Ways of making time pass were also problematic. If routines were resorted to then there was the terrible danger that these might degenerate into obsessions; instead of helping to pass the time they might speed the process of degeneration. A commitment to work also raised its own problems. What exactly did work mean in this context, when that which was called work in one prison – the making of children's toys – was presented in another as an example of a hobby which the prisoner might enjoy?

What then should you think about work; what was the appropriate attitude? There were differences between the men in the choice of solution, but for all of them with varying degrees of explicitness, it was a problem which had to be resolved. Some prisoners decided that work, for all its incongruity in prison, could not be ignored: it was an element which demanded attention. But this did not mean that they gave themselves over to it, became committed or spontaneously involved within it. Instead they might undertake it in a distant cynical style, a mode of relating to reality which allowed them to stand back from what they did, to preserve their identity from any contamination which might result from taking such absurd matters seriously. Others decided that some spontaneous involvement in work was the only way to make time pass, so self-consciousness would be suspended and they would try to become immersed in the task, whilst keeping a wary eye upon themselves lest their chosen way of time-wasting developed into an obsession.

Work, time, deterioration were then some of the everyday matters which intruded into consciousness and which had to be controlled and attended to in particular ways. Neither was it just thoughts about the external world which had to be monitored – purely internal reflection also had to be scrutinized. Certain imaginings and fantasies could be embraced but others must be rejected; some might induce a dangerous depression, prove so compelling that they shattered an already tenuous link with reality. The temptation to slip away into fantasy had to be actively resisted. Only by continuous cognitive engineering could consciousness be constructed in such a way that life remained bearable.

We were beginning to modify our interest in those who sought to declare dramatically their total disenchantment with society. We were becoming intrigued by the much more routine ways in which people periodically distanced themselves from a world which they found too much for them. And instead of assuming that such distancing was explicable in terms of the men being in some crude way, anti-social, we now looked for different modes of consciousness – ways of thinking about how to think, which informed such distancing.

Some of these matters were raised in the book that we wrote about our prison research,[2] and we hoped to develop them further in later interviews with long-term prisoners. But the wing at Durham closed and the Home Office refused to allow us to continue interviewing elsewhere. We ended our book by disparaging the metaphor of 'life as a prison': the literary exploitation of prisons, TB sanatoria, asylums, labour camps to make statements about the human predicament. Such metaphors, we thought, stripped the prison predicament of its unique phenomenal qualities. But as we left the prison world behind and returned to our families, jobs, friends, leisure activities, we were slowly beginning to understand the general sociological implications – by no means metaphorical – of the peculiar prison experience.

Although the prisoners had gone away, the problems they had raised remained with us. The glimpses that we had been given of the complex cognitive engineering which was required to get them through the day, the subtle ways in which they wrestled with the distinction between themselves and the prison world, the use of strategies of dissociation to deal with everyday problems, all of these matters seemed to have relevance for life outside prison.

Everyday Life

We recognized that the problems which occupied consciousness in the outside world were very different from those selected in prison. Such matters as time, work, privacy and deterioration might still be attended, but in the outside world they would lack the salience they had for the men in E-Wing. It is not that they go unattended but rather that attitudes and beliefs about them have already been constructed. The passage of time, for example, is not a topic which continuously presents itself to consciousness. We will periodically reflect upon it – but most of the time 'it just passes'. Those who try to bring home to us the facts of deterioration and death have to contend with minds which are already 'made up' in a way which keeps such ideas at some distance. The message of the wayside pulpits that 'death is at hand' can be maintained at the very edge of consciousness because of our central involvement in continuing life projects which give the phenomenal lie to any ideas of anything coming to a sudden end. We close the gaps between our present and our end in such a way as to reassure ourselves about the significance of our present involvement. We hold ourselves within the present and the immediate future, reflecting upon those limited spans of time which are related to specific projects. As Philip Larkin has written:

> Truly, though our element is time,
> We are not suited to long perspectives
> Open at each instant of our lives
> They link us to our losses . . .[3]

The prisoners who faced thirty years did not find their vision blurred by an immediately visible web of developing prospects but instead could stare right across the void of their sentence into the eyes of death itself. For them death and deterioration had suddenly come into perspective and they wrestled with ways in which they might again be placed on the periphery of consciousness.

There is a density to everyday consciousness which at most times gives us a sense that 'life is going along', 'things are as comfortable as could be expected'. There may be moments when we look around and wonder where we are or what we are doing but we soon pick up the threads again and get back to the rich fabric of life. For much of the time we're propelled by rituals and conventions; if the day begins to go stale on us, to seem slow-moving or pointless, then soon we will get caught up in a minor flirtation, a meal, a journey, a family visit. Not that everyday life would be tolerable if it merely consisted of the uneasy passage from ritual to ritual, from convention to convention. Such a life would be difficult to distinguish from that served by the long-term prisoner. However, we do not typically see our own life as a mere succession of discrete events, we recognize that our activities, rituals and conventions are fastened firmly to a set of structured ideas. Of particular significance are the various timetables and careers within which we are located.

We stand at a certain point in our occupational career, aware of our chances of promotion or retirement ... 'Will Spencer eventually decide to go to Australia and allow us to take over his job and secretary?' We are caught up in the career of our marriage, how well it is going at the moment, its prospects for survival ... 'Did Janet really mean what she said last night about a divorce?' We are involved with the educational career of our children, our leisure career, the state of excellence that we have attained at golf or amateur dramatics. At times we will allow our mind to wander over the state of our sexual career – are we really getting our share, is our virility declining or increasing? – and linked to this will be thoughts about the developing state of our body, the loss of old defects, the emergence of new: our adolescent acne has made way for middle-aged gingivitis. Economic timetables also stand as background items in consciousness: the present state of our bank balance, the current market price of our house. Readers interested in 569 pages of self-conscious description of such problems are referred to Joseph Heller's novel, *Something happened*.

It may be just possible – although we doubt it – to get through a day without allowing any such matters to impinge upon consciousness, but as soon as some slight change or development occurs in our life – even something so trivial as a minor illness – then elements relating to several of these career timetables begin to invade the mind. Although the relationship between them may never be the subject of consciousness, nevertheless they provide the background against which everyday life is apprehended, against which its routines and conventions make sense. Taken together, we may talk of them as our 'life plans'. 'The life plan' is: '... the totalization of all the relevant timetables, their grand sum and their integrative meaning ... the life plan is the basic context in which knowledge of society is organized in the consciousness of the individual.'[4] Consciousness of an everyday world in which life plans already exist is very different from one in which they have to be constructed. There are no clear-cut intersecting career timetables for the long-term prisoner and therefore no immediately available context in which to organize his knowledge of the world. The only timetables which are available – training for careers, working for A-levels – are those offered by the regime, and must therefore be embraced with care lest they produce the type of machine-like conformity that the men observe in other prisoners.

For most of us, however, reality appears relatively friendly. Most of the time the world looks and feels like our own. We pass our time in it with the help of a set of established constructions which allows us to see it as stable, orderly, even 'normal'. With a certain amount of licence we will borrow Berger and Luckmann's term 'paramount reality' to describe the sum total of these constructions:

> This is the reality of everyday life. Its privileged position entitles it to the designation of paramount reality. The tension of consciousness is highest in everyday life, that is, the latter imposes itself upon consciousness in the most massive urgent and intense manner. It is impossible to ignore, difficult even to weaken in its imperative presence.[5]

Interruptions or breaks from paramount reality don't last long: 'The paramount reality envelops them on all sides as it were, and consciousness always returns to the paramount reality as from an excursion.'[6] But that is only one side of the equation which was referred to by the prisoners when they discussed their predicament. It was not just reality and their sense of the world which was problematic but also their relationship to that world; the problem of the tension between self and reality. For we do not simply have to get through life; socialization isn't just a matter of learning how to do reality work. We also require a sense of ourselves as a person who is getting through life in ways which are at times quite distinctively different from even those who follow very similar life plans. We may look at society and see nothing but sets of uniformities: groups of students, or stockbrokers, or labourers, all dressed in a manner appropriate to their role, all adopting appropriate styles of dress, speech and manner. But that surface uniformity merely provides the backdrop against which identity is created, against which we display our differences from others around us.

Living in contemporary society involves us in 'reality work' *and* 'identity work'. We have to build up stable constructions of the world with the help of such structured features of existence as 'life plans' and simultaneously present ourselves as a distinctive individual. The relationship between identity work and reality work is complex, at times complementary, at times antithetical. The prisoners in E-Wing, for example, initially had to contend with the problem of constructing paramount reality in such a way that it might be compatible with identity work. To accept the prison timetables or work schedules or systems of rewards uncritically, threatened the possible development of identity; they could not readily show their uniqueness by accommodating to the 'reality' which the regime presented. Once, however, they had constructed some type of alternative reality – cleared some small subjective spaces which were relatively uncontaminated by the institutional reality – they then had sites upon which identity work might be mounted. They could display their specialness within the very style of dissociation from the regime.

But this hardly resolved the problem of identity work. Most prisoners were engaged in dissociation, few chose to realize or to display themselves in terms of commitment to prison life. In order to establish the sense of difference which is so much the criterion of 'felt' individuality in our society, other resources were required. And, of course, these were far from being freely available. They could not draw upon clothes, leisure pursuits, hair styles, distinctive hobbies, special friends, in order to display differences. The symbolic resources for differentiation were scarce; there was the continual problem therefore of resisting the sense that they were only prisoners. Even their old identities as criminals were not readily available for the construction of a present sense of uniqueness; there was a general agreement that their external career was an inappropriate resource once they were inside.

In everyday life the twin problems of structuring day-to-day existence and simultaneously constructing our identity appear less serious. As we have seen, much of the reality of everyday life already presents itself to us in a structured form. Paramount reality is given. And in addition we are presented with a massive array of symbolic resources out of which we may construct our identity. The market place is full of clothes, books, records, ideologies, commodities, goods, services: the whole spectacular display of a market society is devoted to our identity. It provides badges, props, markers, symbols and allegiances.

But the presence of these 'givens' does not make everyday life unproblematic. Contemporary man is prey to a recurrent sense of dissatisfaction. He is intermittently bored, frustrated and neurotic. Life is only occasionally there to be simply lived. Much of the time its structures demand immediate remedial work; we continually call upon philosophers, moralists and therapists to provide appropriate facilitating devices to help us through the day; we demand new ways to make sense of the existential predicaments we encounter, new cures for the sickness unto death. These therapies ('mysticism with all the metaphysical commitments drained off'7) have come out onto the streets: there they are in the astrology columns, the advice pages, the evening-institute class on sociology and self-improvement, the paperbacks of Berne, Ardrey and Spock.

The major source of our anxieties is to be found in the peculiar nature of the tension which exists in contemporary consciousness between our sense of paramount reality and our notion of what constitutes identity. In some traditional societies identity might readily be constructed out of the material of paramount reality. Individuals could display themselves by showing commitment to the arrangements and routines of everyday life. But contemporary consciousness is informed by a sense of reality as something which is not completely our own. We are able to reflect upon our life plans, are able to see them as relative by observing the existence of other dissimilar life plans. Such reflexivity and relativity promotes the sense, whether it be occasional or frequent, of our separateness from the world in which we live; its arrangements are somehow not entirely *our* arrangements.

There will, of course, be many times in which we happily accept the identities which are offered to us by virtue of our membership of particular parts of the social world. We just ride along, allowing ourselves to be taken as a typical father, husband or businessman. But often, we will share with the prisoners the sense that our identity is only satisfactorily accomplished by drawing upon our sense of distance from the reality we experience. Even to be able to distinguish between our sense of the world (paramount reality) and our sense of identity is a core source of unhappiness, for this is to admit that the world is not our own. It is to say that identity work has to be done against or in spite of the institutional arrangements of society. There is a life plan, a career timetable, roles, statuses, responsibilities, even preferred identities, but these are not what we really are. The more dense is paramount reality, the more elements there are to distance ourselves from; the more highly developed our identity resources – through a literature, mass culture and therapy whose stock in trade is self-consciousness, reflexivity, relativity – the more ingenious our identity work has to be. For so many others are involved in this work, that it itself takes on collective forms which themselves become part of reality rather than the stuff which allows any sense of distance from that reality. Our individual and collective forms of resistance – the escape attempts of this book – draw their sustenance from the very air of the prison itself. At times it is impossible to know which is the problem and which is the solution. It is this historical paradox which makes our book possible.

We want to show just how massive is the presence of paramount reality, and how ingenious, complex and even desperate can be the identity work which seeks to evade its clutches. Some of this work will require no more than shifts in modes of consciousness, some will require the adoption of new forms of behaviour, new locations, new partners. Some will involve resort to fantasy, imagination, even a total life commitment to the search for an alternative reality. But all of it is premised upon that strange feature of the consciousness of modern man, that persistent sense that he is more than the arrangements which he lives, that he stands apart from reality rather than within it, the belief, in John Barth's words, that 'reality is a nice place to visit, but you wouldn't want to live there'.

When we talk of strategies, tactics and plans for escaping and resisting reality, the reality we refer to is that of contemporary Western society. We take this society as given only in the sense that in writing about how the prisoners coped, we took the prison order as given. This does not mean that we think the social order is immutable, any more than we think that prisons can't be abolished. But this is not our subject matter. What concerns us are the ways in which we make sense of ourselves and our life within the structural walls of society. Our subject matter is self in spite of the structural order, not so much the possibilities of self in another social order. It is appropriate that we should have reached this interest from our research on long-term prisoners. Erving Goffman arrived at a similar sense of the tension between self and society from his own research into total institutions:

Without something to belong to, we have no stable self, and yet total commitment and attachment to any social unit implies a kind of selflessness. Our sense of being a person can come from being drawn into a wider social unit; our sense of selfhood can arise through the little ways in which we resist the pull. Our status is backed by the solid buildings of the world, while our sense of personal identity resides in the cracks.[8]

This book is an investigation of the interstitial establishment of identity, but also an account of how the interstices themselves are constructed by man, or are routinely provided by society itself. We are not the only ones involved in this enterprise. There is an explicitly new component to the great revolutionary movements which have traditionally been concerned with the bricks and mortar, with changing the social structural and institutional arrangements in order to create a world without injustice and deprivation, a world of material plenty and spiritual fulfilment. Identity problems are no longer regarded as psychological residues which can be dealt with after the revolution. Identity work has either been more explicitly added to the revolutionary agenda or in the face of massive structural complexity and immobility, structural work has been abandoned and replaced by attempts to construct new symbolic models and meanings within the old order. The identity workers of the world are beginning to unite. This work in our society takes the form of resistance and escape.

It is by looking at these forms of resistance and escape that we can maintain our original interest in struggles against society, in the articulation of alternative realities. Our heroes though are no longer criminals, outsiders, revolutionaries and cultural critics. Men in this book are only occasionally to be found at the front of revolutionary armies, fighting in the streets or raving from their asylum cells. More often they are discovered at home with their hobbies, at the pictures with their children, or on holiday with their girlfriend. Their fights against reality are rarely frontal assaults, running battles or planned campaigns. They are more often interruptions in the flow of life, interludes, temporary breaks, skirmishes, glimpses of other realities. This is the story of just how significant, ubiquitous, heroic, comic, powerful and pathetic, such attempts can be.

2

The Mental
Management of
Routine

The life plan maps our existence. Ahead of us
run the career lines of our jobs, our marriage, our leisure
interests, our children and our economic fortunes. But
sometimes when we scan these maps, traverse these routes,
follow the signs, we become strangely disturbed by the
predictability of the journey, the accuracy of the map, the
knowledge that today's route will be much like yesterday's.
Is this what our life is really about? Why is each day's
journey marked by feelings of boredom, habit, routine?
We feel dissatisfied with our marriage, our job and our
children. The route we take to work, the clothes we wear,
the food we eat, are visible reminders of an awful sense of
monotony.

For some people such feelings may be so in-
tense that they are led to search for alternative realities;
they set out to change their whole world. But for most of
us, the periodic sense of dissatisfaction is related not to
marriage, work, children as such; we do not wish to rid
ourselves of these involvements altogether. What we object
to is the sense that we are sinking into a patterned way of

existence in all these areas; that they no longer appear to us as fresh and novel. They are becoming routinized. They no longer help us to constitute our identity.

The Flywheel of Habit

Even men who claim that life is a series of original and exciting adventures are happy to admit that there still exists some degree of regularity in their own lives. They allow habit to dominate the way in which they dress and undress, brush their teeth, wash up after meals. All of us move through such chained activities with little pause for reflection, rarely worrying that our unthinking involvement within them in any way imperils our personal freedom or our opportunities for expressing identity. These are regularities which we happily accept as part of life. It is not we who have made them into regularities; there is simply something about such matters as brushing teeth or putting on shoes which is inescapably habitual; it is the same for all men and freedom is not diminished by subscription to such a predictable set of actions. We will call this more or less automatic, unthinking way of comprehending these aspects of the everyday world *unreflective accommodation*. This is a mode of consciousness, a mental technique for managing aspects of paramount reality.

In such examples of domestic hygiene as we have given, if a sense of regularity arises in consciousness, it is accepted with this accommodative attitude. We embrace the regularity without further reflection – in no way sensing that this is a part of everyday reality towards which any more active or critical stance is required. We don't have to do any mental work to regard hand-washing as routine; no other accommodation seems appropriate to the task. Indeed people who do regard such habits as requiring mental management are seen as mad; textbooks refer to them as obsessive–compulsives or phobics. Special mood-altering drugs have even been invented to help these unfortunate people to get through their daily routines. On some days, however, these routines and regularities appear as difficult problems to all of us. They reach out from the bathroom into the kitchen, the living room, the bedroom. They may even follow us to work, accompanying us during the day, and escort us home at night. We appear to be living our entire lives unreflectively; outsiders may see our whole day as consisting of simply sets of habits. A hippie describes his father's life:

People are becoming automated. Take my father. Get up, 7.30 breakfast, out at 8; get the 8.30 train to Charing Cross, gets on the tube, off at Oxford Circus, walk along to Hanover Square. He goes upstairs, he sits there all day; he goes out for lunch – gets himself a beer and sandwich, comes back, carries on work, 5.30 he packs in, gets the tube back to Charing Cross, train home. I mean what a life! Where does it get you?[1]

When we ourselves begin to perceive our own life as stretching out in this patterned way we may, like the outside critic, question its meaning – where it gets us. The regularized nature of our life begins to loom within consciousness as a cause for dissatisfaction, as a reason why we feel that something must be done about it.

We talk of routines as dull and dreary; phrases like 'breaking out of routine' suggest their oppressiveness, whilst a reference to something as 'just routine' decreases the significance of the activity so described. Life surely must be more than routines – large sections of it should not be allowed to slip past us without reflection. For the more predictable the life plan appears, the less we are able to sense ourselves as individuals possessing unique identities. Identity within our society cannot be wholly constructed within the life plan, it must also be realized, and realized self-consciously, against it. When the unreflective domain looms large, we have to work hard to dispel the apparent ways in which our sense of individuality is being threatened. We have to retain a vision of ourselves as only partially determined creatures.

One way is to reflect that although much of our life certainly does look like routine, a series of sequences through which we pass in a relatively unreflective, unself-expressive manner, that nevertheless these are adequately balanced by those areas of freedom and spontaneity that we have constructed for ourselves. To feel that many aspects of our existence are routine is tolerable as long as they do not usurp such free domains. We rationalize our way of life by declaring that the ideal state is some equilibrium between the routinized and indeterminate aspects of our existence; if too many of our actions feel repetitive and determined then we become 'fed up' and feel the need to break away a little, to shake off some routines. However in so doing we must not make the mistake of abandoning too much of our regularized behaviour. Even philosophers – those experts on happiness – support this elaborate rationalization. If one part of life appears habitual and routinized, observed Bertrand Russell, then the other should be open and indeterminate.[2] A routinely regarded job should not go hand in hand with a routine marriage or vice versa. Neither should there be a lack of a sense of routine in all the major areas of one's life. Unless the correct balance is achieved, unhappiness will result.

But although our occasional restlessness about the extent of habit in our life may be temporarily banished from consciousness by recourse to some such quantum theory of human happiness, it may return as we reflect upon the sheer predictability of our lives. However much we revolve domestic, occupational and leisure images in consciousness, we still come up with patterned pictures. As in a kaleidoscope, the colours change, but the symmetry persists. Our house appears too much like one of the little boxes in the song, our relationship with our wife and children indistinguishable from those paraded in the soap operas of radio and television. Our job comes straight out of the textbook discussions about alienation at work. We appear to live by order, moving from black-and-white to colour television, from gramophone to stereo system, from refrigerator to deep freeze, along the market tramlines of consumer society. How may we declare ourselves still free and indeterminate, individual and unique, when uniformity asserts itself so massively within our daily life?

There is one way out; we can not only accept

this increase in uniformity as real, but proclaim it as a pre-condition for freedom. Far from encroaching upon freedom, habit makes room for it. The more we are able to view inessential elements of our life as unreflective chains of behaviour, the more we can concentrate upon self-expression in the remaining areas. We can allow the advertisers to stock our cupboards and kitchens and garages, we can happily buy mass-produced clothes off the hook and become lost in the anonymous ritualized journeys to and from work, for we know that this surrenders nothing that is important to ourselves. We do not live or do identity work in these places; real life is elsewhere. 'The standardization of certain patterns of behaviour not essentially significant in human intercourse liberates the attention for more important considerations'.[3] We may all look like uniform beings but that is an illusion. Differentiation and diversity are occurring elsewhere. 'The routinization of lower-level choices' is actually increasing our 'opportunities to be different at more meaningful levels'.

If man had to reflect upon the act of driving every time he entered his car, if he were forced to ponder the significance of work every day at the office, then he would have no time for the more important matters of life. An unreflective approach to some behaviour is a route to emancipation rather than a badge of servitude. We can relegate habits to the lower part of the brain and reserve the higher regions for innovation and originality. Shovel away the flotsam of day-to-day existence and then we get down to real living.

Now all this looks optimistic. We seem to have provided a recipe for dodging accusations about the habitual nature of our lives. The hippie can go hang himself. His father's habits are really roads to liberation.

Sometimes however our dissatisfaction may be founded upon a sense of life as so ubiquitously routine that not even notions of residual areas of freedom may be entertained. Instead of being grateful that unreflective accommodation to routines allows time to pass, helps to get us through the day, we become disturbed by the ways in which we can allow ourselves to be swept along so easily by the mundane, the trivial, the readily predictable. Like the long-term prisoners, we fear that 'giving in' to habit could be a symptom of a more total deterioration, a disintegration of ourselves into automatons.

At this point habit appears not just as a feature of everyday life but an existence itself. This is the experience we call boredom, monotony, tedium, despair. On all sides of us lie invitations to action. The record-player lies unused on the shelf beside the darkened television. The phone rings unanswered in the hallway. The novel beside our bed, the crossword on the table, the sounds of the children upstairs and of our wife moving around the kitchen are merely reinforcements for our condition rather than spurs to action. If we move then we know the way that things will go, we have travelled all the lines before, been to all the stations, investigated all the sidings. Only complete inactivity can save us from the desperate dissatisfaction of routine involvement. It is not that there is nothing to do – 'There is always something to do,' as parents tell their little children. It is only that what is to be done is already too well known to be done again.

At such times words like 'freedom', 'spontaneity' and 'indeterminacy' seem empty slogans. The only freedom lies in doing nothing, in standing still. The habitual stretches out like a contagion into every region of life; it feels inescapable. This is the world despaired of by the existentialists, the empty hollow nothingness of a Beckett play, in which no one moves, nothing changes, and no one comes. It is also the world charted by social scientists – a universe of intercrossing regularities which, whilst pretending to offer man the prospects of travel, merely imprisons him upon a circular track. 'Habit is the great flywheel of society,' wrote William James, 'its most precious conservative agent.'

It alone is what keeps us all within the bounds of ordinance, and saves the children of fortune from the envious uprising of the poor. It alone prevents the hardest and most repulsive walks of life from being deserted by those brought up to tread therein. It keeps the fisherman and the deck-hand at sea through the winter; it holds the miner in his darkness, and nails the countryman to his log cabin and his lonely farm through all the months of snow; it protects us from invasion by the natives of the desert and the frozen zone. It dooms us all to fight out the battle of life upon the lines of our nurture or our early choice, and to make the best of a pursuit that disagrees, because there is no other for which we are fitted, and it is too late to begin again.[4]

On the days when this vision of the world invades our minds, our sense of routine ceases to be based upon an observation of the patterned nature of activities in the house, the office and the golf club. It is no longer simply an aspect of the world which is a cause for despair, the basis for a pessimistic life philosophy. Instead, we begin to see that the routine nature of the world emanates from ourselves. Our personality – that last apparent repository of individuality and spontaneity in a predictable world – is itself the source of the problem. It is we who bring routines to the world; our characters have set like plaster and we can behave in no other way. When this view overcomes us, even the real diversity of our activities, the multi-sidedness of our character, the range of roles we are involved in, offer little consolation. This diversity itself is patterned and predictable: what are we but the sum total of separate constituents called father, husband, lover, chartered accountant, cricket-club secretary? That which at times we thought to be really ourselves – individual, spontaneous, free – was simply bourgeois father playing out his lines or loving husband enacting the rituals of married life. No wonder that we can scarcely move from our chairs on days when this view of life presents itself to consciousness.

Management through Distancing

Paradoxically, such bleakness, such awareness of predictability, may slowly lift us from our state of boredom, lead us back into interaction, into life. For our very reflection upon the determinacy of life, pushes us back into an area of freedom. We create a zone for self, an identity domain out of our consciousness of our very ability to reflect in this way. If we can see this determinacy, detect the ubiquity of routine, of role, then this gives some sense of separation from the activities of life which is not enjoyed by those who unreflectively commit themselves to life's regularities. We can distinguish ourselves from such people, reflect upon their unreflective practices, show some sense of self in what we do.

Now, of course, self-consciousness is a universal feature of contemporary man's existence. It is not however exercised in every part of our life, neither is it necessarily used as an escape attempt. When, for example, we talk intimately with the one we love, we often show our sensitivity by self-consciously reflecting upon our own relationship – 'Our relationship must look conventional to others; but I know, and so do you, that it is not like that at all.' In this case, and others like it, self-consciousness is actually a way of showing commitment to the task, a demonstration that one is qualified as a lover by virtue of such interactional sensitivity.[5] In these cases identity work involves being seen to embrace paramount reality rather than to resist it.

But self-consciousness is a versatile mental device. On some days it may bring us into the world, may provide the proof that we are a knowing and willing member. But on others it stands between us and what we do. It holds routine at bay, keeps convention from the door. It is a mental way of effecting an escape from some of the terrors of patterned living. Instead of playing roles, of acting out routines, we 'play at' or 'act against' roles and routines.

If we can make these mental journeys above the petty arrangements of work, marriage and leisure, what need have we to physically distance ourselves from them? We need not change the patterns, but only the way we think about them. And others who share the heightened self-awareness may join in this transcendent game.

In Sidcup, the wife awaits her husband's return. He arrives home as he always does on the 6.18 Dartford loop-line train. The semi-detached house to which he returns is like thousands of others which present themselves for inspection along the tree-lined avenues of this commuter suburb. The furniture is G-Plan, the pictures on the wall are Impressionist reproductions, the record on the turntable is Tony Bennett, the meal waiting to be served is *coq au vin*. On the table sits the *Daily Telegraph*, on the television the *Radio Times*. Up and down the street the same domestic context is reproduced with only minor variations – beef bourguignonne for *coq au vin*, Sinatra for Bennett, Cintique for G-Plan. The uniformity and predictability of it all might seem to induce an unshakeable sense of routine, a soul-destroying impression of the unmalleability of paramount reality. But when the door is shut against the night, and the two children are safely in bed, husband and wife turn to each other and laugh. They are subscribers to the new self-consciousness, apostles of awareness. Cynically they deride those who share bourgeois arrangements with them, but who do not see the joke. Looking around the room they declare their awareness of their apparent suburbanity, and then with a delicious sense of their own distinctive identities, record their distance from such artefacts. 'We may look as suburban as those next door, but both of us know that we view so much of this life with detachment, with irony, even cynicism.' They caricature their own lives with an easy sense that this lifts them away from the arrangements that they live. For them, it is only others who are truly suburban, who play their roles with a routine orientation, whilst they 'see through' the relativity of the setting, they live against it as much as within it, and thereby preserve their individuality in a conformist world. But although our happy couple may not know it, the trap of routine is not so easily sprung. For meanwhile, on the other side of the Sanderson wallpaper, in the next house, another couple of identity workers are sitting down to start a similar distancing game.

Throughout the land previously disenchanted individuals are busily assuring others that they are more than they do; 'I'm not really a university lecturer,' they confide 'not like the others are ... I see the whole thing as rather an elaborate game.' Dentists, doctors, shop assistants whisper similar self-distancing remarks to appropriate colleagues, unaware that down the corridor their co-workers are busily at work with the same transcending strategy.

The rather pathetic way of dealing with routine by unreflective accommodation is now replaced by the seemingly powerful devices of monitoring and distancing. Through simple self-consciousness, the most insidious of routines can be undermined. Self-consciousness of one's predicament provides the opportunity to establish oneself against it, it protects one from the fear that one's behaviour is determined by the structure and culture of the setting. And as Simmel has observed with the help of an appropriate example: 'For only whoever stands outside his boundary in some sense knows that he stands within it, that is, knows it as a boundary. Kasper Hauser did not know that he was in prison until he came into the open and could see the walls from without.'[6] If our marriage seems more predictable to us than ever, then we may kick it away from ourselves with jokes and mockery. If work seems increasingly routinized, then it can be regarded with less and less seriousness. As soon as a sense of routine threatens to engulf consciousness, then self simply leans back and regards this assault, and in so doing reaffirms its own inviolability. Self-conscious distancing does not take a single form – it does not always have similar identity pay-offs, does not always create the same degree of distance between ourselves and reality. Sometimes, it may appear as sarcasm, at others as irony or cynicism. But in each case the world is put in its place, held apart from ourselves and inspected with varying degrees of dislike and reserve.

Nobody unreflectively accommodates to every aspect of life (even the catatonic is allowed a knowing look by some contemporary psychiatrists), neither does anyone bring self-consciousness to every area (cynicism or irony about matters of personal hygiene is rarely thought appropriate). Different modes of apprehension alternate. This shifting of modes allows man to feel that he is not a creature who is enmeshed by routine; it gives him the sense that there exists a domain of identity development. Not that this heightened self-awareness alters in any way the patterned content of the real world to which it is addressed; the *coq au vin* still sizzles on the table and Tony Bennett still recalls San Francisco through the balanced stereo speakers, but the encroachment of a *sense* of routine has been averted by a strategy of self-awareness. We have found within the manipulation of modes of consciousness a way of beating off the feeling that the world is too much with us. Self-consciousness reduces the press of social conventions by de-mystifying them, by showing their arbitrariness. We seem to have found a crack in the density of social reality through which man may scramble. But while this orientation may look less accommodative to paramount reality than the unreflective mode in that it introduces some distance between self and reality, a phenomenal drawbridge which the individual puts up to keep away paramount reality, it may nevertheless function in a fundamental sense to preserve that very reality. An apparently radical plot can hide a conservative trap.

This is to contradict those liberal sociologists who write about the social construction of everyday life. They tend to see de-mystification of social interaction and social processes as a necessary preliminary to radical structural change. In many circumstances, however, it is de-mystification itself which, by allowing the individual to distance himself from the social arrangements to which he is party, gives him a sense of satisfaction with his own lot which is incompatible with a desire for change. The fact that we can regard with amusement the conventions of university life and our own roles as university lecturers, actually ensures that we remain within those conventions and these roles. Recognition of the arbitrary nature of our domestic arrangements, of our work tasks, of our leisure pursuits does not so much provide premises upon which political action may be constructed, in which the whole concept of work and family might be attacked, instead they give the individual a slightly decreased sense of social commitment, a further warrant for that cynicism about social life which carries with it such a satisfying sense of the importance of oneself as an individual.

Within the maximum-security wing, the prisoners' ability to relativize their experience reduced anxiety and tension. Their recognition that their environment with its phenomenal qualities was one amongst many such environments and their further realization that this recognition guaranteed them a higher degree of self-consciousness than that which had been enjoyed by men in those other environments, proved comforting. Self-consciousness of their predicament provided the opportunity to establish themselves against it, it protected them from the fear that their behaviour was determined by the structure and culture of the setting. It did not mean however that they now acted against the institution, it more usually meant that they went along with its edicts with an easier heart, reassured by the distance which they could mentally maintain from its social arrangements.

We do not wish to take our argument too far. Of course there are occasions upon which de-mystification prompts collective social action, in which irony, cynicism and sarcasm are revolutionary weapons. But these are occasions upon which there already exists a general subscription to an imagined alternative world. In the absence of such an imaginable world (a political or social utopia perhaps) de-mystification serves primarily conservative functions.

Furthermore, the distancing techniques themselves – those apparent guarantees of individuality – can also be experienced as routine. They do not lead us into a special realm which is safe from contamination by regularities, an area of freedom inhabited by higher men who have managed to keep the routine features of paramount reality at bay. The ways of ignoring aspects of our life, the ways of demonstrating that while playing the role we are not just the self that is implied by the role, are themselves finite and predictable: 'When the individual withdraws from a situated self he does not draw into some psychological world that he creates himself but rather acts in the name of some other socially created identity.'[7] In other words, the escapes from the routines and roles are also patterned. We may be startled to find that the person in the office next door, whom we had always pitied as a pathetic 'unreflective accommodator to routine', is not only busy distancing himself madly from all around him, but is doing so in exactly the same way as we are. The frequent use of distancing remarks as a way of ignoring reality, of evidencing identity, may eventually translate them into unreflective features of our everyday conversation. When most people in our office periodically engage in verbal dissociation from its procedures and rituals, it is difficult for us to accord such techniques any special escape status. We are trapped again in routine, the routine of distancing.

How do we avoid this trap? The answer is obvious: we try for another level of self-consciousness, look for a greater degree of distance between ourselves and reality. We start to do identity work on our identity work. Role-distancing or self-monitoring as a way of showing detachment from reality is not conducted just at one level. We not only can show ourselves to be standing outside reality by some comments or attitudes, we can also show that we are aware of ourselves being aware of standing outside the real world, and also show ourselves aware of this awareness and so on. Simmel nicely catches the nature of this escalating self-consciousness: 'The process by which consciousness towers over itself as something known approaches the unlimited. I know not only that I know, but I also know that I know this; writing down the sentence, I lift myself yet again above the previous stages of this process, and so on.'[8]

The areas of life in which demonstrations of this meta-meta-consciousness are required are precisely those where simple processes of role-distancing have been used so many times that they have come to have a routinized nature. So the man who attempts to seduce a girl by simple role-distancing, by saying, 'I'm afraid this looks rather like a casual pick-up,' is likely to be regarded as having a very routine attitude to life compared to the man who is able to declare, 'I'm not going to use that "I'm afraid this looks rather like a casual pick-up" line, for we both know that it *is* only a casual pick-up.'

Role-distancing even at – and perhaps especially at – the meta-level maintains an essentially conservative relationship between the individual and the social fabric. By asserting that his part in it is something more than is apparent, his state of consciousness is frozen or at least can only move backwards in increasingly complicated spirals of awareness, awareness about awareness, distance and distance from distance.

We must now seriously reconsider the use of self-consciousness as a mode of escape. It may well be that for some people to realize the game-like 'unreal' nature of whatever they are doing is a form of liberation, but such extreme self-consciousness may also result in great unhappiness. There are situations in which it is preferable to suspend incredulity and happily play the game.

Of course, such playing can never be completely unselfconscious. For man, self-consciousness is always present and in a sense corrupting. Bateson uses Aldous Huxley's description of this state as a loss of grace to discuss how the artist has to integrate the unconscious and the conscious, the heart and the reason: 'Some cultures may foster a negative approach to this difficult integration, an avoidance of complexity by crass preference either for total consciousness or total unconsciousness. Their art is unlikely to be "great".'[9] By only slightly twisting Bateson's comments on art to fit problems of living, we can also say that a 'crass preference either for total consciousness or total unconsciousness' is unlikely to be a successful escape attempt. Total unconsciousness is more or less impossible for modern man: even the most trivial of routines can become matters for reflection. And total consciousness eventually becomes untenable because of the spirals of meta-consciousness we have described.

Reinvesting in Routine

How may the growth of spirals of self-consciousness in the dominant areas of our life be counteracted? What may we do when having prided ourselves upon our degree of self-awareness, we suddenly begin to recognize that such awareness stands between us and the proper appreciation of our wife or job or child? In these circumstances we cannot slide back and unreflectively accommodate again to routine, for by its very nature such an orientation involves the feeling that life could not be otherwise, and sadly we have already arrived at the position where our self-awareness has destroyed this fiction. There is no going back to such an unreflective condition.

Another escape hatch opens. We may puncture our ballooning self-consciousness by 'reinvesting' in particular behavioural regularities; we summon up the symbols which typically accompany those regularities, we adopt the clothes and the speech and the rituals of those who are routinely oriented to such matters. We allow ourselves to be 'converted' in such a way that we can declare that there was no other path to follow. This is our third way of managing reality, *self-consious reinvestment*. The self-conscious element in this mode of orientation is hopefully limited to the decision to become recommitted or involved; after that commitment we hope that it will recede. So the man who has cynically derided the nature of marriage during many years with his first wife may hope to bury such self-consciousness under the symbolic weight of the marriage arrangements which he undertakes for the benefit of his second. But such self-conscious involvement may not depend upon the availability of new wives, or business opportunities. After years of spiralling self-consciousness with the same person, an agreement may be reached by which both partners dissipate such distancing problems by a declaration that they have at last found each other in a completely new way. 'Do you know, my love, after all these years of discussion and argument and cynicism, I suddenly realize that I love you just like I did when we were very young – let's live that way, shall we?' Similarly, after spending some time in a job where we have been surrounded by cynicism, we may resolve to tackle our new position with a proper sense of commitment. We self-consciously ignore the clever chatter around us and concentrate upon the task.

The stranglehold of self-consciousness may however be too great to be loosened by a mere verbal reformulation. The wife may be unable to resist the opportunity provided by her partner's naive expression of commitment – 'Darling let's face it – you were never young.' Colleagues at work, with whom we've been through layers of cynical distancing routines will understandably be sceptical of our sudden declaration of interest in giving lectures or marking essays. Self-consciousness reasserts itself and the prospects for reinvestment recede.

The problem is that so many demonstrations of a special identity, so many jokes, so many enjoyable arguments depend upon displays of self-awareness that the newly adopted routine commitment may be difficult to sustain. In addition there is the problem that others will not recognize the recommitted nature of the new subjective attitude. Instead, they will regard it as an example of an unreflective accommodation to life, and will therefore seek to undermine such a position by discussions about how relative are such matters as love and work. Those who have reinvested must then either choose to be mistaken for such constitutionally unaware beings, or else round upon their would-be educators with a declaration that they have been through all that self-conscious experience and have now moved to a higher stage. (However, to adopt the latter course is to risk a relativizing of the new position, by the very act of discussing it in terms of former orientations.)

An example from our prison research. Going into the scrap-metal shop in the security wing at Durham raised three possibilities for mental management. Some men at some times approached the work with unreflective accommodation. It was something to be done and that was all there was to it. It was not an opportunity for identity work. But others who reflected upon the nature of the work, who viewed it in relation to work outside prison, and in terms of its meaning in the context of their massive sentences, chose to distance themselves from its demands. It had to be treated as absurd; its routines had to be resisted for the sake of preserving and promoting self-identity and in the hope of avoiding the type of zombie-like degeneration they saw as the product of years of unreflective accommodation. And finally others who had appreciated its absurdity in the past, had held it at arm's length, felt they must now abandon such self-consciousness. Reflecting that work might help to make time pass, might distract them from other anxieties, they reinvested in the task, maintaining a show of commitment.

The Right Mode for the Right Routine

Now these different ways of apprehending the world – unreflective accommodation, self-awareness, and self-conscious reinvestment – may be used in relation to any chain of activity. It is likely that our attitude to such matters as personal hygiene will be one of unreflective accommodation, but suddenly one night you see yourself staring back from the bathroom mirror, a middle-aged man with a green toothbrush. There is a rush of self-consciousness; the activity loses its taken-for-granted appearance and becomes absurd. 'Do you realize', you say to your wife, 'I've stood here every night for eight years at approximately this time and rubbed this spearmint foam around my mouth – is that what life's about?' Your wife becomes irritated by the use of such trivial matters for the expression of personal identity. 'Hurry up my love, I'm waiting to use the mirror.' You bend your head and resume the brushing, perhaps reassured by the ability to stand aside from such universally accepted habits. It is time to reinvest in the activity itself and kick aside your meta-theorizing. After all there is such a thing as making too much of cleaning your teeth.

The relationship between mental-management techniques and the nature of routines themselves is not a straightforward one. The sociologist may observe the existence of regularities in every area of life: work, play, sex, and religion. He may discuss these regularities in a relatively general way, observing for example conventions within the way in which we perform our religious observations, but he may also be more specific and analyse the nature of the family meal in terms of the predictable programme of courses, the regularized way in which conversation is managed, the habitual manner in which knives, forks, spoons, and plates are manipulated. But none of his analysis necessarily leads us to regard any or all of these activities as regularities. And even those which we do so regard may be happily accepted as such – they may be matters for unreflective accommodation.

Man responds differently to the regularities that he recognizes within the world, and his responses are influenced by the ways in which most men regard any particular regularity. We have seen that most people would be happy to regard many aspects of personal grooming as routine features of their life and unreflectively accommodate to them. Work is quite a different matter. Those who work on conveyor belts, or labour at office desks may find it difficult to drive a sense of monotony and routine from their minds. But here it will not be so easy to accommodate unreflectively. For in contrast to personal grooming, work is an activity which takes up a major proportion of our time, it is also an activity in which some declare that they find a chance for self-expression, an opportunity for identity work. This means that for those who see only regularity, an attitude of unreflective accommodation may be inappropriate. To commit oneself to the task now constitutes an abandonment of self-expression, a surrendering of oneself to the motions and pace of the factory and the office. The way is open for an assertion of self-distancing; a statement which indicates that one is above the work that one does. 'Of course', this attitude declares, 'I see the routine nature of the task, but look at how I'm doing it. Watch the way I work on the line or sort the invoices and you will see how far below me I believe the work to be.' On the conveyor belt, distancing from the task is almost an expectation. Anyone who cares about the quality of the manufactured product, who believes in the firm's interest in the worker, in the importance of increased output, is almost a deviant. Distancing is at a premium. Stories about particular individuals who have vigorously demonstrated their contempt for the work by symbolic or actual attacks upon the machinery or management are a common feature of industrial life. These are not necessarily political attacks, they more often involve numerous subtle perversions of the task which at the same time demonstrate competence and contempt.

Within other occupational areas, the limits upon distancing are narrower. So, for example, tasks within a bank which parallel conveyor-belt activities by virtue of their repetitiveness may be less tolerable in that indications of our separateness from them are not culturally acceptable. We are expected to display a certain level of commitment to the task which militates against self-expression. The increasing use of name badges for cashiers in banks can be seen as an institutionalized attempt to suggest individuality within the task, in circumstances where it is not allowed to develop against it.

There are limits upon our chances to show this distancing attitude, however strongly we may hold it within our head. For if our work at the office continues to feel like oppressive routine this may be due not only to the repetitive nature of the task but also to the restrictions upon our opportunity to comment simultaneously upon it. If others are not present during routines we receive no acknowledgement of the fact that we are not thoroughly committed to the task. In the face of contrary evidence, we may be regarded and come to regard ourselves as that which we do. With sympathetic others available, the task can readily be shown to be below our dignity, to be a source of humour, an opportunity to assert special competence, or demonstrate authority. An alternative to unreflective accommodation becomes as possible as it is desirable.

The relevance of the presence of others to a choice of orientation is particularly important in sex. Whilst unreflective accommodation may always be seen as appropriate in personal grooming, and sometimes regarded as acceptable at work, it is usually frowned upon in sexual interaction. Although we may occasionally fuck with no more self-consciousness than we employ when cleaning our teeth, we are likely to be called to account for such an attitude by our sexual partner. We are very much expected to cultivate our identity in sexual work. We must demonstrate manifestly that our activity is not automatic, that it is not something which is just done – 'like a machine' or 'like an animal' – but it is rather a chance to show our individuality.

Within each area of human activity then there is an appropriate mode of mental management for coping with times when a sense of regularity invades our mind. On some occasions we may be confused about the best mode to use: many situations call for rapid and demanding cognitive engineering. At a cocktail party, for example, a sense of monotony and regularity may quickly invade our minds. Self-distancing provides us with no escape from the situation. This is such a familiar technique on these occasions, that its use may actually show predictability rather than self-expressiveness. To comment cynically upon the ways in which people who do not really like each other contrive to talk charmingly is to risk being regarded as boorish, it demonstrates our under-familiarity with the situation rather than transcendence of it. Resort to meta-consciousness may therefore be required, a stance which declares that we are above making comments about the artificiality of the situation. In the event of such meta-consciousness itself being undermined as a source of identity by its adoption by a number of guests, then recourse may be had to reinvestment, in which we now move about the room as though engaged in the unreflective routine performance of an everyday task.

The story is told of the guest who approached the hostess at just such a party: 'I find the whole situation absurd, no one seems to realize the silliness, the grotesque artificiality of their behaviour.' 'Ah,' said the hostess, 'you must join the sociologists in the far corner. The rest of us realized all that long ago but decided to ignore it and enjoy the party.'

3

The Nightmare
of Repetition

The mental management of routines, however existentially consoling, leaves the world unchanged and unchallenged. Our daily life retains its behavioural shape for all our mental juggling. We may still live in the same house with the same woman and retain the same job and the same mistress; the only change is in the way house, mistress, job or wife are now regarded. The mistress who was once the object of self-consciously declared mature love, may now be routinely regarded as a sexual object; the job once considered to be an important task in which one should be uncritically involved, now an object for cynical derision, whilst at home there has been a reinvestment in marriage.

These switches in orientation may not always be enough. We may even see through them, recognizing that we are still in paramount reality, still prisoners of routine. We may consider there is a degree of self-delusion in our 'mental escapes'. The obvious solution is to change the situation which we have come to view in this way. We can abandon our wife or husband and seek a new partner, quit our job, get the boat to Australia, fundamentally change our leisure pursuits. What better way to fight the determinacy of the life plan, ensure a space for identity growth, than to shed old entanglements and pursue a new life?

Chasing Novelty

But although we have abandoned a dark-haired slim companion in favour of a squat blonde one, or have left the sugar works in order to take a job in the car factory, given up golf and squash for karate and ballroom dancing, exchanged Leicester for Sydney, nevertheless, we begin to get an uneasy sense that the novelty and freedom for which we searched, the absence from routine, is proving elusive. Something about the way our new companion walks, or uses the bathroom, or dances, reminds us of former routines. Something about the noise of machinery, the ways in which men talk to each other recalls our former job. The queue at the supermarket in the new city looks the same as in the old. Somehow, everything is not as new as promised. These moments may be short-lived, mere sensory coincidences which can be brushed aside, inevitable repetitions in a world which is imperfectly differentiated. But there are other times when the feeling overwhelms us, times when the whole validity of our escape route seems in doubt, times when a sudden sense of *déjà-vu* invades our minds. We have been here before, said the same words, felt the same way, experienced similar irritations, anxieties and ecstasies. We have not swung ourselves away from our former repetitions; here we are, firmly back on the roundabout.

The notion of *déjà-vu* has been typically reserved for the feeling of environmental coincidence, for the moments when we suddenly sense that we have already seen this particular conjunction of buildings, trees and fields. But although we may have a very similar feeling when we sit down to breakfast with our new wife, or push open the swing doors which lead into our new job, we are unlikely to talk to others of this as a *déjà-vu* experience. So great is the stress in our society upon development, upon the movement from the old to the new, that references to recurrent phenomenal features of social occasions are likely to arouse hostility within others. To turn to one's new wife and admit to a sense of *déjà-vu* would be incompatible with the societal notion that each 'falling in love' represents not merely an advance upon the previous emotional commitment, but also entry into an entirely novel set of routines and roles. If a sense of routine is a frequent theme in our expression of dissatisfaction with life, then the achievement of novelty is seen as a prerequisite of happiness. The movement is always forward. However many temporary setbacks may occur, the old is always being abandoned and the novel embraced. It is not surprising then that talk of the *déjà-vu* phenomenon is confined to environmental rather than social coincidences; landscapes and rooms may be allowed to stay still and resemble each other, but people and their relationships are supposed to go marching on. Feeling that we have been here before and saying it are very different matters.

The idea that 'forward' movement and involvement in 'new relationships' is a guarantee of psychic health is fundamentally challenged by the psychoanalytic notion of repetition-compulsion. Here, the 'untiring impulsion' towards change and perfection is regarded as evidence of neurosis rather than health. Instead of a restless quest for novelty, a striving for something better or different in the future, men are told to content themselves with the pleasures to be obtained from simple repetition. They should, in other words, return to the condition of children who 'cannot have their *pleasurable* experiences repeated enough, and they are inexorable in their insistence that the repetition shall be an identical one'.[1] All this in contrast to the adult where 'novelty is always the condition of enjoyment'.

The argument here is that man's attempt to escape from repetition towards novelty is explicable in terms of his repression. As long as man is repressed, his search for instinctual satisfaction will inevitably be futile. Although he believes himself to be moving forward, he remains locked to the past by the permanent burden of repression that he carries with him.

Under conditions of repression, the repetition-compulsion establishes a fixation to the past, which alienates the neurotic from the present and commits him to the unconscious quest for the past in the future. Thus neurosis exhibits the quest for novelty, but underlying it, at the level of the instincts, is the compulsion to repeat. In man, the neurotic animal, the instinctual compulsion to repeat turns into its opposite, the quest for novelty, and the unconscious aim of the quest for novelty is repetition.[2]

This perspective places the idea of repetition at the centre of human life, but it is hardly likely to be invoked by the individual as he encounters changing scenes and relationships. It is the perspective of the external theorizer whose knowledge of human nature allows him to cast an ironic eye upon man's futile search for novelty and progress, equivalent to the sociologist's detection of routine in all areas of life. The search for novelty may have neurotic undertones, but for people in our society it is often the only way to put themselves ahead of reality, to absent themselves from mindless involvement in routine. It may be culturally unacceptable, or at least socially embarrassing to talk of repetitive experiences, but nevertheless they are still an ever-present challenge to our ongoing symbolic construction of present and future reality. Sometimes it is reassuring to be able to reply, 'Much the same,' to those who ask us how things are going. But a sense of repetition can grow and induce depression. It can even become the dominant feature of our lives; the sense of the repetitive may invade paramount reality so profoundly that we are unable to engage in any action whatsoever for fear that it will merely bring us nearer to an act of repetition. A character in Doris Lessing's novel *A Proper Marriage* is in the grip of this private nightmare:

She could not meet a young man or woman without looking around anxiously for the father and mother: that was how they would end, there was no escape for them. She could not meet an elderly person without wondering what the unalterable influences had been that had created them just so. She could take no step, perform no action, no matter how apparently new and unforseen without the secret fear that in fact this new and arbitrary thing would turn out to be part of the inevitable process she was doomed to. She was, in short, in the grip of the great bourgeois monster, the nightmare repetition.[3]

Scripts

Why *do* we have this sense of similarity – what is it about situations or episodes which allows them, however temporarily, to take on a phenomenal unity? Let us go back to the ways in which roles and routines are organized into coherent entities in the social world. We hardly need sociologists to tell us that we play many characters in life, that we alternate between being father, businessman, socialite and adulterer. But too often these roles are presented by the theorists as performances to be simply laid alongside other performances. So we are provided with analyses of the relationship between father and mother, mother and son, businessman and client, which describe the ways in which the regularities associated with each characterization are integrated with each other.

However, this is equivalent to describing the story of Hamlet by listing the responsibilities that the characters have towards each other. It tells us nothing of the feelings of the characters, of the actual plot of the drama, its twists and turns and eventual denouement. Our lives are not lived out by simply playing sets of roles; these roles are located within a series of minor and major dramas. These we will call *scripts* – and it is the sheer fact of their ubiquity, coupled with their finite number which is the source of our sense of repetition when we seek out novelty. Scripts provide our routines and roles with meaning and significance, tell us how we should be acting and feeling at any particular moment, provide us with details of others whom we encounter in the situation and forecast the next move in the game, the next development in the play. The script 'defines the situation, names the actors and plots the behaviour'.[4]

Now for many parts of our daily life, the situation may appear unscripted. Our journey to work, for example, does not involve any necessity to name actors or plot behaviour. However, as soon as we come into contact with others in those spheres of our life which we consider as 'projects', 'key areas', 'where we live', 'life plans' – areas of home, sex, work, leisure, politics – then we are more likely to enter into miniature dramas where defining, naming and plotting are at a premium.

In some cases these dramas are hardly discernible within everyday life; they may appear like natural transactions. But as Eric Berne and others have pointed out there is frequently a plot to such routine interactions.[5] For example he describes what he calls the 'game' of Rapo, in which an individual, usually a female, gives out strong cooperative messages which indicate that she is interested in sexual interaction. The man who has been selected for this attention will soon indicate his interest and begin to commit his attention to the project. Suddenly the woman displays alarm and shock that the man should have behaved in such a manner. He has misunderstood her intentions and thereby shown his animal or sub-human nature. She contemptuously rejects him whilst the man apologizes. Berne is interested in the plot of this story because he detects within it some possible degree of collaboration between the partners, an implicit pact which is made between two people, neither of whom want sex, but are unable to make the point in any other way, or indeed to realize that this is the point they wish to make.

We are not so much interested in crossed transactions and their interpretations but rather in the idea that plots can be detected in the most common situations. At times these may be no more than episodes or rituals – the good night kiss, the last waltz, the family meal – but in each case we may detect a number of elements which demand more than a simple description of the behaviour. A strict sequence is maintained in these episodes as it is in Berne's game. Certain members of the group initiate activity and others respond; the female says come on in Rapo, the man leads in the last waltz, father carves and mother passes the plates round during the meal. As the episode proceeds so certain emotions become appropriate, the family at dinner indicate contentment following the meal, the girl becomes more languidly involved with the music as the waltz proceeds, the woman in Rapo suddenly becomes outraged. Emotions are orchestrated for each move in the sequence and for the characters who make them.

A script description of a family meal would go well beyond listing the characters who are present, the food which is eaten, the words which are spoken. It would refer to the notion of what a family meal should be like, a notion which is sensed if not articulated by all those present, a notion which simultaneously allows one to understand the roles which are played, the emotions which are expressed and the way these are orchestrated. If the script is more or less successfully followed, then the episode feels right. It feels right precisely because we have experienced it in the same way before. It is an example of a repetition which demands no comment for no novelty was expected or desired. Indeed any novel or unexpected element in the script can be a source of anxiety.

However, it is when we enter a situation to search for novelty and then encounter a sense of familiarity that the nightmare of repetition looms. The sense of *déjà-vu* – of repetition – which invades our consciousness at these moments derives from script recognition, from seeing that although the cast has been changed, the scenery reconstructed, and the properties refashioned, that nevertheless the situation, the plot and the parts played by the actors are fundamentally the same. The fit is not between concrete persons and events but between our symbolic comprehensions of such matters. The frequency with which such script recognition occurs is evidence not of an inner psychic compulsion to repetition but of the limited number of scripts our society provides.

There are, for example, only a limited number

of sexual scripts. As with other scripts, we may find that all of these are known about quite self-consciously by some members of society, but that others may know only one script, and regard that one as 'natural', 'the only way to behave'. The 'noble savage' script, for example, is one in which a large range of situations may be defined as sexual, in which one actor plays hero and another plays passive victim. The script goes wrong if the hero cannot proceed quickly to orgasm, or if he verbalizes any interest in the other person's feelings. The action is vigorous throughout and orgasm is reached rather like the finishing line at the end of a cross-country chase. After orgasm, that is the end of the matter. The script stops there. The sexual situation is over. Notice that the script does not just define the behaviour. It is not that one goes in for different anatomical stances during the noble-savage script, but that one becomes a brute, acts like a brute, and gets one's physical response from reflecting upon oneself as a brute.

Even such an apparently simple script as the one that we have described above involves detailed learning. As Gagnon and Simon observe: 'Scripts are involved in learning the meaning of internal states, organising the sequence of specifically sexual acts, decoding novel situations, setting the limits on sexual responses and linking meanings from non-sexual experience.'[6] There are no 'natural' sexual feelings, or 'natural' sexual situations, or indeed 'natural' sex behaviour. People who use such peculiar words as 'natural' in this context, reveal only their ignorance of alternative arrangements.

Neither are there natural domestic feelings which simply pop out as we sit by the fireside with Ovaltine and television, or natural occupational or leisure sentiments which are inevitably elicited by particular situations. In learning our lines for the varieties of dramas in which we appear we have to learn exactly how we should be feeling within a specific situation and at a certain point in the development of the plot. For in any social situation, an analysis of one's emotional state has high priority. 'Am I happy?', 'Do I feel sad?' are typical questions that we ask ourselves. But in fact we are really asking 'Should I be feeling happy?', 'Should I be feeling sad?'. This cannot be determined by an examination of some inner visceral state but only by reference to the script in which one is immersed. The full question becomes – 'Given that I am at this stage in the script, and playing this character, then how should I be feeling?'

No situation elicits totally novel feelings. We cannot simply have new experiences; it's not possible to suddenly become a marijuana user, any more than it's possible to suddenly fall in love, or become a mystic. These experiences demand not simply a new set of techniques which can be learned rather as one learns to drive a car, but also a new sense of ourself as a character in a different drama, an appreciation of the plot of this new drama, an ability to name internal states as 'high' or 'ecstatic' or 'sexy' depending upon the stage of the event-sequence, a competence at orchestrating all these matters with the feelings and meanings of others who are present, and the ability to bring the experience to a recognizably successful conclusion.

There are certain ways of using drugs, falling in love, looking after the children, having days in the country, nights out on the town, and being mystical which are incorporated into mass culture. These constitute the master scripts to which all other occupational, leisure, romantic, domestic scripts must attend. This is not to say that we necessarily *follow* these scripts. What we are describing is our potential for becoming aware of them, a potential which exists because of their general availability in our society. In many cases we may consciously construct scripts against such master scripts, actively announcing our disenchantment with the customary plots and characters. We may, for example, tell those around us that when we fall in love we will not go in for all that moon in June nonsense. However, as we shall see, the counterscript which is constructed as a result of that determination draws its character from the master script.

The devices we use to distance ourselves from

that master script – jokes, irony and exaggeration – only provide further evidence of its salience. Just as habit and routine followed us into areas which we thought to be 'free' and 'indeterminate', so then do scripts intrude into the most meaningful and personal parts of our experience. Emotions and meanings, relationships and experiences, conversations and conversions, are not free-floating ingredients which can be mixed anew by every individual in his search for novelty; they are rather embedded within finite sets of symbolic frameworks whose elusive shape may at first seduce us with the promise of novelty. But the illusion is often temporary. The distinctiveness of the new world disappears. It was after all only part of the mainland.

I used to imagine life divided into separate compartments, consisting, for example, of such dual abstractions as pleasure and pain, love and hate, friendship and enmity; and more material classifications like work and play ... That illusion, as such a point of view was, in due course to appear – was closely related to another belief: that existence fans out indefinitely into new areas of experience, and that almost every additional acquaintance offers some supplementary world with its own hazards and enchantments. As time goes on, of course, these supposedly different worlds, in fact, draw closer, if not to each other, then to some pattern common to all; so that at last diversity between them, if in truth existent, seems to be almost imperceptible except in a few crude and exterior ways: unthinkable as formerly appeared, any single consummation of cause and effect. In other words, nearly all the inhabitants of these outwardly disconnected empires turn out at last to be tenaciously interrelated; love and hate, friendship and enmity, too, becoming themselves much less clearly defined, more often than not showing signs of possessing characteristics that could claim, to say the least, not a little in common; while work and play merge indistinguishably into a complex tissue of pleasure and tedium.[7]

Script Origins

We have so far referred in a rather cavalier way to 'external models', 'master metaphors' and 'master scripts' from which domestic, sexual, occupational, leisure and life scripts are derived. We must now be more specific. What is the source of these scripts?

The most obvious progenitor is popular culture. In any single day we absorb countless dramas all with carefully delineated characters, plots and climaxes. Some of these models are explicit. The strip cartoons in the morning paper, the magazine stories in the weekly journal, the novel we consume at lunchtime, the short story in the evening paper, the thrillers and comedies which occupy our evening viewing, all present a structured sequence of events relating to home, sex, work and leisure.

Apart from these dramas in which plots and characters and denouements are explicit components there are the multitude of dramas which are daily presented to us by news-broadcasting, by astrological columns, by advertising. Sociologists have done much to uncover the heroes and plots of these particular dramas, showing how even the most straightforward of news stories contain distinguishable characters who perform in predictable ways with determinate consequences. And although sociologists may be needed to demonstrate the presence of scripts in such materials, there can be little doubt that they are often experienced as dramas even by those who could not explicitly describe their theatrical components. Sometimes we may even feel that what is happening to us is just like a newspaper story or a television commercial, but even when that feeling is not present, the model still reinforces our tendency to bind sentiments and activities together in a dramatic way.

The presence of so many scripts has a double impact. Not only does the universal existence of this dramatic form influence the ways in which we organize our daily events but the actual plots themselves become adopted as the specific templates to which the events of everyday life are referred.

Families start behaving like the Garnetts, marriages take on the *Who's Afraid of Virginia Woolf?* script, a generation of adolescents seem to behave like Holden Caulfield in *Catcher in the Rye*, some women appear to strike poses extraordinarily like Anna Karenina, Madame Bovary and Hedda Gabler, middle-class intellectual males start acting like Herzog. So familiar in fact has the actualization of fictional scripts become that comments about this become commonplace – 'Are you going to do your Madame Bovary scene again?' – and indeed has become in a meta-meta-way an art form in itself. We have John Barth's characters continually feeling that they are characters from other peoples' novels, and movies about men who live their lives along Humphrey Bogart scripts. Such models increase the dangers of *déjà-vu*: we have been there before only the 'there' is something that has happened in a movie. The experience of 'familiar reality' for the man who wakes up in his lover's bed, is brought a cup of coffee, goes to the bathroom to shave in front of a cracked mirror occurs not just because it's happened before – perhaps it hasn't – but because he's heard Dory Previn's song about it.

In many ways our notion of scripts is close to Kenneth Burke's 'dramatistic pentad' – act, scene, agent, agency and purpose – for all of these elements are certainly fundamentals of every script.[8] Burke found these elements in all the basic forms of thought through which men experience the world: 'in elaborated metaphysical structures, in legal judgement, in poetry and fiction, in political and scientific works, in news and in bits of gossip offered at random.' Our interest is more concrete and individualized. We are concerned with those occasions in which an individual consciously apprehends dramatic qualities, when he senses that the symbolic relationship between act, scene, agent, agency and purpose is something that he has experienced before, whether in dreams, or in the past, or in some external cultural source.

Script Awareness

There are times when we become highly aware of the dramatic construction of certain important areas of our life, times when we draw a proscenium arch around a set of routine behaviours, casting them into a dramatic form.

There are certain aspects of life which may appear scripted to all people. It is difficult for example for participants in weddings, funerals and honeymoons to ignore the dramatic quality of the occasion, the sense that the scene is being 'acted' rather than simply occurring. But it is also possible to recognize the bounded dramatic quality of far more 'natural' events such as job interviews, domestic life, courtship, days out in the country. Some people, because of their position in relation to these events, may be more likely to sense their scripted nature than others:

The theatrical quality of life, taken for granted by nearly everyone, seems to be experienced most concretely by those who feel themselves on the margin of events either because they have adopted the role of spectator or because, though present, they have not yet been offered a part or have not learnt it sufficiently well to enable them to join the actors.[9]

We recently tested the everyday ability to become script-aware by using a questionnaire prepared by Eric Berne in which people were asked, 'If your family were placed on the stage what type of play would it be?' There was little difficulty in dealing with this imaginative problem. A variety of standard responses were quickly produced – 'A horror movie', 'a domestic comedy', 'a farce', 'a kitchen-sink drama', 'a bloody tragedy', 'a comedy of manners', 'theatre of the absurd'. It seems that many of us are able to cast complex sets of relationships and behaviour into a theatrical convention; we recognize that it is possible to see life as a series of dramas, each with its set of characters and its typical script.

We should not be surprised at this ability to describe domestic life in dramatic forms. For such models are not merely abstract ideas, they are actually referred to during the daily round of family life. Members of the family behave with reference to scripts which always reach out beyond the individual situation. Their 'borrowed' component aids their very enactment and enhances their significance. The man in his noble-savage script is away from his semi-detached house and out with Steve McQueen screwing all the women of the world, the mutually tender lovers have drifted away from their bed into a great pantheistic ball with the earth and sea and sky. Meanwhile mother and father and children sit down in the sunlight to their early morning breakfast – the start of a Kelloggs's happy family day – whilst upstairs their adolescent son prepares for the morning by adjusting his Holden Caulfield face in the mirror. The existence of so many cultural models enables an increasing number of everyday experiences to be given this symbolic elevation. In each case the external models may only be improperly realized; a slight defect in the setting, an inappropriate line, a failure by one member to recognize the way the plot develops, can disrupt the scene – with comic or tragic consequences. But then it does not matter to our argument whether or not a script is ever enacted in its perfect form. The point is that the pervasiveness of scripts means that those engaged in interaction have frequently to take account of them.

As long as we embrace repetition unquestioningly, then our occasional sense of enacting a familiar script will not be problematic. It may even be embraced for the symbolic heightening of experience which it provides. However, it is when we seek for change, when we select new partners and circumstances in our quest for novelty, and yet are still confronted by a sense of repetition, that we become anxious about this persistent element of regularity in our lives, this form of symbolic organization which places the stranglehold of the past around that which was to be our new future. Suddenly 'spontaneity' and 'originality' begin to appear unobtainable. They are not simply options which we have previously declined to exercise.

So, whilst the presence of models outside the setting always provides a chance for elevation of routine experience and so looks like an escape from routine, at the same time, their very insidiousness threatens the novel status of situations which have been constructed by individuals anxious to escape from customary arrangements.

Managing the Script

However much we may switch our sexual partners, our jobs, our hobbies, our favourite holiday spots, we may still be faced by the intrusion of former scripts. These on the whole will just refer to single areas of our life: the novelty of a new wife may be undermined by the sense of repetition which arises from finding that the scripts for domestic, leisure or sexual interactions are still the same. But at times all areas of life, no matter how we may switch the internal components, remain at the mercy of what Berne has called the life script – that script which contains not just stage directions for sex, work and leisure, but for the whole development of our personality. Existing models such as marginal Jewish intellectual or lapsed Catholic sinner may infiltrate individuals' lives to such an extent that no amount of role-switching or routine-substitution does anything to reduce the feeling that this path, for all its situational and behavioural unfamiliarity, has been trodden many times before.

The recognition of familiar dramatic patterns in that which we had optimistically hoped would constitute a novel experience need not, however, produce inevitable disenchantment with the project in hand. Scripts like routines are amenable to mental management. If what at first appears natural is now imbued with a sense of *déjà-vu*, novelty can still be attempted, the world held at bay, and identity work renewed, by a shift in the mode or orientation to the ongoing drama. We can return to the falling-in-love script for an example.

Here the sequence of behaviour, the meaning attributed to internal states, may be quite finely orchestrated with reference to widely known cultural models. But despite the popularity of the script and therefore the massive availability of scenes and properties which will help to sustain it (lovers' lane, moonlight, fast cars, soft music) there are still strong pressures to regard the script as unique. We are expected to be 'naturally' in love, and also to be somehow the only ones who are really in love. However, whilst this routine unreflective and committed style may be culturally approved for the first run-through of the script and indeed may be abided by, even if with some difficulty, it will be less readily sustained during the second performance. For the falling-in-love script is so saturated with notions of uniqueness and novelty, that even partners playing it for the second or third time are still called upon to demonstrate the presence of something entirely new. Paradoxically for so 'natural' an area, this novelty may be attempted by the introduction of a degree of self-consciousness. The behaviour does not differ greatly but the participants declare this to be different from the previously played script by their mutual ability to speak some of the lines in a distancing manner. When the moment comes for a declaration of love, for example, the man may ironically go down on one knee, or affect a Charles Boyer accent. The declaration is still being made, and may be accepted as having been made, but the couple have a sense that they have somehow evaded the stilted conventionality of 'falling-in-love' scripts, where such matters are handled with displays of hesitation, embarrassment, and commitment.

The third style of mental management might be introduced when the self-conscious playing of the 'falling-in-love' script has in turn lost its own novelty. Thus we may find middle-aged partners who, after several self-reflective 'falling-in-love' performances, will now abandon such an ironic stance and declare that such self-consciousness reduces the true nature of the experience. Instead they will suspend disbelief, say the lines as though they meant them, look forward quite happily to the wedding ceremony, and even accept tasteless wedding presents without demur.

It is considerably more difficult mentally to manage scripts than routines, although the techniques are similar. For scripts as we have said, refer to key areas of our life, to 'where we live', whereas routines may more readily be marked off as the necessary flotsam of everyday existence, as things to be done before the 'real living' can begin.

It is not difficult to adopt distancing techniques toward such matters as travelling to the office, or working on the conveyor belt, for such routines are not regarded as natural or as necessary to our self-realization, as sites for identity, our development as a person. However, the opposite is true in the case of scripts; their mental management involves the need to introduce a sense that 'things could be otherwise' into settings which have often felt most natural, most self-expressive. Additionally it demands that we become conscious not just of the patterned qualities of a set of activities (as in the mental management of routines) but also of the symbolic network which holds those activities together, and of alternative scripts which are every bit as culturally saturated as the one to which we adhere at the moment.

The transcendence of dramatic sequences (the good night kiss) or simple social dramas (the family dinner) by mental management is relatively simple as long as these miniature scripts are seen as self-contained. In this sense, to escape from the nightmare of repetition which scripts induce, is always possible. But they seldom are self-contained and moveover the individual realizes that – just as his role-distancing was patterned and routine – so does his script management occur in highly predictable ways. The marginal Jewish intellectual, for example, will suitably manage the tasteless Christmas ceremonies which his more integrated children demand, but how does he get out of the marginal-Jewish-intellectual script? He is helped, naturally, by relativizing this life script, but no amount of reading of Roth, Bellow and Richler will work unless he can find a new script that leads him out of his present cycle of repetition.

Let us construct a familiar scene in order to show the management of scripts at work. We are drinking in a pub on Saturday night. A friend enters and scripts the scene for us. 'Ah, Saturday night out with the boys.' We counter by showing we can distance ourselves from that classification. We escape one script by our awareness of another, 'Not at all, just drowning our sorrows in drink.' On this occasion our friend is unhappy to allow us such a script, 'More like two middle-aged sociologists playing at meeting the natives.' In circumstances where we could not name other scripts in which our behaviour might be placed, we would be left with the alternative of either accepting the newcomer's dramatic framing, or denying that there was anything scripted about the situation at all. 'We just dropped in for a quick pint on the way home.' In other words, our actions have no particular significance and are therefore unsuitable for any of the preferred symbolic frameworks. They are just routines.

We need to recapitulate. We have so far in this chapter been concerned to add to the density of social life. Whereas in Chapter 2 we trapped man within his routines and roles – only allowing him to wriggle free for brief moments by recourse to different modes of subjective orientation – in this chapter we have locked him into an even more elaborate maze by showing that even the abandonment of particular roles and routines does not enable him to spring the trap. A sense of *déjà-vu* can always invade his novel circumstances, and that which was spontaneous becomes only a variant on an old theme; the new partner begins to speak familiar lines, and the acts unroll predictably. Again our beleagured individual wriggles. As his awareness of the script increases, so does he strike different attitudes towards it in order to demonstrate his freedom.

Evading and Switching the Script

Fortunately the nature of scripts creates the possibility for more escape devices than was the case with routine. We cannot, for example, readily change our habits and routines by reordering them. It would make little sense to try to escape routine by walking to work backwards, by opening your morning mail in the evening, or by saying 'good morning' to everyone at work as you leave. (We should however credit Luke Rhinehart's Dice Man – one of the heroes of our book – with having tried, in his 'National Habit-Breaking Week', these and other escapes: pissing in flowerpots instead of lavatories, jogging backwards to work, trying to fuck his wife *under* the bed.)

Matters are different with scripts. Participants who know all the lines in the drama back to front, may take licence with the play, acting it in a variety of styles, substituting lines and switching characters. Causal sequences may be reversed: we may start a 'falling-in-love' script by proposing marriage, even though the acquaintanceship is only a few seconds old. Character reversal may occur, as during a sexual script when the female climbs on the man and behaves as though having a masculine orgasm. Elements from other scripts may be briefly introduced, as when a marijuana smoker passes the joint around in mock imitation of drinks at a bottle party, or lovers play briefly at doctors and nurses or little children. Such improvisations occur within master scripts, partners return to the basic plot after the symbolic excursion, satisfied with the demonstration that their falling-in-love, sexual intercourse, or marijuana smoking, is more than the determined activity which they assume it to be for large numbers of others.

Within this type of script manipulation there is considerable opportunity for the participants to demonstrate several varieties of self-consciousness about the project-in-hand. They do not simply indicate that they can monitor their own performance of the script, but also display a variety of styles in that monitoring. So, for example, participants may agree to approach the situation ironically, sarcastically, or with cynicism.

It is not infrequent to encounter cynical or ironic subcultures at parties or ceremonies. Members of these groups will indicate to each other during the evening that they are playing with the script. Excessive politeness

may be shown, or banal conversation deliberately cultivated. After the scene is over, members of the subculture
will retire to another setting for a brief conversational
celebration of their script-awareness. Matters are often
more subtly handled; the irony more difficult to detect and
only existing to provide an individual character with reassurance about the uniqueness of his involvement within
the familiar script. In other cases characters will 'play
blank', giving indications in perfectly familiar situations
that 'they do not know what to do next', and relying upon
their partner for prompting.

Script switching is an alternative device for
assembling a sense of originality in conventional situations.
It is a way in which new emotional colouring can be
grafted onto traditional arrangements, novelty reasserted
in face of repetition. Such switching may serve, for example, an erotic function, as in the practice recommended by
marriage manuals to reinvigorate a jaded sex life. Husband
and wife are told to enjoy a formal evening out in town
with theatre and dinner and then instead of returning
home, book into a sordid hotel for an evening of prostitute
and client. Everything will be geared to emphasizing the
juxtaposition – the hotel may be selected for its contextual-
ly absurd name or location (Mon Repos Guest House,
Clapham), the wife may remove her wedding ring, false
names may be adopted for the hotel register. The problem
with such script juxtaposition is that it may lead to
anxiety about the status of the different scripts. The hotel
example may work well enough as long as it does not
impel the woman so wholly into the prostitute script that
such features of the married-sex script as mutual understanding and tenderness are no longer tenable. Playing at
prostitute and client is fine just as long as at the end of it
the man does not pull on his trousers and walk out into the
night.

On other occasions, script switching may introduce comical, even hysterical toning into normal practices.
A single element from an alien source may be enough to
trigger this 'holiday from script'. The wife sits at the

kitchen table about to begin the evening meal. Husband enters with a bottle of wine, walks round behind her, and in the manner of a wine waiter, proffers the bottle for inspection. An invitation has been issued to a script evasion. If taken up (and of course it may often be refused – 'Don't be silly Michael, sit down and pour it out'), it may incorporate any number of odd events. Objects may be transformed (baked beans into caviare) or used in incongruous ways (coal scuttles as violins, chairs as dancing partners), standard domestic roles reversed or mocked, special names invented.

Although the participants in these examples of script juxtaposition and switching may experience them as absurd, ludicrous, incongruous or 'out of character', nevertheless their novelty derives from the complex ways in which they juggle but at the same time maintain some of the essential elements from the parent script to which they are contrasted.

It's not surprising that these techniques occur to those who seek some escape from scripts. For script switching and juxtaposition are standard elements in so many of the dramatic models that we referred to in our discussion of the origins of scripts. Comedy routinely relies upon placing a character from one script in the middle of another; the bedraggled hippie in the cosy suburban parlour, the aggressive proletarian at a society ball, are visible reminders of the joyous experience of evading the script. And comedy, as psychoanalysts are fond of telling us, represents a temporary freedom from constraint, a sudden opportunity to 'break script'. But such whimsical, surrealist, bizarre moments are necessarily short-lived; they are fissures within the symbolic map of men's lives, breathing and laughing spaces which can only exist by courtesy of the symbolic boundaries which they ignore.

Freedom from Scripts

But most of our life is lived well within the boundaries. Those who set out to seek novelty encounter their persistent presence as soon as a sense of repetition begins to invade their consciousness. Even the script evasions draw their strength, their sense of surprise and excitement from the manipulation of enduring master scripts. They are not spontaneous and novel. They are common patterned practices which are resorted to after a history of standard scripted performances.

Nevertheless there are those in contemporary society who, despite, or perhaps because of, their awareness of the repetitiveness of life, still set out in search of spontaneity. Every day, so the escape promise goes, can be the beginning of a new adventure. There are a wide variety of religions, therapies and cults (examined in Chapters 5 and 6) which promise such a treasured commodity as a payoff to extended self-examination and an abandonment of old ways of living. But really all that such graduates display is their mastery of a spontaneous script.[10] They have learnt a series of cues which will help to facilitate particular script evasions, but ironically, it may be the case that their increased self-consciousness about the 'naturalness' of such behaviour reduces its escape qualities. In any case such spontaneity can only emerge against existing scripts. Those who choose to play at spontaneity all the time would presumably arrive one day at a stage where psychic variety might only be obtained by a quick bout of rigid adherence to a traditional script.

This might sound an excessively cynical line to take. It looks as if, not satisfied with the way in which routines and roles lock the person into the prison of paramount reality and act as an impediment to identity work, we are adding the script as a further barrier. But nowhere have we said that behaviour is *determined* by scripts. Quite the contrary, the script allows us to elevate routines, regularities and mere behavioural sequences in such a way that we can assert our superiority over the everyday world. To say that there are only a finite number of scripts is no more 'deterministic' than to say that at any one time an artist has only a limited range of forms, materials and techniques to employ for self-expression.

Nevertheless, the availability of a large range of scripts within our society creates a peculiar paradox for today's identity workers, for those who seek an assurance that they are somehow above mundane reality. For, on the one hand, the presence of these scripts provides an excellent opportunity for escape from routine life. We no longer fall in love, or have children, or succeed at work, like others around us, but may elevate our experiences by referring them to the master scripts created by films, novels, plays and superstars. And in so doing we may feel that we have not only removed ourselves from the banal conventions of our everyday setting, but have also effected an identity transformation. We have at least for a short time stepped outside the identity thrust on us by our life plan. But the paradox for those who elevate their experience by reference to master scripts is that strict acquiescence to such existing templates simultaneously induces a sense of the predictable. The scripts are available to others who seek similar transformations of identity and experience; they are a common cultural resource. Reality catches up with us: our unique identity development is threatened. The only way out is to invoke various modes of mental management, script switching and script juxtaposition. By juggling the elements of the script, we hope to persuade ourselves and others that we still remain in possession of a unique cultural package. Ironically we end up by feverishly distancing ourselves from that which we once embraced, pushing away the script with an even greater contempt than we typically show to habit and routine.

The script then is simultaneously a launching pad for identity work and a battleground on which to fight for a separate identity. Evading and distancing ourselves from each script or compulsively racing from one script to another, we confuse the temporal sequence of our voyages. To avoid the nightmare, the movement should really be backwards not forwards, to that still point of childhood where security is obtained from sameness and repetition.

4

The Inner Theatre
of the Mind

'I don't want realism, I want magic,' says
Blanche Dubois, in *A Streetcar Named Desire*. This
chapter is about magic, the mental magic of fantasy, and
about the ways in which it is an escape from reality and,
paradoxically, also a support for that reality. In real life as
well as fiction the notions of escape and resistance are most
explicitly used not for monitoring, distancing, self-
consciousness, script evasion or even the attempted movement into new scripts, but for such particular forms of
consciousness as daydreaming, imagining, fantasy, longing, wishing. For as we go through our routines, play our
roles, follow our scripts, there is always the possibility not
just of re-aligning the action to our sense of identity or
'real' self, but of introducing imagined elements into the
action, letting the mind drift elsewhere. In theory at least,
there can hardly be more radical a way of escaping the flywheel of habit and the nightmare of repetition than by
subverting realism altogether, by imagining that this world
of objects and consciousness is not really where life is.

The notion of escaping from reality through the use of fantasy does not only look radical but also looks a particularly accessible and easy way out. Why go through elaborate techniques of managing routine, time-consuming and precarious attempts at script switching or evasion if all one has to do is remain perfectly still, conjuring up in the mind the possibilities of an alternative and extravagantly different reality? For surely the mind is the last and only domain of privacy, an internal space quite safe from the intrusions of the vulgar world? Here we can go ahead, quietly busy at our identity work, conjuring up visions of ourselves, our wives, work, home, sexual prowess, physical attractiveness, talents, as completely different from what they 'really' are.

If we consider those whose contact with reality is so impoverished that they appear to have a greater need for fantasy than the rest of us, we can readily observe how potent an escape device it is. The world of the long-term prisoner for example is so circumscribed, so lacking in variety that he is permitted, indeed even expected to have some sort of fantasy world into which to retreat, some private unobserved place for identity work. (The most elaborate example of the construction of just such a fantasy world is provided by Genet: squalor, degradation and monotony are transformed into delights of orgasmic intensity and baroque complexity.)

Most prison fantasies are more mundane but equally effective in keeping reality at bay. The standard one is the straightforward leap-over-the-walls scenario. Prisoners have an enormous range of 'looking outside' fantasies; there are conventional styles of doing all right, like the swinger style (a straight job but high action in leisure), the playboy style (abundant wealth and contact with glamorous and promiscuous women), the rich-old-lady fantasy which involves capturing a wealthy woman and living the good life. There are marginal styles, such as kinky occupations, bohemian, student intellectual, expatriate, revolutionary. And there are full scale criminal styles – the big-score plan, the hustles.[1]

In prison it is easy to observe the expression and regulation of fantasies, primarily because other forms of escape – breaking routine, self-monitoring, script evasion – are extremely limited. Fantasy works at every level: to help time pass, to provide psychic excitement in situations with little perceptual variety, to keep sexual appetites alive. Even the looking-outside fantasies, although not in any direct sense realizable in the prison can allow at least some planning and rehearsal for another world. So the prisoner setting up the intellectual style can spend his time reading and studying and prisoners fantasying the expatriation style (building a boat and sailing it to the Caribbean) can make extensive preparations for its execution, studying navigation, boat design, perusing travel literature, dreaming of ocean sailing.

These mental rehearsals might not subvert prison reality – they might even be condoned by the authorities to keep the prisoner's mind off his immediate surroundings. Subversion only occurs when the fantasy is lived out: either by short-circuiting the gap between what is, and what is possible – you act out the escape fantasy and start digging the tunnel – or when like Genet you actually believe or act as if what is, is really something else. How do these relationships between fantasy and action obtain in the world outside prisons? Is fantasy primarily supportive or subversive of paramount reality?

Fantasy is Everywhere

The major obstacle to answering such questions is not the obvious one that the outside world is more complex than the laboratory-like situation of a security prison, but that there is a peculiar lack of acknowledgement by every man and his sociological observers alike that fantasy is indeed a salient feature of everyday life.

For although the content of fantasies may be the 'magic' that Blanche Dubois contrasted with realism, the ability to fantasize is not at all esoteric or reserved for such reality-impoverished groups as long-term prisoners.

Our lives are run through with fantasies: they invade our work-place, our kitchen table, our marriage bed. At any moment it is as though we can throw a switch inside our heads and effect some bizarre adjustment to the concrete world which faces us – make horses fly, strip the women, assassinate the bosses – or else conjure up an alternative reality which has apparently little connection with our present situation. Fantasies are always on the tip of our mind, about to enter consciousness. They squeeze themselves into all those moments of our lives when we are not fully engaged by the demands of the concrete world. They provide a continual possibility for the blurring and distortion of the clear predictable lines of paramount reality.

Not that one would realize all this from reading sociological texts. Their paramount reality is far too secular and rational, too concerned with the material goals and conventions associated with status, self approval and material advancement to allow any place for mere mental wonderings. We wish to reinsert the fantastic into the everyday so-called rational world. For although fantasies may often lack the coherence of organized religious beliefs and might only be markers towards an external reality rather than fully constructed maps of Heaven or Hell, they are still ominipresent 'inner worldly' and at the same time 'other worldly' realities which accompany and influence most aspects of our daily behaviour.

The resistance we have encountered to discussing fantasy seriously outside the prison situation has almost made us think that we are the only people in the world who can't get out of bed in the morning without a fantasy about what might drop through the letter box, who can get through boring meetings only be imagining that we are sitting in a Hollywood board room casting a ten-million-dollar epic, who walk around the streets conjuring up erotic possibilities from all conceivable stimuli. But we now know after years of drawing out our friends, students, and colleagues, that fantasy, perhaps under other names, is an ever-present thread in all lives. Even those whose lack of insight or whose romantic ideas about 'spontaneity' lead to emotional resistance to seeing their lives in terms of scripts admit to its significance in their personal lives – particularly if they include such experiences variously described as 'daydreams', 'reveries', 'brown studies', 'woolgathering', 'building castles in the air'. And we frequently enough talk of people 'drifting off into worlds of their own' or 'not quite being with us'. Consider a standard definition of daydreaming:

... the word is used to mean a shift of attention away from an ongoing physical or mental task or from a perceptual response to external stimulation towards a response to some internal stimulus. The inner processes usually considered are 'pictures in the mind's eye', the unrolling of a sequence of events, memories or creatively constructed images of future events of varying degrees of everyday occurrence.[2]

Those who have studied fantasies in such settings as prisons refer obviously not just to the actual perceptual shift from the task in hand – whether it be sewing mail bags or walking in the exercise yard – but the ways in which the 'picture in the mind's eye' conjures up another reality. For fantasy is more than imagination. It is not simply the representation in the mind of objects not present but a representation which may be so 'out of this world' as to be incompatible with paramount reality. It directs the flow of imagination and conjures up territories in an alternative world. It is not just a matter of monitoring or distancing but of projecting the activity or the self into something quite different.

Here are some trivial examples from outside the prison: the child dawdling at his dinner heard softly imitating the sounds of Indian war whoops and pioneer gunfire; the executive contemplating a forthcoming romantic rendezvous while reading over profit and loss statements; the harried housewife who while stirring the soup sees herself as a member of royalty at a gala affair.

Each of these daydreams or conscious fantasies is of a slightly different kind: the child is somehow *pretending* to be an Indian warrior, the executive is *mentally*

rehearsing a script which he has reasonable hopes of finding himself in, the housewife is *indulging* in what we
would see as highly 'unrealistic', in the sense of unrealizable, fantasy. All of these interfere with involvement
in reality. They are relatively incoherent reveries, streams
of association, internal monologues, and are all evoked by
particular situations.

For the infant most of activity has a play and
almost dream-like quality. For the older child fantasy
might be diversion from domestic routine or transformations of this routine: playing with toy boats in the bath,
dressing up for dinner, inventing an imaginary playmate.
Gradually the world of fairy tales, adventure stories,
romances, pop heroes gives fantasy a richer quality: we
can deliberately act as if we are someone quite different.
Very little is needed to trigger off this type of fantasy, and
once the images get going, they can be of a totally absorb-
ing or even obsessional kind: the fourteen-year-old who
plays out for five days against a chalked wicket on a back
wall every minute of an international cricket match; the
sixteen-year-old girl who surrounds herself with and even
takes on the props of her favourite film or pop star. They
may grow into more elaborate structures, like the classic
heroic fantasy of the Walter Mitty type, a fantasy world
with such coherence and density that it continually
threatened to prevent Walter from actually operating in
the real world at all.

Some private fantasies – for example sexual –
are highly esoteric and assembled in idiosyncratic ways by
the individual. But the stock of most fantasies is drawn
from patterned cultural themes or even – if we are to
believe Jungian psychologists – from an archetypal collective unconscious. The fact that one's private fantasies are
shared with others might surprise or even shock. 'Exposure of private fantasies is painful not only because it
reveals inner dynamic trends ordinarily concealed but also
because it exposes the soap-opera, cliché-ridden quality
of much thought.'[3] The standardized, even cyclical nature
of the soap opera of one individual's life fantasies is shown

beautifully by Luke Rhinehart. We summarize the Rhinehart Power Pattern for Men, the predictable pattern of the
average American male's fantasies from childhood to
death:

Daydreams begin sometimes in the child's first
decade, usually around the age of eight or nine. At this age the
boy inevitably projects himself in terms of raw power. Frequently he is faster than a speeding bullet, more powerful than a locomotive and can leap buildings at a single bound. He becomes
the Genghis Khan of the fourth grade, the Attila the Hun of the
local shopping center, the General George Patton of Cub Scout
Local 216. His parents are being tortured to death in a horribly
creative way . . .

By the age of thirteen the scene has usually shifted
to Yankee Stadium, where the boy, playing for the hopeless
Yankees, with the bases loaded, two outs and his team trailing
by three runs in the last half of the ninth innings in the seventh
game of the World Series, manages to stroke a 495-foot drive
off the highest part of the fence in right center field and, with a
fantastic flash around the bases and an impossible headfirst
slide, just touches home plate with the extended uncut finger-
nail of his left pinky . . .

In the world of sport, girls are absent, but by the
age of sixteen or seventeen the stroke of a baseball has been replaced by other strokes, and the only ones intercepting passes
are female. The boy has become a man, and the man is com-
mander-in-chief of a harem. Here things go on beyond the
wildest imagination of anyone – except that of the boy doing the
dreaming. A woman, panting helplessly, flings her nude body
onto the hero, who, puffing nonchantly on a Corsican cigarette
and tastefully sipping a glass of rare New York State wine, and
steering his Aston-Martin at 165 miles per hour down a rarely
used road in the Alps, manages to give the girl the most exciting
love experience of her life . . .

But by the age of twenty-one our male is either engaged, married or sated; the world he wants to rule is a new
world – he has become Horatio Alger. With grim determination
and uncanny acuity he invests fifty-six dollars in the stock
market and after buying and selling with cool nonchalance over
a period of six months, finally sells out, pocketing a cool
$4,862,927.33. When the Board of General Motors is panicked

by the threat of disarmament he calmly presents his invention of an inexpensive jet sportscar built in the shape of a Polaris missile and getting fifty miles per gallon of jet fuel. In three weeks he is on the covers of *Time, Fortune* and *Success*!

But in the next few years he is earning a modest salary as second clerk at Pierce, Perkins and Poof and is upset at the injustice and hypocrisy that exist in the world: a world in which some men are athletic stars, James Bonds, and millionaires and he is not; he is morally appalled. In his dreams he recreates the world, righting all wrongs, eliminating suffering, redistributing wealth, redistributing women, ending all wars. He becomes a reincarnation of Gautama Buddha, Jesus Christ and Hugh Hefner. Evil governments topple, corrupt churches collapse, laws are revised, and Truth, written in Xeroxed tablets of stone by our hero, is presented to the world. Everyone is happy.

Except our hero, whose income continues to be modest. At the age of twenty-five he has reached the first apex of the Rhinehart Power Pattern for Men: the dream of reforming the world. By the age of twenty-eight or -nine regression has begun . . .

At the age of forty-one it is complete; the male, once again dreams of conquering the world. The accumulated bitterness of the years asserts itself, he becomes as fast as a speeding bullet, as powerful as a locomotive and can leap buildings with three powerful strides. He becomes a General Curtis LeMay and bombs China back into the Stone Age. He becomes a Spiro Agnew and puts the blacks and hippies and liberals firmly in their places. His wife and children are being tortured to death in some horribly creative way . . .[4]

We are not suggesting that there is a statistically average fantasy sequence like this in any population. What is clear though is that it is difficult to talk meaningfully of there being such an ideational element as an individual fantasy. There is rather a common stock of symbolic material out of which all our fantasies are fashioned. Even when the fantasies are not as grounded as some of Rhinehart's American male power patterns, even when tigers speak, people fly, planets explode, buildings topple, these are not specialized experiences. Fantasies may break down standard everyday beliefs about the defining characteristics of everyday objects, about the ubiquity of cause and consequence, about the constraints of time and space, nevertheless they directly exhibit affinities both of structure and content with aspects of a world which has been recorded for centuries by writers, poets and artists. The world of fantasies has a vocabulary and grammar as certainly as the world of material objects and events.

The Expression and Regulation of Fantasy

Despite the ubiquity of fantasy there are strong social taboos upon the reporting of individual fantasies, a fact which ensures that this private world remains largely private. However, there are public occasions upon which a certain release of elements from that inner life take place. This occurs when we are placed in a situation with others and made aware of an element of their fantastic life, which has affinity with our own. The common nature of the experience provides a licence for private revelations; at such moments the shared nature of fantasy life is manifested. We recognize a degree of intersubjectivity which is lacking in conversations concerned with the manipulation of objects and events in the 'real' world. This intersubjective expression may demolish the fantasy (we have often been grieved to discover that somebody whom we thought extremely boring shares our same unique fantasy down to the last detail) – or else reinforce it, by the realization that our shamefully sordid fantasies are after all acceptable.

Fantasy chains may emerge in a group when suddenly everyone begins to talk at once; there is a marked surge of excitement and a rapid escalation of ideas. Then suddenly the moment is passed. The chain of fantasy has been allowed to go far enough. The members of the group have felt a sudden moment of intersubjectivity as they enjoyed awareness of the way in which others could share in that which was formerly personal to themselves. They then retreat from any further escalation and get back to instrumental shuffling of elements in the real world.[5]

We referred earlier to the taboos on the expression of fantasies. These are stronger than the prohibitions against breaking out of routine or exhibiting distance rather than commitment. Our strugglers and escapers, coping with a world which they see as uncomfortable, oppressive or constricting, by dreaming and fantasying are told, as it were, to keep their subversive or dirty thoughts to themselves.

In some cases we find moral injunctions about the types of fantasy that we should entertain. Certain fantasies it is argued should be pushed out of mind because even the consideration of these provides an immoral source of satisfaction. The Catholic religion, for example, places great stress upon the need to banish bad thoughts, suggesting that these are placed there by alien sources (the classic illustration is the Devil's temptation of Christ in the desert) and that, therefore, even to give them house-room is to yield to the influence of evil. The view that fantasies provide a source of satisfaction is standard Freudian dogma, although here the content of fantasies is seen as providing clues to the existence of a private libidinal world, rather than as evidence of the subtleties employed by members of an alien demonic one. Again in the Freudian view the appearance of fantasies is not a cause for concern but rather relief. They are cathartic. In Saul Bellow's phrase 'A thought murder a day keeps the doctor away.'

In both the Catholic and Freudian view, fantasies are objects of interest in their own right whether they lead to action or not. But it is this possibility of a link between fantasy and action which lies behind public disapproval of strong involvement in fantasies. We are all allowed 'dirty thoughts' or 'wild fantasies', just as long as they are not obsessively cultivated. Occasional fantasy as a way of absenting ourselves from routine is permissible: we can be 'away' from the conveyor belt by thinking of other worlds, build up through a hobby or pop music a considerable fantasy investment. But at some point this goes too far; the point at which we no longer occasionally evoke a fantasy world but appear to be living in one. The poly-morphous nature of everyday fantasies – we might meet this exotic woman on holiday, we might shoot a hole in one – are not condemned; what is thought deviant is the single-minded obsessiveness with which some fantasies are constructed and the apparent lack of distancing techniques with which they are pursued.

We make allowances for those, like long-term prisoners, whose contact with reality is so limited that they can be said to have a greater 'need' for fantasy than the rest of us. But – as we described – the way the authorities allow for and even encourage such fantasies, might suggest that fantasy is not as radical and subversive an escape route as it might at first appear. Could it be that the taboos on the expression of fantasy – like the many other repressions and prohibitions of our civilization – are gigantic frauds, unnecessary mystifications? And that if we lifted the barrier there would be nothing on the other side and certainly not a secret passage out of society?

Fantasies as Social Supports

When we begin to examine how fantasies are actually used, we indeed see them operating in facilitating or supportive ways which (as in the management of routines and scripts) far from disrupting paramount reality, actually may bear a conservative relationship towards it. Take these constructions, close to simple daydreams, which are used to accommodate the self to monotonous or routine tasks. The worker on the assembly line, the juror sitting through a boring court case, an audience hearing a lecturer drone away, the commuter standing in a long bus queue, will either involuntarily drift away or else consciously resort to fantasies, daydreams, mind games. The content of such fantasies may be purely past directed, it may contain ele-ments of wish fulfilment and future planning, it may be banal or extravagant, but the point is that such fantasies are summoned up to facilitate the daily round and they are strictly rationed into certain parts of that round.

We have only to note the positive recommenda-
tion of fantasies like these by clinical psychologists to
recognize their non-subversive functions: 'Daydreaming is
a neutral skill available for adaptive enrichment of the life
of otherwise ordinary persons as well as being a manifesta-
tion in many persons of escape, evasion of responsibility
or self-dissatisfaction.'[6] The young housewife who copes
with the monotony of baby care and the repugnance of
dirty nappies by a fantasy about what to cook for dinner
and how she will spend the evening with her husband, is
supposed to have her mood altered, be allowed a more
flexible response to the immediate task. But if her fantasies
are unrelated to the task they can still be used in a
functional way: she might have romantic fantasies (lying on
a deserted beach with a handsome tanned stranger),
women's-liberation fantasies (successful career woman
while husband is at home doing the housework) or combination romantic/women's-liberation fantasies (herself as
Jane Fonda, striding towards the White House) but as long
as she rations the fantasy, is conscious that it is a fantasy
and cannot immediately embed it in any ongoing life script,
there is little room for subversion.

We can distinguish between different types of
functional fantasies, *starters*, *stoppers* and *maintainers*.

A starter fantasy is one which enables us to
begin a task, experience an emotion, register a perception
by importing some new element into whatever segment
of reality we are confronting. The typical starter fantasy
occurs in the sexual realm. We might only be able to begin
a seduction move, have an erection, experience an orgasm
if some reference to another reality is introduced into the
situation. So the woman is transformed into Brigitte
Bardot, your mother, the girl next door, your secretary,
your first love or – in the banal but appropriate phrases –
'whatever gets you off' or 'gets you going'. In the non-
sexual realm we might think ourselves into taking a job,
going on a holiday, setting off on a journey by fantasying
what these might hold in store. The simple act of getting
up in the morning is often accompanied by starter fantasies.

Lying in bed, in the moments after the alarm clock has gone off, we summon up fantasies of what might happen during the day in order to nudge us into some movement. This might be the day when the aloof blonde in the train compartment will at last smile at us, when the boss calls us to his office to announce a promotion, when the morning mail will bring news of an unexpected inheritance from a distant relative. All over the country, people are now dragging themselves out of bed every morning to see if any of the letters dropped through the door will bring some news to change their lives.

Stopper fantasies can also be observed in their simplest form in sex. A common technique of preventing premature ejaculation or of increasing pleasure by delaying orgasm is to fantasize doing something extremely boring or even unpleasant. This technique is explicitly recommended by sex instruction manuals where the favoured fantasies include playing chess, watching cricket or filling out one's income-tax return. Fantasies are also invoked to stop, delay or inhibit other less physiological sequences. The standard invitation, 'Why don't you come round for a drink at my place tonight?', instead of triggering the culturally expected starter fantasies has often evoked enough instant images about the apartment, the bed, the bathroom, the paintings on the wall, to effectively kill this course of action. Similarly we have been inhibited from accepting lecture invitations by conjuring up the whole scenario of a long train journey, a bad dinner desperately trying to make small talk with the local students' sociology-society committee, a lecture to a bored and half-stoned audience, endless rounds of half-pints in a stuffy union bar, a cramped night on a sofa or the guest room of a university hall of residence, endless correspondence about travelling expenses . . .

A maintainer fantasy involves either continuing the starter fantasy into the activity itself or else struggling to 'get through' an activity by using fantasy (as in our example of the bored housewife desperately getting her mind off the household routine by projecting herself into other worlds). These fantasies are really mind games. They go beyond most starters and stoppers; they are not just mental rehearsals of unplayed scripts, but accompaniments to normal life scripts. Indeed the script might become dependent on maintainer fantasies; Gore Vidal talks of our reliance in sex on 'an inner theatre of the mind to keep things going'.[7] When we use fantasies in this way – simply as private accompaniments to our work, domestic, sexual or leisure scripts – none of our fellow players need know about our lack of involvement. Indeed we might have to take great pains particularly at work to conceal our daydreams and pretend to be really occupied by the task at hand. At times though we might want to exhibit our fantasies in public; factory workers, for example, invent elaborate fantasy games in which the room is transformed into a football pitch and each man on the conveyor belt given a named part in an imaginary league game. It helps to pass the time.

Another example: we found ourselves with two hours to wait for a plane. Sitting on a bench in the concourse we invented with manic ease a game in which at five-minute intervals we each had to nominate a woman crossing a particular point of the building as being a desirable sexual object. We had only one turn each and at the end of the five minutes we had to agree on whose nominee was the best-looking prospect.

This was a relatively simple fantasy game. Its content was drawn from one of the most banal and conservative components of contemporary mass culture, the male-chauvinist-pig fantasy of sexual conquest. It was used for two fairly clear reasons: the intrinsic fun it provided and the way it helped pass the time during a boring period of waiting. It hardly undermined the realities of either our personal lives or that of the airport lounge, although it could have done both if we could have stumbled on a convenient script in which to proceed to embed the fantasy.

Maintainer fantasies then make the present enjoyable or more tolerable by transporting the self to a reality of delight, to a different modality of experience. This is more self-conscious and controlled than a schizophrenic dissociation from reality: there is indeed a split from the real world, but this split appears to be manageable. The content of these summoned-up fantasies might relate wholly to the past; they might refer to a plan or project dreamt up to make future action easier or they might be wholly self-contained trips into another world. We see ourselves – usually as heroes – in the script of a play with mythical partners and a mythical audience:

> The transition between realities is marked by the rising and falling of the curtain. As the curtain rises, the spectator is 'transported into another world' with its own meanings and an order that may or may not have much to do with the order of everyday life. As the curtain falls, the spectator returns to reality, that is, to the paramount reality of everyday life by comparison with which the reality presented on the stage now appears tenuous and ephemeral, however vivid the presentation may have been a few moments previously.[8]

The sense of having been somewhere else during these fantasies is often so acute that we may refer to them as transformers rather than maintainers. Reality has changed. An escape has been made. But we always return: unless, that is, either the inner trip keeps going (via the scripted path of mysticism or the less scripted path of madness) or – as we will consider in the next sections – we can find a script actually to get the fantasy working *within* our paramount reality. Otherwise the fantasy is the psychic equivalent of Simmel's adventure where there is no continuity with life:

> The adventure lacks that reciprocal interpenetration with adjacent parts of life which constitute life-as-a-whole. It is like an island in life which determines its beginning according to its own formative powers and not – like the part of a continent – also according to those of adjacent territories.[9]

Institutionalized Fantasies

The fact that many fantasies are supportive rather than disruptive of reality readily explains why so many of them have taken on an institutionalized form. This commercial routinization of fantasy, contains the same double-edged opportunities as the greater availability of such escape routes as role-distancing. On the one hand it is easier to get the fantasy going, to sustain it, to embed into an appropriate script, but on the other the actual fact of institutionalization can strip something from the experience. We are not arguing that the fantasy of adultery, for example, is *necessarily* less tenable as an escape because of the existence of wife-swopping clubs, key parties and swingers' directories, but that this transforms the experience into a qualitatively different mode. Liberation and escape can indeed be found by the suburban swinger, but the very ease with which the fantasy can be realized makes it very different from Madame Bovary's escape. Our next chapters will be devoted to the consequences of the institutionalization of free areas in which people are allowed to encourage their escapist fantasies.

We would not know how to find evidence for historical changes in the use of fantasy. Certainly there is a greater public accessibility to a wide range of fantasy material formerly only hinted at. Sexual fantasies of a previously taboo kind are now the bread and butter of mass culture. This might mean that there is less room for the active exercise of fantasy.[10] This tendency has already been picked up by popular psychology which, having already tried to get people to live free and authentic – that is, non role and non script-bound lives (an enterprise which, as we pointed out, is doomed to failure) – is now trying to encourage people to get into fantasy. 'It's more important today than ever that we should all enjoy the process of fantasy,' argues Dr Herbert Otto in his book *Fantasy Encounter Games*, parts of which have appeared in such popular magazines as *She*.[11] The argument is that limiting our fantasies cuts out humanity's creativity and eternal hopes. Fantasy, far from being an escape can '. . . even act as a stepping stone for reality – through the process of speaking out our fantasies we reveal them and through doing this can ultimately recognize them as goals'. Fantasies are also recommended as ways of achieving a deeper level of self-understanding; such techniques as fantasy encounter games are aids to this process of self-discovery, creativity and personal growth. The content of most of these games are banal enough although demanding a fairly sophisticated degree of self-monitoring: in the Cosmic-Visitors'-Arrival Fantasy, for example, two partners are assumed to be cosmic visitors from another planet arriving on Earth and inhabiting the bodies of the two persons reading about the fantasy; in the Loving Fantasy you are instructed to have a fantasy about a particular person in which you ask yourself the question, 'Supposing I had the power of a magician or wizard, what is the most loving gift I could give this person?', and the Disaster-Survival Fantasy, in which one fantasizes having survived a major disaster in the company of a band of others you've selected: you are elected as the person in charge and can reshape the environment.

Standard critiques of mass culture invariably make a great deal of the escape status of fantasies disseminated in films, plays and comics, implying that the depiction of excessive hedonism, violence, promiscuity, sensuality or whatever can undermine people's attachment to paramount reality. But no such undermining can be assumed: the fantasies of popular culture may, on the contrary, support and enhance paramount reality. The advertisements for rum, cigars or perfume which are set on a white Jamaican beach might indeed provide the source material for fantasies but they hardly send people rushing to Jamaican beaches, for they provide no script for such a journey.

Similarly, the James Bond movie, one of the more explicit fantasy elements in popular culture, gives no stage directions for people anxious to act in a Bond-like manner. It is, paradoxically, those advertisements, plays and films which are apparently low on fantasy and tie in well with existing scripts that are more likely to provide useable tools for distancing and identity work. The advertisements which show the products set in the local pub or high street, the television films such as *Dixon of Dock Green* which take place in familiar settings, all have a fantasy component, an elaboration of reality, but in these cases this elaborated reality seems within reach. It is just around the corner and we can use our existing scripts in order to get there. Policemen do not have to invent new scripts, in order to act like Dixon or Barlow, doctors may readily regard themselves as Kildare or Finlay. It is strange that so much attention has been lavished upon the possibilities of individuals 'escaping from reality' by identifying with such grand fantasy figures as Bond, Superman, and de Sade when the pavements are crawling with individuals who have identified themselves with the more readily scripted and easily assimilated fantasy figures of Dan Archer, Mrs Dale, Ena Sharples, Steptoe and Andy Capp. Such fantasy living is regarded with only mild amusement by others and hardly more noteworthy than the existence of large numbers of people who apparently believe that the characters of radio and television soap operas actually exist and write weekly letters to the BBC giving the Archers, the Dales and the inhabitants of Coronation Street advice on running their lives.

Mass culture might suggest the content of new fantasies but it also might provide the script for a fantasy which the individual previously regarded as being his own and not only unsharable but unrealizable. This is particularly evident with sexual fantasies. It is banal enough to talk about the use of pornographic photos or writing as fantasies to reinforce conventional action; what is more interesting is how such material opens up the windows to alternative and novel actions. When esoteric sexual practices are described in detail in the pages of freely available literature such as *Playboy*, *Penthouse*, *Forum* and *Mayfair*, they serve both to guide and to normalize the individual's own fantasy life. This is especially so if the descriptions are conveyed not in dramatic forms but in such styles as letters to the editor or highly scientific looking 'surveys' – like the 'Quest' series in *Mayfair*. When sadists can buy their Gestapo uniforms by mail order, when rubber fetishists can attire themselves at the local boutique, when you can buy parlour games called, Libido, Diplomacy and Fantasy, and when intellectual women describing themselves as 'highly sexed Germaine-Greer-type females, aged 35', can search for a 'middle-aged sensual Herzog type' in the columns of the *New York Review of Books*, then indeed fantasy has become part of the fabric of life – as supportive of reality as the most everyday routine.

Transformer Fantasies

The problem for those who would rely upon the inner life as a sanctuary from the routines and repetitions of life, as a private site where personal identity might be assiduously cultivated, arises not only from the ways in which society regulates and shapes the nature of that inner life, but also from the difficulties in effecting continuity between our imaginings. We experience the external world as bound together by space and time, it spreads before us in an ordered and predictable manner. But often the purely inner life is far more random and inchoate. Sometimes we literally cannot get our fantasies going. We lie back and wait but they will not unroll, our inner eye refuses to travel, remaining myopically fixed upon a single obstinate image. We respond by feeding it with further stimuli, we gaze at pictures, read books, assemble relevant properties. We try to facilitate the appearance and development of our fantasy by constructing a compatible external world.

By resorting to such activities, we reveal the unsuitability of fantasy as a means for genuinely transforming our lives. It is only in rare circumstances, and amongst rare beings, that fantasy life feels solid and continuous enough to constitute some sort of alternative world, some escape from paramount reality, something which is more than Simmel's 'island in life'. Much of the time its transformative effects are more limited; it allows us to think what we may not say, to see what is not there, to mentally compensate for some of the aesthetic or erotic inadequacies of landscapes and lovers.

This is of course the role that is played by fantasy within the scripts that we described in the previous chapter. All scripts have a fantasy component, in that they refer to something outside the situation, something which is only imaginatively present to all the participating actors, for example, a conception of how true lovers should behave in the countryside, a notion of the ideal family breakfast, the most satisfactory night out on the town. Again fantasy is playing a minor transformative role, blurring some of the cruder edges of reality, and giving routine experiences a more elevated status. It is so regularly called upon that it eventually becomes part of the scene, an old friend that we turn to for help at particular moments. We can even catch ourselves invoking fantasies at times when quite specific reality transformations are required. So the lover who is already involved in a particular script with definite fantasy components – he may, for example, be identifying with some other master lover, imagining himself in some arcadian setting – will suddenly have to invoke another, possibly unrelated fantasy in order to deal with certain situational contingencies, the need to maintain an erection, to prevent premature orgasm. The fantasy is quickly summoned, fulfils its function by transforming the situation in such a way as to enhance its erotic elements, and then again retreats to the margins of the mind. The 'inner theatre of the mind' becomes a complicated business when we are mentally juxtaposing the image of ourselves playing cricket in the backyard (a specific stopper fantasy) with an image of ourselves as a D. H. Lawrence lover exploding in mystical communion (a specific sexual script).

So much have fantasies been neglected in discussions of everyday life, that it is common to encounter resistance to such descriptions of their role. It is as though we do not like to believe that we are continually modifying the here and now by the use of imagination, particularly when the imaginatively transformed situation is one that is regarded as spontaneous or natural. And although we may laugh at the story of the lover who turns contentedly to his partner after consummation and says, 'You tell me your fantasies and I'll tell you mine,' or nod knowingly when we hear Freud's comment about sexual intercourse always involving at least four people – the two lovers and the two imagined lovers – nevertheless we are cautious about admitting that fantasy has quite such salience in our own life. We acknowledge by our relative silence, the strength of the cultural pressures which insist that fantasy must be kept in its place, that it must not be allowed to 'run over us'. There are spatial and hydraulic metaphors which convey the need for control: we must be careful to open the sluice gate to fantasies only at the right places, the right times and let in the right amount.

Much of the time this mental management creates no problems. We summon and dismiss fantasies whenever some minor blurring or partial transformation is required. Even when they are not self-consciously invoked – but somehow 'come over you' – like the almost reflexive male-chauvinist sexual fantasies – you quickly become aware of what is happening. You move in on your thoughts and take charge of them. Paradoxically then, that domain of experience – fantasy – which appears in common sense to be the closest to the unconscious is in fact saturated with consciousness, at least in its appearance in the daily round. Needless to say, the familiar paradox of consciousness still applies: fantasy is a way of getting away from the world, but as soon as you know this – as you must – the world again announces its presence.

Nevertheless, the sense of our control over fantasies is far from complete. Our unreadiness to discuss them openly is no doubt related to our feeling that they are dangerous allies. In some circumstances, they can be happily summoned to fight on our side, to transform dull, ugly, routine situations, but then they may reappear quite 'inappropriately' in circumstances where we wished to call attention to 'the here and now'. And they may also 'run away with us'. Instead of fulfilling their minor blurring or transformative function, and then departing, they begin to dominate our lives, standing between us and reality instead of facilitating contact.

In Malzberg's novel *Screen*, the hero has been carried away by his fantasies into the world of the movies. We all use picture-houses as fantasy factories, places where we can sit back for a limited period of time and allow our imagination a holiday, a brief respite from its busy task of complementing our daily activities. We identify with the hero or heroine, imagine ourselves riding alongside Lee Marvin, lying beside Elizabeth Taylor, shooting it out with Jack Palance. Malzberg's hero has however gone further than most of us. His fantastic identification takes him right into the screen world. He is transformed into Brigitte Bardot's lover, Sophia Loren's husband. Only a few seconds of the movie are required to prompt this transformation; just a few frames and he is into his fantastic sexual world.

At home his fantasy life is helped along by 16-mm movies and pornographic magazines. Into this world comes a real girl, someone who insists that 'reality' is more important than the movies. Our hero is tempted by the reality she offers; he concentrates his mind upon her appearance, her body, and begins to make love to her. As he does, he keeps a wary eye upon the contents of his mind. There are no fantasy figures in sight; he begins to believe that this act will therefore be a transformation, a glimpse of life without fantasy, emancipation from the world of movie stars. But gradually the images begin to appear:

They began on the offstage of consciousness, dry, subtle, almost imperceptible and then, as I increased my speed and moans, trying to throw them off that way by putting myself in an isolate pocket they came in nearer and nearer, working to the midpoint and then the forefront of the cerebrum and the voices were the soft, urgent voices of women.[12]

Row upon row of fantasy figures, whispering his name, reassert their importance in his life. His hope that he might live without them is promptly abandoned. In the evening he eagerly propels his girlfriend to the local movie-house where he happily drifts back into the screen world, and into the arms of Doris Day.

Clearly, some fantasies do take on this obsessive quality. Instead of transforming some aspects of the world, they make whole areas of that world untenable. But to allow them to 'get out of hand' in this manner is a dangerous way to effect an escape from reality. It is the pathway to madness, for it eventually breaks down the distinction between the inner and the outer life in such a way that visions and hallucinations, images and reality, delusions and beliefs, become indistinguishable.

Our sense of the specialness of our inner life, coupled with our fears about allowing it to 'run away with us' may lead us to attempt transformations of reality by bringing our fantasies into the real world. In other words, instead of allowing fantasies to be mere adjuncts to existing scripts, we actually set out to script our fantasies, to give some concrete expression to our imaginings.

But the possibilities for transforming reality by such techniques are limited by the reluctance of others to aid our fantastic performances, and by the unsuitability of the settings in which they must occur.

There are many historical examples of individuals who had sufficient resources to script their private fantasies, who were able to assemble the scenery, the properties and the cast of supporting characters. However in everyday life the unavailability of such aspects, means that fantasies are enacted less publicly; they take a form which is co-terminous if not compatible with daily existence. And often the chances of their being enacted depends upon the presence of another person.

Take the Humphrey Bogart fantasy. I start identifying – with a greater or lesser degree of self-consciousness – with his screen personality and life style. I imagine what it would be like to live my life like that. Gradually I begin to work up a few Bogart poses: light my cigarette in a particular way, turn my lips into the right evil smile. Girls friends are cast into Lauren Bacall figures and my local is transformed into Rick's bar in Casablanca. But there are definite limits to how far I can go with all this. Self-consciousness soon enough calls my bluff as I catch a glimpse of myself in the mirror or somebody laughs as they see me watching myself. But above all, I cannot really continue my fantasy, thoroughly invest in it, unless a stage, script and props are provided. Conceivably I might be able to command the financial and other resources to mould the world according to my fantasy: like the hero of John Fowles's *The Collector*, who starts catching women and collecting them like butterflies. If everyone, he observes, had more money and more time, this sort of thing would happen more often.

As we have argued, for much of the time we keep our fantasies to ourselves. Those that we do discuss with others are likely to be the less extreme or eccentric imaginings – ones which by virtue of their compatibility with aspects of paramount reality may be accommodated within existing scripts. However, on occasions, individuals will come together and find that they share each other's bizarre fantasies. The fantasy ceases to be a personal mental resource to be drawn upon intermittently during the course of everyday life; now it can be elaborated with the help of another and may shift into the centre of our lives. The classical clinical description of this phenomenon is *folie à deux*, a situation in which two individuals actively cultivate their extreme fantasy to the point at which scripts may be assembled for its enactment.

So those who find they share a megalomaniac fantasy may consciously start organizing its elaboration. They may gradually acquire a range of properties which help to constitute it as a possible reality. Alongside the shelves of books by Hitler, de Sade and Nietzsche will be pictures of death and destruction, perhaps some actual objects related to the fantasy: knives, guns, uniforms. The fantasy is still a long way from being embedded into a script which would facilitate megalomaniac behaviour. Indeed, whilst it exists in this state of elaboration its 'fantastic' nature may be weakened by its dependence upon conventional philosophies and material artefacts. Nevertheless, it has come out of the mind and into the world. Collective behavioural 'eccentricity' has taken over from private mental obsessiveness.

These then are some of the times when fantasy slips out of its accustomed role; when it interferes with the typical complementary relationship between imagination and reality, when it creates a special world of its own, or an enclave in the real world to which we may periodically retreat when paramount reality appears oppressive.

But such illustrations are not enough to allow us to accord fantasy any magical escape status. For much of the time fantasies merely help us through the day by providing the questionable reassurance that there is some portion of ourselves which is not fully committed to life's routines and habits. Even this consolation can be rapidly undermined by any knowledge that we acquire about their dependence upon the common cultural stock.

It seems that we have a poor legacy from the imaginative riches of childhood. The external world is now firmly separated from the inner, leaving behind a few mundane series of associations, a set of B-feature movies to which we periodically attend when short of external stimulation, or when we are so self-deluded as to believe that there is still an inner sanctuary in which we can hide from the hard world of reality.

5

Free Areas,
Escape Routes and
Identity Sites

With reference to the existence of at least some order and predictability in the natural world, Einstein is said to have remarked, 'God is subtle but he isn't plain mean.' Similarly, however subtle the social order may be and however odd the escapes from it may look, it isn't so mean and perverse as not to provide distinguishable patterns of solutions to the very problems it creates.

Relativism and self-awareness will not always solve the problem of being unhappy with our routines and our scripts. And our life scripts will not always make room for our fantasies. We look elsewhere to cope with routine, boredom, lack of individuality, frustration. We want a genuine escape, a flight to an area in which we can temporarily absent ourselves from paramount reality, find ourselves out of play, and assemble our identity in peace or with new and more powerful symbolic resources. Society creates just such areas and assiduously signposts them. Indeed it signposts them so well that they become, as we will describe in this chapter, part of paramount reality itself.

These areas represent society's anticipation of

the fact that its arrangements must be toyed with, its rules relaxed, its gates opened. And because fantasy is added to the script which accompanies such provisions, we can even talk about these areas as places in which paramount reality is allowed to slip away.

We need such arrangements because of the limitations of such techniques as monitoring and self-distancing. These, we suggested, may even be counter-productive in that the realization of self against tasks and roles draws attention to the lack of a sector of life in which we are really at home, ourself, free. Self-consciousness may render the fabric of work and family even more routine and unbearable. The distancing techniques become more desperate as the individual strives to convince himself and others that he is more than just worker, husband, father. To show that we can do more than tease and pick away at the fabric we try to create new parts and to enter into specific escape scripts. The idea is sustained that there should be some activities, some roles to which we are fully committed, which are sufficiently compatible with our identity, to enable that identity to be realized in their very performance. We also look for areas in which we don't experience any massive tension or disruption between fantasy and script: the free area is a place where we can act out our fantasies or where the action doesn't need any extrinsic fantasies to transform it.

We simultaneously occupy several worlds and move into different activities each of which may be distinguished by the degree of individuality, at-homeness, freedom from constraints which can be experienced. These are areas in which the actual performance of the task is regarded as self-expressive, areas in which indications of distance are often inappropriate and where assertions of the meaninglessness of the activity are virtually taboo. These routes are institutionalized, not because we experience them as such, but because this is how they are categorized by society. These areas, although licensed by society as safety valves, have, like fantasy, to be carefully regulated and patrolled. For in these areas, reality may slip away too far, providing glimpses of alternative realities which can have radical consequences. The 'taste of freedom' provided by a prisoner's release on licence, can very much change how he sees his prison. Visiting a free area, then, involves some risks. There is a slight gamble in these temporary absences from everyday life, even though the return route is clearly mapped out and the excursion is at the most only to the edges of alternative reality.

Some very odd and apparently completely dissimilar areas of life come under our heading of free areas: from collecting bus tickets to undergoing psychoanalysis, from taking a package holiday to going on an acid trip, from playing roulette to joining a commune. They all share a similar escape meaning: they are routes out. They also share a peculiar tension between the known and the unknown, the safe and the dangerous, the innovatory and the conventional. When we opt for any of these activities we might be buying some quite standard elements of everyday life. The time and money we invest in a hobby might only buy what looks to others like another job. Our holiday cheque will get us sun, beaches, and food. Our stake at the gambling table buys sociability, a pleasant way of spending time and the possibility of some financial gain. When we light the joint or swallow the tab of acid, we are buying relaxation, heightened sensitivity and a variety of pleasurable physical sensations.

But many of these packages have risks attached to them. Indeed, they are marketed by reference to these risks: if you take this holiday, place this bet, swallow this pill, then something out of the ordinary might happen to you. Your life might be transformed by the sudden discovery of a new cultural world while on holiday, by the dramatic translation from poverty to wealth after a pools win, the mind-blowing discovery of your real self after ingesting a chemical.

It is difficult to find any intrinsic behavioural characteristics of free areas – so diverse are they in content – other than that of voluntary participation. These are the areas in which man does not sell his self. They might best be classified not in terms of their own features – which might be wholly mundane and uninteresting – but in terms of the area of paramount reality which the individual is trying to edge away from and to put on the line. There are *activity enclaves* in which people try to dig out, through hobbies, sex, games, sport, a safe place for self-expression and identity work; *new landscapes* in which people use holidays and adventures to get away from the routine world, to find a setting for acting out their fantasies, and *mindscapes* where the voyage, with the aid of drugs and various therapies is an internal one.

ACTIVITY ENCLAVES

Hobbies

The hobby is one of the purest types of free area. The actual activity itself is unimportant: almost anything will do as long as we voluntarily submit to its rhythms and demands. The home decorator, the gardener, the modeller, the philatelist, may all be engaged in tasks which are identical to those which call for routine accommodation or self-distancing by others. But they are distinguished by the individual's assertions that this is where he really lives, where he suspends self-consciousness because the activity in itself provides an adequate opportunity for self-expression. We may be surprised to hear that someone collects used matchboxes or old beer tins as a hobby, but would never declare that this was not a hobby as long as we could see that it was voluntarily undertaken and quite separate from his working life.

The hobby is a free area which is very high on routine and relatively low on monitoring or awareness. Typically, this is a world of non-human objects – stamps, butterflies, flowers, wood, boats, electric wires – and indeed much of the hobby involves organizing, classifying, arranging, recording and eventually mastering this inanimate world. The hobby is a microsphere of manageable objects like the child's world of play and it is obsessive and ritualistic. We can happily suspend consciousness for there is rarely anyone else around with whom to interact. The manuals, television programmes and guides to good gardening are directed purely towards improving techniques, towards mastery of the world of seeds, slugs and compost. No one is concerned – and therefore you need not be – about your style, your feelings, whether or not you are spontaneous and warm. The other people present in your hobby world – the dealer you buy your stamps from, your fellow competitors in the best daffodil collection – are present in purely functional roles.

Hobbies are sometimes conceived of as sacrosanct escapes from the daily round – the spatial location of the enclave in the garden, the games room, the cellar or attic reinforces this – and also as ways of dislodging the weight of everyday routine. But they remain, behaviourally and subjectively 'at home' for most people. The gardener, philatelist, pigeon breeder, trout fisher, model-train enthusiast, is not pitting himself against a hostile and alien world. He is carving out some free areas within that world. Even if he were now and then to conceive of the world as a prison, he would see such areas as ways of making prison time pass in a more relaxed and easy-going way.

Precisely because such free areas are inside the normal life plan they are not free from contamination. People certainly can become wholly absorbed in their private hobbies in ways that they would not at work yet there is little reason to suppose that because these areas are classified as 'leisure' and are characterized by the crucial fact that the person is not actually selling his time, energy and self, the same self-consciousness which monitors other areas of life will somehow be suspended. Even if there is no one actually present, the world will still not leave you in peace. The triggers to such self-consciousness are many: the banality of the activity itself (is one really finding one's true self by sticking postage stamps in albums or growing large leeks?), the awareness that so many others might be involved in the same thing, the ritualization of the experience by the mass media, the highly commercialized and patterned form in which one is urged to enjoy one-self in magazines, clubs, newsletters, do-it-yourself kits.

In other words, any one of these enclaves can be invaded by the same awareness which makes for cynicism and distancing about the 'non-free' areas of our lives. The tenuousness of these free areas arises from their co-existence with other phenomenally dissonant worlds. They represent the attempts of man to preserve an area of 'natural' behaviour at a time when the multiplicity of roles and activities available threatens to render everything relative.

At times, though, these special worlds will be preserved by the presence of a group ideology which en-shrines their intrinsic significance, their potential for self-realization. Heroes will be cited whose personality can only be understood in terms of their complete identification with the activity in question. Most hobbyists have their specialized equivalent of the Guinness Book of Records: a mythology in which prodigious feats – the largest leek, the blackest rose, the most matchbox labels – proclaim the reward in store for the faithful.

The difficulty still remains, though, of sustain-ing the integrity of the self-realizing enclave within the 'real' world. Is it becoming just another routine or another activity *against* which one asserts self-hood or do we find our identity *within* it? The integrity of the free area is even more fundamentally threatened by the cultural adoption and promotion of the activities it contains. The introduc-tion of competition for example pollutes the free area with vindictiveness, spite, jealousy, as in the perennial allega-tions that the champion marrow grower or dog breeder has been cheating. Again, the private world of the philatelist, the model builder, the amateur keep-fit expert may sud-denly be held up for mockery by those daily television and radio comedies, whose humour relies so much upon teas-ing out the intimacies of everyday domestic life. It is just a little more difficult to return to our matchbox collection in the attic after having seen such an obsession mocked for the delight of millions by television comedians.

Routine and self-consciousness can both constitute threats to that part of our life which we characterize
as more 'real' than any other. The acceptance that much
of the activity is trivial, lacking in 'meaning', makes it
liable to be viewed as routine – as a task which is hardly
appropriate for involvement or for identity work. It becomes 'below our dignity' – 'mere repetition'. On the
other hand, the intrusion of self-consciousness renders the
activity one amongst others, it distances us from it so that
its self-realizing function is undermined. We start 'escaping' from that which was to be our escape. This undermining is more or less inevitable, but matters less to those
who invest their hobbies with only the minimal degree of
resistance or escape status. Someone with an esoteric
hobby, such as collecting matchbox labels or constructing
boats in bottles, far from being filled with angst and
despair at the thought of appearing on a television show
or being entered into the Guinness Book of Records may
be delighted at such recognition. One man's cultural co-
option may be another's sense of individuality.

Routine, self-consciousness and co-option then
are always lurking outside these activity enclaves, always
threatening to burst in and announce their unwanted
presence. They are the representatives of the world of
instrumentality, the very world which the hobby has
sought to undermine. The child's play world is safe from
such intruders: in an inchoate world he willingly embraces
routine and repetition; self-consciousness and absurdity
never disturb him; he is immune from co-option.

Such threats become quite different matters
when the 'light-hearted' hobby is taken too seriously. The
hobby is usually a relatively safe escape route. There are
risks, though, when it becomes an obsession and the
fantasy element threatens to take over. Comic literature is
full of characters whose hobby becomes an obsession
which encompasses their whole life: like Kirby Groom-
kirby in N. F. Simpson's *One Way Pendulum*, who devotes
his life to teaching weighing machines to sing. ('It's a form

of escape, of course. Escapism,' remarks one character benignly of Kirby's hobby.)

Bill Shankly's classic reply to the accusation that he regarded football as being as important as life or death, was that football was '... far, far *more* important than life or death'. Taken literally, this becomes a prescription for a somewhat different script for relating one's hobby to one's life. Something fantastic, as we will see in Chapter 8, is now possible.

Games

Hobbies are not the only things going on in our activity enclaves; they are also places for playing games. Games, of course, like hobbies, can often be solitary – patience or crossword puzzles – but unlike hobbies someone else is usually needed either for collusion or competition.

Those with a low fantasy component and with little connection to any significant scripts are not used to subvert paramount reality. They are merely ways of passing time: playing Scrabble, badminton or dominoes is invested with little more meaning than this. But most competitive games and sports whose action might be just as banal or trivial can become the scenes for much wider social dramas. It has become the stock-in-trade of even the less sophisticated commentators on our leisure activities to see in the world of chess, golf, football, cricket and poker, metaphors and meanings which go way above the immediate activity and project the player into a world of the spectacular, the tragic, the ironic, the heroic, the comic, the melodramatic.

The escape status of games is related both to how much is invested in them and to the degree to which fantasies are called for. At the lowest level, games like Scrabble and dominoes not only call for no fantastic investment, but allow little room for identity work. There are no compelling cultural scripts at hand which could carry us away from the world. At the next level there is the vast majority of sports and games which are also carried out for non-escape reasons – keeping fit, building character, passing time – but which can be seen as activity enclaves in which some sense of self-expression is possible and which generate their own dramas and draw on cultural dramas. *The Hustler*, *The Cincinnati Kid*, Hemingway's bullfighters, Mailer's boxers, Bukowski's jockeys, are all acting out scenes of passion, conflict, sexuality and terror far beyond the simple behavioural sequences of the game. And this is why, as anyone who plays games with any level of commitment knows, it is not just a matter of two grown men standing on a platform hitting each other, not just kicking a leather ball about, not just riding a horse along a track. Only our old enemy, self-monitoring, forces such definitions on the players. They can only be rescued – like the hobbyist – by an appeal to fantasy, to legendary per-formers and players, to master scripts. The Goal of the Month, Match of the Year, Hall of Fame, the chronicles, photos, posters, biographies of the great, keep intact the possibility of transcending the banality of the activity itself. And, paradoxically, the very force which generates these scripts – commercial co-option – also reminds us that individuality, mastery of objects and self-expression can just become commodities sold by professionals.

In most conventional games and sports people can decide how much fantasy to invest in the activity. You can either just hit somebody with a padded glove or be striking a blow for black emancipation. But some games are much more explicit in exploiting fantasies. The adult parlour game is a good example. Playing Monopoly is virtually impossible if you play it just like draughts or snakes-and-ladders. You are expected to project yourself into the identity of the millionaire property tycoon, to create some sort of imaginary world (however tenuous) out of the symbols provided. Reality doesn't matter in the way that it does in conventional games where goals, knock-outs, check-mates, and fastest times are the 'real' objects of the exercise.

Adult parlour games have recently embodied more elaborate fantasies than the conventional one of business success. Diplomacy games, spy games, war games have all offered up new ritualized fantasies. Even the previously taboo area of sex has been used in games such as Libido. 'Dare you play Libido?' the advertisement reads and, of course, we dare, because in addition to the strong, if short-lived, sense of relativity and freedom which characterizes all institutionalized escapes, the game at the same time prescribes that the successful player must also be fiendishly busy distancing and monitoring.

Less safely packaged sexual games, like wife-swopping and key parties throw up the more subtle limits of such escape routes. Certainly they provide a ritualized way of enacting the common fantasy of taking home a strange woman from a party or screwing your best-friend's wife, but folklore and research on these activities indicate that self-consciousness very soon catches up and the enclave is riddled with the very forces – guilt, anxiety and a sense of the absurd – which pervade 'normal' sex.

There is another category of games which we will be examining again in the context of therapy: mind games, socio and psycho dramas, fantasy workshops and the like. Taking seriously the neo-Freudian enterprise of nudging consciousness towards some state of pure play and innocence, unencumbered by the hang-ups of industrial society, some popular therapies have directed escapers towards finding liberation through games. The most developed version is the mind game: mental exercises which offer such extraordinary options as being able to die and look back on your own life, relive experiences you had as a small child or transform yourself into a mythical animal. Clearly the claims for such games and the motivation of those who play them are much more grandiose than those associated with playing bridge or racing motor cars. But more often than not, as we shall see, the contrived nature of the game is deliberately directed towards accommodation rather than resistance to paramount reality. In the same way as the public-school ethos held that playing rugby was good for the character, so the mind games suggest that by the male acting out the role of bored housewife, the marriage can become stabilized.

But the very fetish which is made of authenticity in the mind games shows how vulnerable this activity enclave is. The aspiring cricketer is told that he should bat *like* Gary Sobers, not become Gary Sobers. But the mind-games player is enjoined to actually pretend to be someone else, like his wife, his boss or his father. This hardly subverts reality unless of course the pretence continues when the game spills out of its enclave into daily routine. It is all very well for the prison officer and prisoner to swap roles under the guidance of their Moreno-trained group therapist, but they all know that when they leave that part of the prison where such dramas take place (usually, significantly, the hobbies or games room), the game is over.

Gambling

In many of the games that we have discussed, an element of gambling is involved. Many of them depend upon the readiness of the players to risk something of their identity, their grasp of paramount reality. This notion of offering ourselves or part of our world to chance is not, however, confined to those structured occasions we call games. Notions of luck, chance, fate and risk may permeate our everyday existence. Life's routines may be dull and monotonous at the moment, but there's always the possibility that something will happen. What better escape from paramount reality could there be than to be suddenly kidnapped by Lady Luck or Dame Fortune and transported to a novel world?

But although we may believe in chance, invoking it to explain incidents in our own and other people's lives, it is difficult to lay ourself open to its intrusion. The idea that it will simply force its attention upon us without any prompting is little more than a recurrent fantasy which helps the day along, but which remains stubbornly unscripted.

Our hope that chance will subvert reality therefore leads us out into enclaves where the appropriate rituals of invocation may be performed. These enclaves immediately circumscribe the part of our world that may be placed on the line. Pure chance might transform us into a king, convey us to a desert island, free us from our family, friends and work. The structured chance that we encounter at bingo halls, casinos and racetracks pays out identity dividends for some and cash dividends for others which provide the means for transformation and not the transformation itself.[1] The unpredictability is still present, but the cultivation of unpredictability in a predictable fashion now makes chance reconcilable with other features of social life. Its pursuance within institutionalized contexts allows the ideas which inform its pursuance to be coterminous with life rather than subversive of it. As Simmel notes, 'The gambler, clearly, has abandoned himself to the meaninglessness of chance. In so far, however, as he counts on its favours and believes possible and realizes a life dependent on it, chance for him has become part of a context of meaning.'[2]

Nevertheless, the subversive element of fantasy still exists in gambling. Instrumentality, despite the acknowledged existence of 'skills', the conscious exploitation of a system, is often low. Even the most skilled of gamblers operates with magical notions about the way the numbers are running, the way the cards are falling. Self-expression and the cultivation of style is all important: the epic poker, dice and roulette games of the movies are constant external reproaches to those who would try to manipulate the cards, dice or chips as they would operate a lathe or balance a set of accounts. The escape theme is reinforced by the tacit agreement not to let the stuff of paramount reality trickle into the enclave.

However, the fantasies may be difficult to sustain, for all the efforts of betting shops and casinos to exclude the comings and goings of everyday life. Similarly, in many contexts where the insulation from the everyday world is ineffective, the operation of pure chance is further inhibited by the frequent agreements amongst players about the extent to which social conventions should interfere with the extremes of good or bad fortune. The players, as it were, hold themselves back from the operation of pure chance, by the recognition that after the game, both losers and winners will have to be returned to the world in a form which will allow life to continue. There are few ways of wholly immersing ourselves into the gambling world which do not either lead to the action degenerating into routine, or to the exposure of ourselves to other reminders of paramount reality. Nevertheless, as the different reactions of the two characters in the film *California Split* nicely illustrated, there is a possibility that the 'meaninglessness of chance' can at times, paradoxically, provide the only viable enclave of meaning – a true alternative reality.

Sex

There is one other national pastime which must be classed as an activity enclave – a section of our life where we may feel ourselves to be temporarily away from the daily round – an area where we may engage in some identity work without the risk of becoming entangled by routine and monotony. This is sex.

The station bookstall proclaims the popularity of one of its major cultural forms – masturbation. Books and magazines devoted to servicing the needs of wankers far outnumber those available to other hobbyists – the gardener, the train spotter, the stamp collector. And for advanced students, there are specialist bookshops in every major town, with texts entirely geared to the subtle differences in their interests. The gardener who is predominantly interested in growing daffodils may have to content himself with magazines which cover other horticultural preferences, but the masturbator may easily find a publication which concentrates solely upon his own particular way of establishing an erection – female sadism, pederastic homosexuality, lesbian masochism.

Not that such magazines typically announce themselves as catering to the needs of the masturbator. Alternative reasons for the publication of the pictures and stories abound. The most hypocritical rationales appear in mass-circulation newspapers. The nude on page 3 of the *Sun* – attired in her alliterative legend – 'Susan Steps Out', 'Carol Comes Calling' – is there to demonstrate the joys of spring, the first swim of the season, the pleasures of holidays abroad. The bookstall nudie magazines are more explicit about their sexual relevance. Frank letters and articles accompany the pictures. We are told in detail about a variety of esoteric sexual practices – 'Imagine my surprise when my girlfriend's sister walked into our bedroom, took off her clothes and climbed into bed with us. *What a night*. Have other readers similar experiences to report?' – but never about the hobby to which the book is devoted. If you want to know how to grow a champion marrow, then your gardening journal will fearlessly refer you to page 56 for practical help. But nowhere in *Mayfair* or *Penthouse* do we find any reference to the excellent masturbatory aids provided on page 23 by the double photo spread of Tessa – 'Leicester's Lustiest Lass'.

In recent years this hobby has lost its traditional masculine image. Just as the yachting and golfing clubs have opened their doors to women members, so there are now books, magazines and apparatus available for female masturbators. To the list of technological aids available to hobbyists – the power drill, the electric lawn mower, the rotary cultivator – must now be added the vibrator. Everyone can now become a masturbator and most of us happily do.

Like other hobbies, masturbation is typically located in a special setting, not the garden or the attic or the cellar, but the bathroom or the lavatory. There are occasions upon which masturbatory aids are publicly provided – the strip club, the skin-flick movie house – but actual masturbation in such settings is discouraged by the management. It is not uncommon at strip shows for the performers to stop in mid-act in order to censure a member of the audience who appears to be masturbating.

At one session we observed, the stripper broke out of her languid sensuous routine, stepped to the front of the stage, pointed to a member of the audience and denounced him as a 'dirty bugger'. 'Save that for the lavatory afterwards,' she commanded, and slid back into her performance.

For many people, masturbation does not achieve the status of an activity enclave. It remains a peripheral element, having no more escape significance than would such other intermittent activities, as planting a few garden bulbs in spring and autumn, or keeping interesting foreign stamps in our desk drawer. Like the other activities we have described, it only becomes important when it is cultivated as a free area, when it is regarded as a portion of life in which we can feel ourselves free of the routine nature of the rest of existence, when it is accompanied by feelings of excitement and delight. Once so constituted, it can quickly become as obsessive and ritualistic as other hobbies. Certain times of the day may be set aside for it, particular adjustments of clothing and posture may be regarded as essential components. Self-consciousness is avoided. Although we may joke in public about the activity, there will be few occasions when our commitment to it is less than full.

But there is one way in which masturbation stands apart from most other activity enclaves; it is dominated by the fantasy component. What is organized, arranged and mastered here, is not a collection of non-human concrete objects – stamps, butterflies, flowers – but rather an assortment of mental images, which must be arranged in such a fashion as to produce a successful physiological response. Even when books and magazines are used as adjuncts to the act, they are not simply stared at in a mindless fashion, but are rather used as source material for the production of mental images. It has even been argued that the complexity of synchronizing images and behaviour in masturbation makes it an important apprenticeship for that general mental manipulation of symbolic material which is required in everyday life.[3]

It is this high fantasy component which ironic-

ally raises the chances of the activity enclave being pene-
trated by aspects of paramount reality. For it is difficult to
maintain the sense of individual specialness about our
fantasies when we observe their institutional promotion in
books, magazines and films. As soon as we sense that
'Leicester's Lustiest Lass' is in several million lavatories
and not just our own, our enclave may begin to feel less
personal. Nevertheless, if this sense of intrusion is threatening, it can be held at bay by our continuing belief in the
'unique' characteristics of our own fantasy work upon the
source material, aided perhaps by the promoters' tactful
silence about the actual practice for which their packaged
fantasies are intended.

If masturbation is accorded a place within
activity enclaves, then there is no evident reason for ex-
cluding that other form of sexual activity – intercourse
itself. It is perhaps more rigidly confined to a spatial location than masturbation and is certainly more temporally
circumscribed. The bed at night time is the standard setting and one to which most of us aspire, however much we
may have been forced by circumstances to use alternatives
from time to time. And, although sex-making may become
part of the routine of life, a mere aspect of paramount
reality, it is persistently regarded as an activity in which we
may 'be ourselves' or 'get away from everyday life'. Indeed, it is difficult not to feel that its status is undermined
by crudely slotting it into 'activity enclaves' along with
other hobbies and pastimes. Even more than with masturbation, there is the sense that this is an activity which
resists such compartmentalization.

We tend to talk as though sex just *is*; it is
saturated with notions of privacy, spontaneity and naturalness, each of which separates it from the public, determined
and artificial nature of much of the rest of our social life.
We may allow that there are cultural features which give it
a certain relativity, for example, the degree to which
individuals and societies vary in their emphasis upon the
need to choose partners of the opposite sex and in their
emphasis upon certain approved styles and techniques for

reaching orgasm. But, these are peripheral items of cultural relativity. They may be attended or disattended without any critical difference being made to the idea that there is something called sex which has a natural *and* special quality. At times this sense of the natural quality of sex-making has generated major theories which suggest that a concentration upon sexuality might lead to the subversion of the whole nature of paramount reality. Sex has been represented as the key which unlocks the door to total escape. 'Making love is posited against "making war", the creativity of the natural against the destructive, death-dealing power of the technological-bureaucratic world.'[4]

But what aspects of sexual activity allow us to describe it as so special? The behaviour looks perfectly compatible with many other aspects of paramount reality. It is extremely difficult to view contemporary attitudes to sex as unrelated to the consciousness which characterizes our involvement in the other aspects of life. Sex, for example, involves the participants in adhering to a formal sequence of activities; there are stages through which the partners go, which, although amenable to a certain amount of shuffling and skipping, nevertheless follow the basic pattern of foreplay, intercourse and orgasm. It is orgasm which constitutes the end of the activity, the product which is created by the combined work of the participants. Failure to achieve orgasm is related to faults in the earlier process. Measurement of success at sex is increasingly dependent upon the number of orgasms achieved by both partners. Marriage and sexual manuals are preoccupied with the ways in which production norms in this domain might be increased.

Clearly, this concern with stages, techniques and end-products has affinities with the world of work and production. This is to reverse the psychoanalytic tendency to treat sexuality as a source of meaning which informs other worlds, and to suggest instead that meanings and cognitive styles from other worlds may invade the 'natural' area of sex. None of this means that such alien modes of consciousness will *dominate* our sexual lives, any more than they will usurp our hobbies or games; they are simply elements which may invade this free area, and threaten its unique, self-realizing status.

This may do something to undermine the 'uniqueness' of sexual consciousness, but it does little to take away its 'specialness'. Our actual experience of the activity still sets it apart, it 'feels' different, however much it may be apprehended through alien categories.

But do these qualities reside in the activity itself or are they somehow cultural accretions? Gagnon and Simon have set out to establish the latter by proposing that the *special* feelings associated with sexuality arise from the guilt, fear and anxiety which surround the act.[5] They are not declaring that all sexual feelings are produced in these ways, but only the special feeling which sets it apart from such other activities as gourmet cooking (the simile is theirs).

Their argument starts with childhood. For the young child, they argue, there is no such thing as specifically sexual behaviour. Stimulation of parts of the body is a general source of pleasure and stimulation of the genitals is merely one aspect of this auto-eroticism. However, the young child is very soon made aware that genital stimulation must be marked off from other forms of self-stimulation; a sexual vocabulary is placed upon a localized aspect of a general activity. This is the period during which the sexual world emerges, a special life world stocked with taboo words and actions, a world set apart from others by the especially strong emotions which are accredited to it. The child is not naturally a sexual being, for the child sex is not a discriminated activity, either behaviourally or experientally. However, it soon becomes so and in so doing acquires a distinctive set of emotional responses, that special feeling.

Of course, there will be those who claim that sexual activities provide them with special feelings whilst denying that such activities are accompanied by guilt, fear and anxiety. We could only claim in response that everyone's sexual activities have at some time been characterized by such emotions and that therefore the denial of their contemporary presence needs to be taken with some scepticism. We can argue another way by referring to those cases in which the sexual behaviour is described as most special. These appear to be the very occasions upon which guilt, fear or anxiety might be expected to be at a premium – the first girlfriend, the first mistress, the first homosexual adventure, the times that new perversions have been practised, the occasions upon which sex has taken place in unusual circumstances or at unusual times.

We are not asserting that sex in other circumstances is lacking in pleasure, but simply that the 'specialness' of the experience, and therefore its potential escape status is oddly enough related to the degree to which it is accompanied by fear, guilt and anxiety.

The manufacturers and salesmen of pornographic films, photographs and magazines appear to know this only too well. The covert ways in which such products are marketed are guaranteed to arouse the very emotions which create the sense of specialness. The back alleyways, dimly lit clubs, posters which 'dare' you to step inside, advertisements which warn you that you must be over eighteen, are all there to reinforce the childhood guilts and fears, which we might all like to feel we have left well behind.

This is of course the paradox involved in talk of sexual liberation. If the specialness of sexual activity depends upon such emotions as fear, guilt and anxiety, then a society where sex is treated as merely one activity amongst others, will be one in which the behaviour comes to be experienced like other pleasurable activities. This will mean the abandonment of any notion that its specialness might allow it to disrupt contemporary reality. For the freeing of sex from the guilty back alleys of our minds and our cities will destroy its unique potency. It will then be as absurd to look to sex for the subversion of paramount reality as it would be to look to gourmet cooking or stamp collecting.

Now, lest this seem an unnecessarily cynical

position, we would re-emphasize that we are referring to sex-making as it has come to be constituted and experienced within our society. We are talking of a phenomenon which like hobbies or holidays, or drug taking, has been squeezed into a concrete and phenomenal enclave; a phenomenon which like the others we have described does not take its shape wholly from its intrinsic nature but is rather partially determined by the intrustion of alien elements from paramount reality.

The use of such words as 'natural' and 'instinctive' may at first suggest that sex-making occupies a very special free area within paramount reality. But we have tried to show that it is no less immune from the intrusions of routine and excessive self-consciousness or from temporal and spatial localization, or from invasion by modes of consciousness from paramount reality, than any other of the free areas we have described. This is not to say that sex-making provides no relief from the daily round, no sense of occupying a slightly different plane of reality. It is rather that the nature of the activity – *as it has been constituted by society* – is such that this sense will be temporary and precarious. Those who attempt long-term absences from paramount reality through sex-making are unlikely to be any more successful than those who attempt it through landscaping or mindscaping. They will come to be viewed as absurd; for they have not learnt that sex, like hobbies, and the other institutionalized escapes we will discuss – *has its place and its time*.

NEW LANDSCAPES

Holidays

Hobbies and games are forms of shuffling about within the domain of paramount reality. If we look at them using a prison metaphor, they appear simply as ways of making time pass. Within this same metaphor there are also outside working parties, visits, weekend leaves, release on licence. People can be at home in this world but feel the need to 'get out of themselves'; they can cope with the daily round, but every now and then 'things get on top of you'; the familiarity of the regime can be endured, but sometimes 'you have to get away from it all'; self-discipline is tolerable, but you have to 'let your hair down'. The most conventionalized routes which our society provides from all these impulses is the holiday. It is a setting in which constraints can be relaxed if not rejected, identities slip if not disappear, a place where lives are rejuvenated if not changed. The holiday is the archetypal free area, the institutionalized setting for temporary excursions away from the domain of paramount reality. More than digging out an activity enclave you literally create a new landscape. The efforts which go into this creation can be truly epic; sending away for passports, suffering injections, queueing for coaches, trains and planes, sweating for hours in traffic jams, laying in stocks of suntan oil, insect repellent and Entro-vioform, buying special clothes and suitcases, arranging accommodation for the cat, dog, and budgie who are left behind. Martian visitors observing the ten-mile bank-holiday queue of cars loaded with silent grannies, whimpering children and bursting suitcases would be forced to assume that some great god was beckoning his followers. What else could inspire such patience, devotion and endurance?

More than any other everyday escape, the holiday is a small-scale replica of the great escape messages of our culture. Reverberating right through religion, folklore, artistic expression and mass culture, are powerful symbolic and allegorical messages around the theme of a move to a new land. Pilgrims and seekers after spiritual enlightenment must move to new landscapes: somewhere outside the walls of the prison is the Holy Grail, El Dorado, Shangri-La. And even those whose search is inwards use the metaphor of a physical journey to describe their quest: one goes on a *trip*, on a *voyage* of self-discovery. The themes of quest and refuge, episodic excitement and release from constraint are deeply rooted in our culture.

But we will concentrate on holidays rather than

114

the carnivals, feasts and celebrations which have been escapes in other societies. And while package holidays to the Costa Brava, day trips to Margate, pony trekking in Wales, skiing in Switzerland, hardly sound the stuff of which legends are made, they couldn't survive without the legends.

Escape is the explicit message behind the packaging, selling and arranging of such holidays. Travel brochures and advertisements are densely saturated with escape messages: get away from it all, relax, be yourself, leave your worries at home, enter a new, exciting world. 'The urge to escape comes to most of us at some time or another. No more office politics, dreary train journeys, boring strikes, power cuts and nasty colds. Just one long, pleasant life in the sun, dispensing booze to happy customers and chatting up vulnerable female tourists,' writes William Davis, in *High Life*, the magazine published by British Airways and given free to travellers, but, 'It usually stays a daydream.' And then he counts the practical cost of ever getting this particular dream scripted. Potential landscapers are warned that they might have to work hard on their fantasies.

As the producers of such messages become conscious about the public's possible disbelief that holidays will actually provide these meanings, so they stumble over themselves to devise new messages playing down the conventional holiday – as satirized in folklore and stage humour about the package holiday – and offer new potentials. And as these become more sophisticated, so too does the meta-message that even the new experience can be a let down. We will let you into our fantasy landscape, but remember that it is just a fantasy.

The difficulties of landscaping can be seen in the new ways of attracting middle-class consumers who want more from their holidays than relaxation, who want an *authentic* experience. 'The concern of moderns for the shallowness of their life and inauthenticity of their experience parallels the concern for the sacred in primitive society.'[6] Thus sightseers and tourists are motivated to see life as it really is and to get in with the natives. The term 'tourist' even becomes a derisive label for someone who seems content with the obviously inauthentic experience of the staged flamenco dance or the watered-down native food. Advertisements then stress getting off the beaten path and tour managers elaborately create staged back regions: spaces for the outsider to view the inner operations of various commercial or domestic institutions, for example, the cooking and preparation of local food: 'Entry into this space allows adults to recapture original sensations of discovery, or childlike feelings of being half in and half out of society, their faces pressed up against the glass.'[7]

Another part of the sales offer – almost the opposite of the promise of authentic experience – is the stress on fantasy, the possibility of excitement, action and adventure. British Airways' Minitrek brochure offers an 'action holiday' because 'we believe that there's also a bit of the explorer in everyone's character'. It quotes satisfied customers who saw the expeditions across the Sahara as 'romantic trips', holidays which 'should attract the traveller who had done everything else'. The Minitrekker in fact is a 'particular kind of person', young men and women 'with a high sense of adventure willing to have a go at practically anything so long as it's exciting or unusual'. Much more, indeed, is offered; Laurence Durrell is quoted to sell the Greek Minitrek: 'Other countries offer discoveries in matters of lore or landscape: Greece offers you something harder – the discovery of yourself'. A territory especially created for identity work. What more alluring prospect could there be?

In searching holiday advertisements for such messages, we were delighted to find one whose name was created before our own book's title: 'Escape Routes Limited'. It addresses its prospective customers as 'Dear Adventurer' and offers escapes to 'experience our Wonderful World', with Land Rovers, cosy 'tents for two' and expeditions to remote corners of the world in which 'the journey is as important as the destination'.

The fantasy element in such cultural packaging is explicit. There is the possibility of excitement, fun, and more specifically, sexual adventure. The greater openness with which cultural escape routes are now being mapped, has allowed the previously tacit functions of the holiday to be laid out more clearly. Thus the holiday romance or affair is the stock-in-trade of jokes and television sketches featuring Spanish or Italian seduction scenes. An almost regular feature of holiday literature (such as *High Life*) are guides – often written by celebrities – on how to actually set up, manage and eventually safely terminate the holiday affair.[8] The right hairstyle, the correct opening gambits (' "Didn't I see you on the Rome flight last week?" is as good an opening as any. You are fairly safe with Rome as most airlines go there.') are carefully set up. And the script always contains the provision for ensuring that the fantasy doesn't go too far.

Whether the advertisements are believed in or not, whether the holiday actually provides these experiences or not are altogether open questions. There is no reason why everything we have said about self-monitoring, meta-consciousness and role-distancing should not apply to the free area of the holiday and transform it into the routine, the ritualized. This is precisely the safety-net function which holidays perform: after the trip one returns home. The prospective holiday-maker glancing through the brochure is not as dumb as the satirical sketches about the package holiday would have us believe. In spite of the photos in the brochure of seductive flamenco dancers, he knows that he is much more likely to be sitting in a crowded bar with a secretary from Leicester; despite the precision schedules, itineraries and timetables he knows that meals, tours and aircraft departures will be late; despite the extravagant descriptions of the hotel he almost expects that it will be half-built. The very prose of the holiday brochure contains within it the seeds of its own destruction. The promise – of a world in which one is constantly basking idly on the parched decks of a yacht bobbing softly at anchor in some neglected Mediterranean cove, a bronzed companion in one hand, a Martini in the other, pausing now and then to flip into the water – is just too good to be true, just too fantastic to be scriptable.

The point though is that because people not only learn, but learn about learning, they can monitor the package holiday, the weekend by the sea, the night out, in such ways as consciously to project themselves into the fantasy, nudge it even further away from reality. The fact that the holiday becomes a commodity, that it follows patterns and rituals, that it can be satirized, does not strip it of its escape functions any more than is the entertainment provided for the professional wrestling fan lost if he knows that the match is fixed. The fan can assert his independence from the ritual precisely by being in the know, and showing that he is. Thus, the intellectual's critique of tourist settings for being elaborately contrived artificial mirages, 'insufficiently policed by liberal concerns for truth and beauty' is misplaced.[9] Tourists even when searching for authenticity are capable of ironically commenting on their disappointment in not finding it: they see through the staged authenticity of the tourist setting and laugh about it. An exposure to the back region – that is, an awareness that things are not quite what they seem – is a casual part of the tourist experience: 'What they see in the back is only another show: it does not shock, trick or anger them and they do not express any feelings of having been made less pure by their discovery.'[10]

We arrange the new landscape according to our fantasies and so what actually takes place there is not so important; the holiday experience can be transformed into something which looks like the cultural message it offers. It would not be going too far to suggest that the standard holiday folklore about things going wrong – the half-built hotels, the bus going to the wrong place or leaving us behind, the lost suitcases, misunderstandings about the language, the unpalatable food and tummy troubles, how we were cheated by the locals – exists only because people actually make things go wrong or embroider on these stories afterwards. People not only see through such institutionalized escape routes, but go on to inject more than is provided.

This might be observed in accounts of the typical 'adventure holiday'.[11] If we have been on the trip before, we do not believe the adventure promise too sincerely and go for other reasons, such as the presence of friends. But the raw recruit does accept the possibility that something might happen. On the expedition though, reality might intrude in an unexpectedly unpleasant way. When the Land Rover gets stuck in the sand (a contingency the brochure offers as an adventure), it is actually experienced with great anxiety, fuss and distress. On returning home, though, the fantasy element is reinjected and minor incidents (such as accidents or illnesses) are elevated into grand proportions. The adventure came true. Similarly the quest for a new self is fulfilled: the 'adventurer' often consciously sheds layers of his old self – posing in the anonymous free area of the holiday as someone else. At group reunions after the holiday, the expedition's barrister or journalist is shamefully revealed as a bank clerk.

It is the rare holiday, as it is the rare hobby, though, which totally transforms our mode of being in the world. Holidays are just – literally and metaphorically – excursions from the domain of paramount reality. The changes they lead to hardly imply the creation of alternative realities. We can go away from home, but change only one part of the home such as the weather. This is presumably what is involved in self-catered villa holidays in the Mediterranean where the family is greeted by a hamper of English food and shops selling tea like mother makes. And although we might return feeling relaxed and unburdened, all that we have to prove this is a suntan rather than a new self. And although the prison might temporarily have been left behind, the final irony of the market economy triumphs: the benefits from the holiday simply strengthen our ability to accommodate again to the reality of work.

Some explorers, voyagers and adventurers have tried to make themselves immune from being caught up by the world. There are those who deliberately set out to give up comfort, routine, family, friends, safety, to test their strength, faith and courage against a hostile and alien environment.

But while the epic voyagers and explorers of the past might indeed have escaped, it is very difficult to get such trips going now. Adventures have become packaged to look like little more than holidays. On commercial safaris, participants are encouraged to faithfully simulate the real scripts. In the packaged hunting expedition into the deepest jungle, the professional leader elaborately hides away with his weapons in order to give the hunters the impression that they are alone in their confrontations with wild beasts. Affluent business executives are known to put up with a subsistence diet and excessively spartan living conditions to recapture the spirit of adventure, man alone against nature. Such trips are subject to the same possibilities of reality slipping as govern the more conventional holiday. We pretend, but sometimes we have to pretend to pretend because real physical risks might actually intrude.

At a different level of motivation, much exploration and adventuring is carried out in the spirit of competition and conquest and in this respect it is hardly very different from competitive hobbying. Scaling a particular mountain, trying to break an endurance record for living in an underground cave, taking part in a cross-Atlantic sailing race might be objectively more dangerous than fishing, stamp collecting or leek growing but their functions as escape routes are quite similar. The differences are that the exposure to risks may be greater than are bargained for, that the activities are impregnated with values which do stress alternative realities and that legendary or actual exemplars of these values are being constantly referred to.

If it is sometimes difficult to see the standard hobby or sport as a way of finding ourselves or glimpsing alternative reality, this is by no means the case with adventuring and exploring. For the archetypal voyager the promise is that somewhere – in the bleakness of the Arctic night, the loneliness in mid-Atlantic, the blinding heat of the desert – he will be stripped of his protective layers of civilization, freed from boredom and routine to discover an alternative reality. Sometimes the reality is one of simple cultural diversity – the noble-savage theme – at other times it is of a more transcendental nature – a cosmic consciousness or an awareness of the insignificance of the self. While such adventures are by no means impossible today, it is very difficult actually to assemble the stage and props for the script, without becoming culturally co-opted. Voyaging alone around the world is slightly less of an escape if we are sponsored by Pepsi-Cola and followed by a five-man BBC television crew. The great adventure may slip back into being another holiday.

It is Simmel's characterization of 'The Adventure' which perfectly captures the way in which all such holidays – like other free areas – are simultaneously continuous and discontinuous with paramount reality:

> While it falls outside the context of life, it falls with this same movement, as it were, back into that context again ... it is a foreign body in our existence which is yet somehow connected with the center; the outside, if only by a long and unfamiliar detour, is formally an aspect of the inside.[12]

Mass Culture

We have already considered mass culture as a source of scripts and fantasies. But of course the creation and consumption of the products of mass culture serve as free areas in their own right and because of their saturation with fantasy elements such products have a high potential for reality slipping.

The recognition of such potential has been the key argument in the standard critiques about the escapist nature of mass culture. We are told – with the implication that this is a bad thing – that people can escape from the 'real' problems of everyday life by immersing themselves in the fantasy worlds of movies, comics, television, novels and art. This is the conventional 'opium of the masses' argument. Our interest is not a polemical one to argue for or against this position but to analyse the precise senses in which mass culture might serve escape functions or – more generally – might situate the person in a different relationship to paramount reality.

Our concern with mass culture as a vehicle for institutionalized reality slipping is related again to its subjective meanings rather than its overall societal function. On the societal level we would agree with the Situationist critique of mass culture: no form of creativity, innovation, revolution, escape is immune from being absorbed into the dominant ideology as just another package to be bought in the cultural supermarket. Even art forms such as the blues, which once had a potent liberatory and escape function for its producers and consumers, can be stripped of such meanings by commercialization and routinization. They may no longer offer an even temporary absence from the fabric. Debord is correct: 'The entire life of societies in which modern conditions of production reign appears as an immense accumulation of *spectacles*. Everything that was experienced directly has been distanced in a representation.'[13]

But while plastic might not be the real thing, it is clearly something; while fantasies might be synthesized and reduced to the level of the market, they are still available and people *can* 'experience directly' in their ceremonies, spectacles and rituals a sense of alternative realities. The argument is similar to that we used in discussing authenticity in tourist settings: it is not that people are dummies being hopelessly manipulated in the carnivals and side-shows of capitalism but that there is no guarantee that once having seen the trick – it's all done by mirrors – they won't continue participating. The fact that people can experience mass culture (as they do their family, their work, their hobbies) through different modalities and can bring to the experience distancing and self-consciousness, means that a crude communication – audience model of mass culture won't work. The medium is neither simply message nor massage: it is a free area in its own right, an escape route to other areas and the force that charges up our fantasy batteries.

What, for example, is involved in a night out at the movies? At a primitive level the experience itself might be a literal free area: away from home and work we can sit quietly in the dark, relaxed, out of play and anonymous. Hyper-awareness of this experience can destroy it: this is me sitting in a dark building in a seat which I've paid 80p for and watching some images flickering across a screen. For those who feel at home in the world, for those who simply want a temporary release from pressures and are not investing too much in this escape, there is little reason why such forms of consciousness should intrude more than momentarily. They can easily be accommodated to, and for the more sophisticated (as any reader of *Cahiers du Cinema* or any of the other numerous intellectual guide-books on how to enjoy the movies will know) going to movies can be elevated to a fetish, an object of worship. There are well-known scripts for this: the fanatic, the film goer, the buff. The scripts have their own special stages as the National Film Theatre, film clubs, with props such as pin-ups, biographies, complete movie scripts and – more recently – long-playing records of entire sound tracks of cult movies such as *Casablanca*.

These three levels of involvement – just going to the movies, distancing and becoming a film goer – correspond to the ways in which we relate to the actual fantasy component of the movie. At the primitive level we simply enter into the fantasy: we are literally – as the advertisements promise – transported into other worlds. During the hours of the movie and the subsequent hours, days or years of fantasies, we are in the world of duels, fast cars, secret agents, gangsters, shoot-outs, beautiful women, tragedy, drama. All magic and myth is there. What happens though, when the tricks are exposed, the myths destroyed, the fantasies brought down to earth? For some, the process of seeing through the illusions is critical and the movie-goer is urged to realize the essential un-reality of his experience. In some quarters, for example, the Hollywood dream machine is criticized for pretending to ignore the presence of the spectator, pretending that the cinema reflects reality. A typical such critique from this quarter accuses the bourgeois cinema of playing on the spectators' emotions and capitalizing on his identification and projection mechanisms 'in order to induce him subtly, insidiously, unconsciously to participate in the dreams and fantasies that are marketed by bourgeois capitalist society'.[14]

This critique demands ultra self-consciousness and is a rationale for such aesthetic innovations (mirroring the Brechtian theories of drama) as those in Godard's later movies where, for example, the sound and sight of a clapper board is introduced to remind the audience that they should be aware that they are watching a film, in other words, to dislocate their subliminal acceptance of the fantasy as being real.

The problem with staying at this stage – in simple escape terms – is that like other forms of meta-consciousness, it can become extremely boring. We have somehow to climb off the consciousness spiral and enter again into the fantasy. This, presumably, is what Pauline Kael meant by saying that 'a movie is only a movie when you can pretend that it is not a movie'.[15] So we reach the third stage: climbing off the spiral staircase of self-consciousness, we pretend to believe the fantasies are as real as anything else.

The movie illustration can serve as well for any of the other entertainments and spectacles of our time. Even those forms of consumption like reading, listening to records and the radio, watching television, which don't involve any literal moving to new landscapes, are free areas and they project fantastic scenes. Consider how much we invest in these free areas: the morning newspaper arrives with a story about Richard Burton's latest romance (sexual and success fantasies flicker across); turn to sports page where last night's goal by Keegan is described as 'ordinary' (briefly angry, get into complicated script of writing another description of the goal, worry how Keegan must feel when he sees newspaper); then listen to radio in car on way to work (record request played for couple in Stoke reminds you of bad evening spent there, music itself, though, associated with old girlfriend); at work, long discussion over coffee about selection of MCC Touring Team (Should Boycott have accepted without being made captain? Will the Australian pitch help our bowlers?); home again in time to watch TV news (warnings of new power cuts; should we get away from it all for a winter holiday?); whole of supper-time now taken up by discussion about possible holiday (will it be a real break if the kids come with us, more privacy if we go to a villa rather than a hotel, but how much of a holiday will it be if we have to cook and wash dishes?), and after dinner off to the local Odeon to see the new James Bond . . .

Such a hypothetical daily sequence shows not only how preoccupied we are with escapes and free areas but just how complex is the shuffling about between our daily round and those other worlds which have their own logic and rules. But this shuffling about is not always disturbing. Indeed it has rhythms which we get used to. Our fantasies and worries about Kevin Keegan, James Bond, Richard Burton and the Australian pitches don't disturb our daily round very much. And this really shows the odd precariousness of these other worlds: the more we can absorb them, the more fragile they are as escapes. If only we could – through the primordial facility the child has to project himself into the world of fairies, princes and wizards – see these worlds on their own terms we could give in to their magical rhythms. The child can realize the magic by interpreting his own world in terms of the 'other one': sister is a princess, the garden shed is a castle, the pet cat is a dragon. We are doomed by consciousness to interpreting in exactly the opposite way: paramount reality supplies the scripts for seeing the other world: Richard Burton has alimony problems, the actor who plays James Bond has now been fired, will we be able to digest the Spanish food on holiday? It needs either a fine calculation not to let these scripts mess up the landscapes of mass culture, or the opposite: such a massive and fanatic investment that these scripts become the free areas themselves.

Art

It is not difficult, given this type of analysis, to slip from the world of mass culture into the world of art. For the traditional attack by high culture (for example from the Leavis position) on mass culture stresses precisely its desensitizing nature. Far from leading its audience into a perspective which lies outside paramount reality, this critique suggests it merely reproduces in an attractive way the more mundane features of that reality. This perspective insists upon the need to maintain an area of transcendental high tar which is not similarly grounded, an area in which sublime truths about the nature of man and his existence may be preserved. The criteria by which such truths may be recognized have been extensively debated and need not concern us here; our interest lies in the notion of a special free area which has been created by the artist, and which may be visited by all those who wish to escape the common round of mundane experience.

We need, first of all, to recognize that this conception of art as existing in a special super- or extra-societal domain, is not an intrinsic development from the nature of art itself. Raymond Williams and others have shown how the notion of an artistic domain was historically related to the development of the industrial revolution, a system of production whose emphasis upon the mass production of commodities, was seen by certain writers and artists as incompatible with artistic creativity.

However, as is the case with all other free areas, the mere indication of relativity is not enough to destroy the possibility that they still provide escape opportunities for those who turn to them for that purpose. And, certainly, there are many who would maintain that their contact with art or their involvement in its creation constitutes just such an opportunity to move away from paramount reality. Art is symbolically a new landscape although for most of its consumers – those who join madrigal groups, record societies, poetry-appreciation classes – it is just another activity enclave.

However, it is not just the domain of high art which is a societal creation, but also the contemporary mode of comprehending that art. There is an artistic attitude which appears to represent a precondition for the appreciation of any work of art. Without this attitude (as the public are warned by those like Kenneth Clark) the possibilities of art serving as a reality-transformer appear to be diminished. Perhaps there are those who accidentally wander into an art gallery, find themselves face to face with a Rembrandt or Van Gogh and then subsequently declare that the experience has given them emancipation from the pressures of mundane life. Or those like the uncultured Leonard in Forster's *Howards End* who discovers an alternative reality in listening to Beethoven's Fifth. However, it is difficult to avoid the conclusion that such experiences are more likely to be recounted by those who have had some opportunity to develop an artistic consciousness, who have 'learned', even in the most elementary way, how to look at pictures, or read poetry, or view architecture. This learning to look involves not so much the mastery of any principles of aesthetics (although of course these may be included) but rather a knowledge of what we should 'get out' of art. The most elementary forms of instruction – the manuals for the aesthetic-appreciation script – advise us to look for something special within the object, to search for an inner meaning. This meaning, we are taught does not come easily, it requires patience. There is therefore an appropriate amount of time to be spent in the contemplation of artistic commodities, and also in the establishment of the right mood, setting and companions. We are programmed then to discover some revelation, some key to life or nature, which will help us to transform ourselves. It is not too surprising then that users frequently discover such transforming properties in art, that they declare their identity to be changed by the experience.

Now we are not being so naive as to suggest that the 'work of art' has no intrinsic potency, that it does not in some way transcend the mundane, but rather asserting that the 'personalized revelation' mode of appreciation is particular to the contemplation of art in contemporary society. The nature of the revelation is bounded by societal conceptions of the degree of transformative power that 'should' reside within art – as it 'should' in sexuality or drug-taking.

Artists themselves are frequently aware of this 'enclave' appreciation and either insist that their works are incomprehensible (that they contain no inner revelation, no messages about identity or reality) or else that their meaning is immediately manifest (it does not depend for its emergence upon the adoption of a special contemplative mode). They may attempt to make their work more disturbing so that the response steps over the institutionalized boundaries of what constitutes an 'artistic experience'. Similarly they may attempt to move outside galleries, or novels, or theatres, in order to evade the customary modes of artistic contemplation. But however much their art may be said to carry intrinsically disturbing visions of alternative reality, the institutionalized mode of its appreciation makes it for many people, not so much a revolutionary impetus, but rather a circumscribed domain in which temporary relief from the daily round may be obtained. And banal as it might be, it is worth repeating the critique of elitist art which asserts that its world is often too remote from everyday life to even look like an escape route. This is what pop artists have realized. But in transforming shoes, soup cans and hamburgers into artistic objects they have simply made *these* objects sacred and special rather than madonnas, landscapes and princes. So pop art's celebrations of mundane objects – unlike, for example, the Dadaists use of 'ready mades' – are accepted as genuine artistic statements. Disgusted with these new developments, Marcel Duchamp wrote to Hans Richter:

> When I discovered ready mades I thought to discourage esthetics. In Neo-Dada they have taken my ready mades

and found esthetic beauty in them. I threw the bottle rack and the urinal into their faces as a challenge and now they admire them for their esthetic beauty.[16]

There is a certain irony involved in our committed artistic recourse to everyday objects as a way of distancing ourselves from the everyday.

MINDSCAPING

The hobbyist goes down to his cellar or garden, the games player strides off to his field or casino, the holidaymaker packs his clothes, cameras and suntan oil, the culture freak runs around art galleries and concert halls – but all round us, men and women are sitting quite still actively resisting everyday life by moving things around within their heads. At the most they might reach out for a glass of whisky or a joint, get their legs crossed into the lotus position or drag themselves to a psychiatrist's office. But for them, the sense of escaping by doing anything, or manipulating objects, still less of actually changing their physical surroundings, is quite alien. The problem is in the head. These are mindscapers.

Drugs

The occasional use of mind-altering drugs is a prototypical illustration of such forms of institutionalized reality slipping. With the widely disseminated cultural knowledge about the effects of such drugs few prospective users can claim not to know the experience they are looking for. The programming of these escape scripts is very explicit. The anticipated effects vary with the nature and intensity of the drug – from the milder effects claimed for cannabis such as relaxation, slight changes of mood, to the more spectacular claims made for LSD, such as ego loss and mystical insight – but they all have in common the aim of going out of play. In this sense drug use is an escape from reality – although the cultural expectations (and in some cases the actual effects) might be to provide a glimpse of an alternative reality or to enhance the existing one. It is of course alcohol – rather than the newer psychotropic drugs – which provides the classic cultural escape route: we drink to get away from our wife, to forget our job, to drown our sorrows.

The 'social drinker' is only in the weakest sense a candidate for reality slipping. What he buys is euphoria, relaxation and a lubricant to keep the wheels of social interaction moving. There is the subliminal promise – sometimes verified by experience – of new insights into the self and others: the classic *in vino veritas* theme, in which real self emerges or we learn who our friends really are. In the background might be the risk of alcoholism, illness, dependence, the possibility that your life will be ruined. But these are risks built in to deter people from drinking, they are hardly ones that attract as forms of escape. The eventual status of alcoholism is a wholly pathological one, while the statuses en route are either despised ('problem drinker') or highly routinized ('social drinker').

Unlike holidays, which are explicitly packaged with the promise of a special escape, alcohol is sold with wholly down-to-earth promises. The man who 'only came for the beer' is going to achieve nothing more than being cheerful and good company. The Martini advertisements promise the good life only in the sense that they use the same idyllic settings as the appeals to buy particular brands of toothpaste, deodorant or hairspray. Those messages which do suggest more radical escape or reality slippage – like the girls in the Smirnoff vodka advertisements who are never quite the same again – are so self-consciously sending themselves up that no one can believe them. Cultural exemplars are few, and only in such writings as Malcolm Lowry's does one find an articulate apologia for alcohol as the path to some transcendence. And these exemplars invariably meet tragic ends.

The newer mind-altering drugs on the other hand, while viewed by conventional society in wholly negative terms, offer to the user the prospects of a real escape. What we buy initially is a solution to short-term problems, a form of relaxation, an easy mechanism for changing moods and this is all the occasional user gets. But the drug culture is saturated with the message of alternative realities. In the various versions found in guru figures like Leary, the hippie's ideology, the identification with Eastern mysticism, the promises are extreme and marvellous: a complete rejection of formal work values, a destruction of the bonds of linearity and time, a discovery of the self, a cosmic identification with the universe. The user knows – like Goffman's gambler – that there is the possibility of some of these things happening, of a 'pay-off to flow beyond the bounds of the occasion'. But there are powerful conventionalizing forces at work which can pull in the opposite direction. The mass-availability and gradual social acceptance of 'soft' drugs make it harder to render the experience a special one reserved for the privileged few. It is explicitly recognized that the drug experience as such might not change these new users; 'A turned-on square', as Mailer notes, 'is still a square'. The activity itself also becomes ritualized and subject to the pressures of a market economy. The drug culture is saturated with problems of supply and demand, paranoia about busts, fear and suspicion. Far from being evidence of rejecting bourgeois consumer values, the drug culture might mirror them: buying a chemical solution to life problems is hardly a move into a different reality.

There are also the negative risks, that the tab will literally blow our mind, that experimenting with hard drugs will lead down the escalator of addiction. Again it is a question of the script which accompanies the escape attempt: the complex symbolic meanings attached to drugs – compared say with hobbies – make it difficult not to pick up a potent escape message. The drug culture is continually putting down those who use chemicals as 'personality props' or just to relax, help time pass, keep social interaction moving along. The vulnerability of this escape route lies in the precarious balance between expectation and effect, a balance which is not always in the control of the user.

Therapy

The overt promise of a holiday (relaxation, getting away from it all) with its subliminal message of risk taking has a curious parallel in the area of personal therapy. Here the overt promise is a healing and reparative one (mending the psyche, resolving conflict, reducing tension and anxiety) but the subliminal message is much more important and constitutes an escape route for the healthy as well as the sick. The promise – and as we shall see – the risk, is no less than that of personal liberation, escape from a prison created by the mind.

Of course, psychotherapy is something other than an 'institutionalized escape route' or free area, but for our argument this is its most significant function. Its spectacular popularity in the last fifty years together with the more recent proliferation of options such as Gestalt therapy, encounter groups, sensitivity training, Esalen, awareness groups, are moves in the overall cultural directions we are tracing. (A recent estimate suggested that as many as six million Americans had participated in some kind of sensitivity, encounter or personal-growth group. And such groups are of course only one part of the therapeutic empire.)[17] Such therapies offer widely different, if not contradictory modes of liberation. To take just one dimension, the classic psychoanalytical message is that the prison is created by the past: as Marcuse puts it, remembrance of things past becomes the vehicle of future liberation. In other therapies however the stress is on the here and now: the patient is expected to examine every aspect of his current situation before an alternative future reality is possible. But stressing the past or the present, exploiting the conscious or the unconscious, using free associations or non-directive probing, talking or massaging, the goal of therapy is to bring about a change of consciousness.

For Freud, such psychic manipulation was not

at all an entry into an alternative reality. He would have been far too pessimistic and sceptical to even contemplate such a philosophy. The classic psychoanalytical message, as Karl Menninger once put it, is that it's not your neurosis that counts, but how you live with it. The newer cult therapies offer something more spectacular. Maslow's Human Potential Movement '. . . more revolutionary than bombs, bullets or slogans . . . deals with non-verbal experience, altered states of consciousness and various techniques, whereby people can find new ways to identify themselves and live their lives more fully.'[18] Autogenic training offers total control of even bodily functions like heartbeat and temperature. Masters and Houston (directors of the New York Foundation for Mind Research) actually sell a practical system for achieving ASCs (Altered States of Consciousness) which results in greater imagination and creativity until 'we one day look back astounded at the impoverished world of consciousness we once shared, and supposed to be the real world, our officially defined and defended reality'.

There is no reason to doubt that some people believe these promises or even that they have such experiences. But we cannot believe that these altered states of consciousness can remain safe for very long from the insistent demands of the paramount-reality police. How do we suspend self-consciousness if the tracks to liberation are laid with ASCIDs (Altered States of Consciousness Induction Devices, which are cradles which immobilize a person's body as it rocks him through space); bio-energetic diets and exercises; orgone boxes; biofeedback electrodes to monitor your own brainwaves; fasting; casting sticks; organic foods; nude encounter groups; OPLSs (Opto-kinetic Perceptual Learning Devices, which are revolving drum-shaped light-boxes); sensory deprivation; progressive massage relaxation; Rolfing (a body-manipulation technique designed by Ida Rolf which 'digs into the muscle linings to get at the soul')?

None of these activities is intrinsically more absurd or capable of distancing behaviour than stamp collecting, playing badminton or pony trekking but neither are they less so. And when they claim to do so much – as many drugs do – they must be very wary indeed of invasions from the controllers of paramount reality.

Cultural co-option of such mass therapies is also a threat. Not only are the how-to-do-it guides marketed in an obviously exploitative manner, but the institutions in which such mindscaping takes place look suspiciously unlike the creations of an alternative consciousness. Biofeedback systems, transcendental meditation, Divine Light and the like are packaged and marketed in the same way as Charles Atlas Body Building courses. (Indeed when we discussed the way long-term prisoners coped with their paramount reality, we considered mind building and body building as – in the beloved phrase of sociologists – 'functional alternatives'.)

The crippling blow to mindscaping as an escape into alternative reality, as a site for identity-work, will come (and in some places has already come) through the harnessing of those techniques to the market economy. Directors, managers and workers are going or being sent to encounter groups, Esalen weekends and sensitivity training sessions to help them perform more adequately. It cannot be too long before work canteens start serving bio-energetic lunches, boards of directors cast the I Ching and assembly-line workers chant a suitably selected mantra.

But even leaving aside the dangers of self-consciousness and commercial exploitation, what liberation does the actual message itself offer? Here the claims of mass-cult therapies and psychedelic drug cultures may be considered together.

All these popular contemporary therapies are closely allied to the very traditional Eastern ways of liberation, not only in the sense that both involve a change of consciousness but also aim to free the individual from various forms of social conditioning, habits and routines. Part of the liberation is from hating the conditioning because the hatred itself is a form of bondage to its object. The patient's troubles are not merely psychological but reside in the social institutions, language, relationships in which he is trapped. The patient's distress, like the un-initiated's troubles arise from *maya*: not just illusion, but the outside culture. 'The aim of a way of liberation is not the destruction of *maya* but seeing it for what it is, or seeing through it.'[19]

Such liberation is similar to that provided by the monitoring, self-consciousness and distancing which we have described in more sociological language. It is equally radical in the sense of opening up the windows to an alternative reality and equally conservative in saying that this is only a window.

> ... The task of the psychotherapist is to bring about a reconci-liation between individual feeling and social norms without, however, sacrificing the integrity of the individual. He tries to help the individual to be himself and to go it alone without giving unnecessary offence to his community, to be in the world (of social convention) but not of the world.[20]

It is precisely the opposite of all this which characterizes the more radical escapes we consider later. These offer little chance of 'reconciliation' between the individual and society; they do run the risk of sacrificing the 'integ-rity' of the individual; the going it alone must give 'un-necessary offence' to the community; we are neither in nor of the world.

Here lies the risk of therapy and other forms of self-discovery aided or unaided by chemical or other techniques. For the reality might slip so far away that there is no route back. If 'there is nowhere to go but in' then the voyage of discovery might indeed parallel the Laingian trip into schizophrenia. The risk, as in gambling, and drug use, lies in taking the message too seriously.

If we submit to therapy in the way characterized by Watts, Rieff and others, it remains a transitional stage, an institutionalized escape rather than the real way. For therapies – especially of the more traditional variety – are escapes purposely constructed to let us back in again. We nestle down in the wooden horse without much expectation that the horse itself will move. It is not just that the thrice-weekly production of 'insights' to our therapist eventually becomes routine and that the spectacle of thousands of suburban housewives studying yoga at evening institutes looks a bit unlike a 'special experience'. The more complicated problem is that the act of submitting ourselves to these treatments, regimes and activities, involves a classic confrontation with two messages which are mutually contradictory. On the one hand is the unavoidable fact that submission is an escape from the real world, on the other there is the frequent admonition in each of these therapies that they do *not* constitute escapes from reality, we will have to return to family relationships, work, where the 'real' problems are. The contradiction in the escape message is obvious even to those who have the most transitory flashes of self-consciousness: we go to the room of a complete stranger, lie on a couch and talk about personal problems; we go into a weekend retreat to get rid of our inhibitions and have our naked body touched by people we have never seen before; we go to our usual 'consciousness raising' Women's Liberation meeting and then return to the home routine. The mindscaper finds – not admittedly, with the same sense of physical immediacy as the landscaper knows – that the escape script is often a homecoming script.

Activity enclaves, landscaping and mindscaping can be seen as well-established tunnels out of paramount reality. But their walls are precarious and they threaten every minute to cave in. Before considering some other routes, we must anticipate an objection to our image of everyone digging away at his own special tunnel. For the fact is that so common are these routes, that we may have tried nearly all of them.

A visit to either one of our respective homes at the moment would reveal a museum of half-abandoned relics from these escape routes and free areas. Here there is a health-food diet book and a half-empty muesli packet left over from the days when rejuvenation through food was eagerly tried. In the desk drawer are fragments of the unfinished novel which meant emancipation from the drudgery of academic life. The bookshelves are full of long-forgotten novels and psychological tracts which at the time of reading seemed to offer the key to personal happiness, being nice to our family and able to cope with life's burdens. Alongside the packets of Rizlas and torn cardboard on the living-room shelf are old boxes of incense sticks to remind us that tonight's taken-for-granted joint was only a few years ago seen as the doorway to new perception. Lying in an old shoe box are photos of the country cottage which was going to be the place to get away from it all. Hanging on the walls are Klee and Picasso reproductions bought in the days when it was important to have our aesthetic sensitivities fully catered for. Stuffed in the sock drawer are a few Indian beads we used to wear to pop festivals. Our annual bank-balance statements reveal payments of stop orders for causes we no longer even remember supporting. And in the cupboard under the stairs lie discarded travel brochures, half-constructed model airplanes, wrinkled dahlia tubers, unfinished water-colours, vegetarian recipe books, the remains of three hand-made candles, a smelly beer-stained polythene bucket, and a nasty pile of fetid mushroom culture. There are even deserted rooms in the house to remind us of the days when the fantasy of providing a communal haven for itinerant hippie student friends was still going strong.

Gloomily surveying the debris of failed escapes, we must wonder if there is some route which is too pure or natural to be spoilt or – failing that – some hope of putting together some of the elements which by themselves have proved so susceptible to subversion, so incapable of furthering our quest for identity. Can there be one composite free area, which will be less precarious, and from which escapes will be unnecessary?

6

Getting it Together

Any reflection on the meaning to the individual of those frenetic activities we reviewed in the previous chapter will reveal an obvious paradox: that the use of all these free areas and enclaves will often not signify a desire to escape. Quite the reverse. It may indicate a profound contentment with our state of current being, with our present accommodation to paramount reality. The regular pub drinker, the family on the annual holiday by the sea, the student smoking a joint on his way to the Saturday-night disco, the husband engaging in a standard flirtation script with his secretary, may all be embracing the diverse charms which paramount reality offers, rather than seeking special areas of immunity.

But each of these activities as we have seen carries prospects of dissociation from the world: hobbies, holidays, games, risk-taking, adventure, drugs and sex are areas heavily saturated with messages of escape and identity-transformation. Indeed, we are increasingly surrounded by an ideology which tries to transform every activity into a potential escape. The mundane world is saturated with escape messages. Look at the new how-to-do-it books in the hip bookstores: Zen is offered as well as fruit pickling, yoga as well as playing chess, sexual liberation as well as badminton. You can even pick up a catalogue to all these activities in such books as *The Great Escape* (significantly classified in the Library of Congress catalogue under the heading 'Handbooks, Vade Mecums') which list escape routes such as ashrams, astrology, autogenic training, bio-energetics, painting, chanting, I Ching, massage, psychodrama, sensuous awakening, women's liberation, yoga, martial arts, dancing, occult, drugs, sexual workshops, discovering wild flowers, eating, boating, fishing, nude sunbathing, parachuting, bird watching, travelling, doing jigsaws ... And for a less esoteric audience, the classified advertisements in such regular publications as *Time Out* sell computer dating and economy package flights along with encounter groups, free universities and the familiar stuff of the commercial underground. Even the 'Accommodation Vacant' column can suggest dense escape scripts (as we flick through it, conjuring up quick *Last Tango in Paris* fantasies of desperate sex in a 'flat to let'). All around us – on advertisement hoardings, bookshelves, record covers, television screens – these miniature escape fantasies present themselves. This, it seems, is how we are destined to live, as split personalities in which the private life is disturbed by the promise of escape routes to another reality – and (curiously) private life itself is held out as an escape.

But to say that everything can be an escape is as unhelpful as it is to assert that there is no need to look for escapes, that life offers everything. The complexities of the life plan do not allow for such simple visions, and the guidebooks, while helping us to travel along each escape route offer no help at all in locking together the various free areas, fantasies, scripts into some overall life plan. The enclaving of the free area, the absorption of the fantasy, the repetition of the script make it difficult to move very far. At best, we will find ways of stitching together a few escapes into some larger domain: holidays may turn into quests for romantic love, sex may be transformed with the aid of psychedelic drugs, spatial and temporal barriers may be broken by extending the night out with the boys into a whole lost week of drunkenness.

But even this compositing of free areas may afford only a marginal increase in the size and density of our escape zone. The complexity of the life plan will resist much further expansion; at home a sick child needs looking after, at work an urgent report has to be written, there's an overdue tax form to complete, the mortgage to be paid, the car to be serviced, the garden wall to be repaired. Paramount reality is a world of timetables, routines, duties, responsibilities, fixed times, fixed places. We have to learn that our temporarily extended free areas are only 'binges', 'arousal jags', 'crazy interludes', 'mad flings', 'escapes'. They are not stageposts on the way to some alternative reality. However consoling they may be, they still remain compartmentalized features of everyday life.

How may this compartmentalization be broken down, is there any way in which the free areas might somehow be merged with the rest of life, or indeed usurp its authority entirely? Is there some way in which on every day, life could be a holiday, a hobby? At the times when we yearn for this possibility, we may nostalgically look back to childhood as a period when we seemed to have no commitments, no responsibilities, a time when the resolute hunting out of escape routes was not such an existential necessity.

Back to Childhood

For the very young child there are no free areas, no enclaves within reality, for reality itself has not asserted any claims to attention. Infancy represents a 'period of privileged irresponsibility and freedom from the domination of the reality principle'.[1] At this time our own body, objects in the world and other people are apprehended through play. Play, during this period of life, is not one separate localized activity or form of experience. It is not yet the play-time that it will become at school, it is rather the general purposeless but meaningful activity of the young child. At this stage fantasy may be acted out without remainder. Objects and persons in the world do not have an immutable and unchanging identity which renders them unsuitable for incorporation within childhood daydreams. Everything is transformable, so that fantasies can be happily scripted with the help of bricks and paper bags and old fireside chairs.

Gradually, this world of play is differentiated. Play, like the other free areas that we have discussed, becomes an enclave within life rather than life itself. There will be a time allocated for play, even a part of the house set aside as a playroom. (Ironically this may necessitate father removing his own free area, the hobby, into the cellar or boxroom.) Children will be told that it is time to stop playing, they will be reminded when calamities occur during their fantasy enactments that it is 'only a game'. This drawing of boundaries around the child's play does not institutionalize the activity in the way in which hobbies and sex-making are later enclaved by their depiction in stage-by-stage charts, do-it-yourself manuals and magazines. But play is now an escape from reality rather than reality itself. Erikson observes that for the young child 'solitary play remains an indispensable harbour for the overhauling of shattered emotions after periods of rough going in the social seas'.[2] This 'enclaving' of play is a prototype of the enclaving of other aspects of childhood consciousness as a result of the conflicting demands of paramount reality.

Hobbies, for example, will begin to make their appearance at precisely that moment when the growing child declares an initial sense of the distance which exists between himself and school-work, which is then no longer seen as self-expressive, no longer voluntarily undertaken. The emergence of these self-conscious stances paves the way for the development of an alternative idea of work which is undertaken 'for its own sake' and in which society allows that there exist opportunities for self-expression. The hobby is born. We typically expect our children to have developed this enclave before they leave junior school. Teachers will ask children to talk about their hobbies; a favourite essay title will become 'My Hobby'. Children's programmes on radio and television are there to assist, with breezy adults initiating their audience into the wonders of cutting, pasting and collecting. By the time the child is old enough to apply for university, his hobbies are expected to be well-developed. The university application form provides three whole lines for their description.

Similarly the emergence of sex-making as an enclave activity is dependent upon the differentiation which occurs within auto-erotic play. The body comes to be viewed not as a general pleasure resource, to be incorporated within daily play, but rather as an object which can be used to obtain pleasurable resources. It is not an end in itself but rather a means to obtain such ends as profit, power and sex itself. Auto-eroticism instead of remaining an adjunct of all other activities, becomes irreconcilable with most, and is transformed into a privatized (bedroom, bathroom) and localized (genital stimulation) activity. Informed by aspects of technological consciousness it becomes a matter of genitals and orgasms. Norman O. Brown summarizes the processes which lead to the creation of the 'sex-making' enclave:

If normal adult sexuality is a pattern which has grown out of the infantile delight in the pleasurable activity of all parts of the human body, then what was originally a much wider capacity for pleasure in the body has been narrowed in range, concentrated on one particular (the genital) organ and subordinated to ... propagation.[3]

Our point is that although certain free areas may show associations with aspects of the uncontaminated consciousness of the child, nevertheless they are in effect mutations of aspects of that early life. They have been transformed by their new role as alternatives to dominant reality, their childish autonomy has been swallowed up in the apparently incorrigible density of contemporary reality. And this reality has become transformed into one which somehow contains more and less 'real' roles, more and less 'free' activities, areas in which to escape. It is perhaps 'our remembrance of things past', our sense that shades of the prison house have grown around us over the years, that leads to a conscious attempt to composite our free areas: drug-taking, work, sex and aesthetic pleasure will all be housed under the same real or symbolic roof; categories will be shattered. The vision is of a world in which no escapes are required, in which identities are happily realized within paramount reality.

Utopias and Eupsychias

This notion of creating a world which is again our own is a familiar theme within revolutionary and utopian programmes. Only a dramatic change in existing structures it is argued can resolve the fragmentation of contemporary man, dissipate his sense of alienation, make him once again into a whole being in tune with his friends, his work, and his world. These utopian visions do not always select the same societal or individual features as impediments to their realization. Sometimes social structural factors are seen as primary; without an end to the class system there is no prospect for the emergence of a new race of men who can pursue their lives without periodic searches for escape routes. This is the traditional nineteenth-century emphasis upon societal change as a precondition for individual change; we will refer to it as the *utopian* vision. In contrast is the view of individual change as either a precondition for societal transformation or as an end in itself; the revolution must occur in daily life, in the nature of our psychic structures, our current identities. We borrow the word *eupsychia* from Maslow to characterize such programmes. Utopian political movements, specifically of the marxist type, have been primarily concerned with social structural transformation as the means to abolish deprivation, injustice and exploitation.

They have always more or less assumed that identity transformations will follow in the wake of the revolution. This is not to say that they have left unexamined the precise psychological metamorphosis that is to occur. The classical marxist literature on alienation is reasonably explicit about the 'natural' unalienated state which existed before the coercive division of labour, a state close to the world of childhood. Here no identity work has to be done, no escapes are necessary because man is identified – is at one – with the fruits of his labour. He is at home in the world.

Almost as long as this revolutionary programme has existed, there has been a counter-critique from those who have insisted that the identity metamorphoses cannot be taken for granted, that the programme has to be clearer about how everyday life itself is to be altered:

> Those who speak of revolution and class struggles without referring explicitly to daily life, without understanding the subversive element in sex and the routine element in the rejection of constraints have a corpse in their mouths . . .[4]

Or, to put it in our language, how exactly will a change in structure and institutions allow identity work to be done always within paramount reality rather than against it? A society in which man does not have any sense of reflexivity, relativity, separateness, is inconceivable, and as long as these properties remain, man has to take some stance in regard to institutional arrangements like work, family, sex and inter-personal relationships. We have to be explicitly concerned with both psychic and social structures, and indeed it may not even be clear to some which is more important. As one slogan puts it: 'We do not want a world in which the guarantee of no longer dying of hunger is exchanged for the risk of dying of boredom.' The response of the structural revolutionary is that the identity metamorphosis is 'inconceivable' in the sense that any eupsychian programme is directed towards a future society which by definition does not yet exist. There *is* no script for how work, sex, relationships, will change. And to concentrate now on cultural domains such as identity is to assume that consciousness about such matters is a free-floating entity which can be altered without reference to structural arrangements. The Women's Liberation Movement presents a good contemporary example of the oscillation between the utopian and the eupsychian: is 'consciousness raising' an end in itself, a prelude to structural change or even something which can be dispensed with entirely in favour of practical reforms?

Crudely, then, three ideologies and movements present themselves: change the structure and identity will look after itself; connect your programme of structural change with an identity programme; sort out your heads first before you change the structure. Because our book concentrates on identity work, we have to look more carefully at the last of these options. What has variously been called the underground, the counter-culture, the alternative life style, has emerged in the last decade as a visibly available programme for those identity workers looking for total solutions. These are predominantly eupsychian movements, although they may vary in the degree to which they view identity transformation either as the key to structural change, or as a revolutionary programme in its own right.

The counter-cultural package stresses the need for the subversion of aspects of paramount reality and for some form of identity transformatian. So paramount reality is attacked by the conflation of certain categories through which the world is routinely apprehended. The taken-for-granted relationship between past, present and future is undermined by a determined emphasis upon the irrelevance of the past and future, and a glorification of the present – the here-and-now experience. Time itself is demoted from its central place as an organizing principle within consciousness; watches and clocks are dispensed with, and the routine divisions of night and day, morning and afternoon, are ignored. Standard divisions between work, hobbies and leisure are denied. 'Work is done only for fun, as a pastime, obsession, hobby or art form and thus is not work in the accepted sense.'[5]

The scripted nature of everyday experience is resisted by an emphasis upon naturalness and spontaneity, and fantasy is promoted by resort to the occult, psychedelics, esoteric Eastern religion, folk magic and a general hostility to rationality. An attempt is made to construct a reality which is script-free, pre-categorial and fantasy-saturated. It is an attempt to revert to the consciousness of the child – the pure world of play, to create an 'irresistible, fun possessed, play-powered counter culture'.[6]

Allied to this attack upon paramount reality is a commitment to identity transformation. The hippie puts his previous identity on the line, he puts himself out for conversion. Sometimes such identity transformation may be promoted by landscaping – by the trip to the East in which it is hoped that you will discover yourself, or the mindscaping of psychedelic use, in which actual ego-loss may occur, the sudden moment when your past identity falls from you as a cloak.

Allied to this internal identity transformation, is the calculated use of symbolic resources to make the transformation evident to others. The hippie cultivates cultural contradictions in his choice of hair styles and clothes, in the manner in which he indicates involvement in social interaction (the emphasis being 'cool'). The essence of the hippie script (or anti-script) lies in 'getting it together', which literally means assembling the reconstructed nature of paramount reality, and the newly-embraced identity, into a master script, nothing less than a new life plan.

The problem with the realization of counter-cultural values is their existence within phenomenally dissonant worlds on which, at the same time, they are parasitically dependent. It is by now a common enough critique of the counter-culture to point to such dissonances: the proclamation of a primitivist anti-technology is made surrounded by hi-fi tape recorders and the most advanced technological gadgets; the appeal to brotherly love and communality is made by those wearing clothes and eating food made possible by the massive exploitation of the poor.

The emphasis upon the insignificance of time, upon the irrelevance of past and future, is made by members of a group which is more rigorously age-graded than many others in society. Chronological features of existence are hardly evaded by dispensing with a watch, if the whole counter-cultural activity itself can be seen to be very firmly located within certain years of a person's life. Neither may the denial of work stand as a unique re-organization of taken-for-granted experience, when there is chronic unemployment among other non-counter-cultural members of the same age group, and when in common with that group, appeal is made to unemployment benefit as a way of financially sustaining the anti-work ethic. It is difficult in such circumstances to show that you are unemployed in a different way to anyone else who is 'out of work'. And if work is undertaken in a spirit of fun or leisure, there are inevitable contradictions with the instrumental features of the work situation. Even the most far-out hip bookshop, or the most esoteric under-ground magazine requires some workers who play down the fun and leisure approach for long enough to ensure the maintenance of a structure in which non-work attitudes may be displayed.

The existence of such incongruities and am-biguities threatens complete commitment to the collective enterprise. It is only possible to promote our identity entirely within the collectivity if a sense of reflexivity and relativity can be held at bay. The presence of contradic-tions raises the possibility that members will begin to en-gage in identity work by dissociation. They will revert to the notion of constructing themselves against the present reality instead of in terms of it. In fact, the whole notion of constituting identity without some type of dissociative, uncommitted activity is a problem for members of the counter culture, or indeed for any ideologically organized 'extra-societal' group. Where commitment is the order of the day, even the most trivial display of identity by dissoci-ation – for example, acting on a 'whim' rather than in terms of group purposes, or using sarcasm or cynicism as a conversational gambit – is likely to be seen as a violation of the conditions of membership.

But we need to go beyond such critiques and understand that they are not simply cynical posturings about the hypocrisy of hippies, and others, or pragmatic points about the difficulty of living alternative life styles, but derive from a flaw in the whole demodernization package. The utopian tradition is correct. We cannot simply adopt counter-cultural values – that is change consciousness – while the institutions on which this consciousness was built, remain the same. Berger and his colleagues give a nice example:

> Suppose you are waiting in an airport lounge prior to going on a plane trip and see the pilots walking towards the plane across the tarmac – two stereotyped counter-cultural types, with shaggy hair and beads, moving loose-limbed to an unheard rock rhythm, one of them puffing on a marijuana joint. Would you take a trip on this plane? The answer, we believe is obvious – no matter how great your sympathies with the counter-culture may be. [7]

This is the type of argument which punctures the notion of the alternative reality as a viable means for transforming the consciousness and identity of all men. It seeks to place the hippie movement into a compartment, into a space within paramount reality. The counter-culture then becomes no more than a site for experiments in reality work and identity work; the symbolic equivalent of other free areas such as hobbies and holidays.

The other problem that makes the counter-cultural programme so vulnerable as an escape route is that the style becomes a saleable commodity – and if it does, it cannot easily stand for a change in values. Free areas like hobbies and holidays are not – as we saw – *necessarily* undermined by commercialization or cultural co-option but the counter-cultural free area is so explicitly constructed *against* the imperatives of technology and the market economy, that any assault from these sources must be especially embarrassing. If love beads can be bought in Carnaby Street, large corporations advertise their products being happily consumed by long-haired freaks, tourists sold 'love burgers' – then where do we stake our claim to a new identity? Even the old hippie trail to the East is no longer sacred: far from the itinerant Hesse-like journey in which you shed your material possessions in search of the true self, it becomes an extended Boy Scout ramble consuming dope instead of baked beans and picking up the money from home at each American Express office en route. The conversion self-discovery script slips into a routine holiday script.

So far, we have confined ourselves to problems of realizing counter-cultural values within conventional society. But the most determined escapers along the counter-cultural route have long realized these problems (they don't want to become turned-on airline pilots) and, abandoning the world to its devices, have set off to composite their whole ideology into a viable entity capable of resisting institutionalization. These are members of the commune movement.

Communes

The new communards explicitly reject the notion that paramount reality may be evaded by simple recourse to one or other free area. They point to the intrusions of technological and capitalist consciousness into sex-making, hobbies, holidays, and drug-taking, declaring that only a society which merges such elements into a collective enterprise has any chance of constituting an alternative reality. So communes may try to break down the symbolic relationship between hobbies and work by allowing members' hobbies – wine-making, gardening, knitting – to constitute the only *work* of the commune. The area reserved for self-expression is dragged out of the attic or cellar and placed at the centre of life. Drug-taking, sex-making and even romantic love may be fused together into a collective spiritual exercise which it is hoped will produce lasting changes in the consciousness of all members. All this integration of free areas occurs in a new landscape, in the belief that physical isolation will help to lessen the concrete and symbolic intrusions of paramount reality.

The commune movement contains many diverse objectives – religious, political, therapeutic, attempts to recreate communal ties, to avoid the stresses of anomic urban life – but we are primarily interested in those communes which contain an explicit programme about resolving the problems of everyday life. There are two key elements in this: the attempt to set up a structure in which the self can be repossessed, in which identity work is done *by* the collective rather than *against* the collective, and the attempt to create an enclave in which categories can be broken down. Here is a typical claim by an enthusiastic contemporary student of communes:

> By offering alternative definitions of reality, by seeking to display that individuals can create for themselves a life where work has meaning, where companionship and individuality can be fruitfully combined, by seeking to live lives which form integral wholes and not fragmented sets of roles to be played at, the communitarians are seeking the subversion of conventional society from within by cutting away the moral cement that holds the existing system together. They are seeking to offer alternatives and working examples of the fact that man can create his own living environment.[8]

Experience of communes and some research[9] has begun to show however that they are not wholly suited to such 'subversion of society from within'; they are far from being perfect experiential sites for self-creation. Their members face the paradox (which we discuss more fully in our final chapter) that the structure of consciousness which makes the very idea of an individual unique self so imperative, develops in structures and institutions which make this very self-realization so difficult. The commune intends to promote values and structures in which people may repossess a sense of themselves as full, rich and unique individuals, but if everyone is searching for their own identity and bringing with them a sense of identity from the outside world, their collective search can become a zero-sum game. What some have, others must be denied.

The core members might be able to appreciate an individual identity, but if they have this and we don't, we have to work *against* it or else leave the group. Communal self-identity is a precarious thing, identities still have to be negotiated and this is even harder in a set-up in which formal structures (like work, marriage, leisure) are deliberately blurred. These structural flaws become experienced as matters of personality and the short-lived nature of many communes is blamed on members who leave because of a feeling that others are too domineering, idiosyncratic or selfish. The cruel irony of self-possession is evident: the search for individualism in the commune is threatened by that very individualism.

The attempt to shut out paramount reality by creating a precategorial enclave is even more obviously precarious than the experiment in identity work. An initial problem for communes is the risk of co-option by the wider and rejected society. The necessity of involvement in some form or another with the market economy, the need to establish criteria of membership, to discipline recalcitrant communards, and to place some regulations upon personal conduct, all bring to the forefront modes of apprehending reality which are at other times treated as unfortunate residues of an alien consciousness. Dominant consciousness splits away from a relationship with the technological modes of production and comes to enjoy a free-floating ideological status, influencing our views of the nature of social relationships, of society, and of man himself. It is difficult to see how its influence may be evaded in a micro-society, whose very existence depends upon a permit from the wider society in which it holds court.

Communards are not of course insensitive to such problems and frequently resort to detailed discussions about the most mundane aspects of life in order to detect within their organization vestiges of an alien consciousness. This distancing from routines and from scripts is conceived of as a way in which ordinary mundane life may be subverted. However (as we have argued elsewhere) self-consciousness is unlikely to enjoy any such transforming power. The situation remains very much as it was; the mundane task has still to be performed but without the benefits to be gained from a routine orientation spiced from time to time with maintainer fantasies. It seems rather silly to try to evade the press of paramount reality by making such tasks as washing dishes and taking out the garbage the objects of extensive self-reflection, discussion and ideological significance they become in the commune.

Take, for example, the way in which commune members allocate work in order not to duplicate the hierarchies, injustices and overall sense of non-fulfilment which the labour market creates outside. One commune has evolved a perfectly rational and efficient system for this by using labour credits.[10] Every week all members must earn the same number of credits, labour credits are calculated by multiplying the hours worked by a factor of ·9 to 1·5 which reflects the desirability of the task to the member: the more desirable the job, the lower the factor. Each Sunday everyone ranks in order of preference a list of up to sixty-three tasks, ranging from laundry to morning milking to washing the supper pots. The preference sheets are given each week to the labour-credit manager and the work then distributed: the person assigned to less preferred work earns more credit.

Now effective and altogether rational as this system is, it is not at all clear how this solves the subjective problem of work, nor what further problems are created by the obsessional neatness of the system. Does it not create a preoccupation with work far more intense than that in the outside world?

The critical problem which has to be faced by such communes is that the 'free areas' which they attempt to composite in their search for a 'integrated whole' have in many cases been constituted *against* paramount reality; they are responses to that reality; their particular form has been conditioned by that reality. To hope that they may be placed at the service of different ends once they have been translated to a novel landscape is optimistic. And, indeed, it would seem that many of the activities do indeed lose their 'free area' appeal once they surrender their oppositional relationship to the dominant reality. For example, hobbies which once stood out in relief against work, lose their appeal when they are translated into the centre of reality. Similarly, sex-making when legitimized within communes by reference to a free-love ethic, may lose its excitement along with its oppositional and covert status. For in a way all involvement in free areas necessitates putting ourselves at risk, it means putting a fantasy on the line, taking a chance that life-buoys from paramount reality will not be available when required. Even a free area so mundane as a hobby involves the continual risk of becoming an obsession, an area of activity which drifts dangerously away from the mainland. The risk element exists by courtesy of paramount reality; when such reality is no longer oppressive then we are left with a number of free-floating alternatives with no prospects of development, for such development depends upon continued contrast and contradiction, irony and resistance, distance and dissociation.

Communes may have made the mistake of taking the things that men do in order to escape paramount reality and elevating these into real human needs. But these free areas are only tangentially related to man's intrinsic nature; they are more fundamentally products of his biographical realtionship with society.

Indeed, we can only fully understand the localized precariousness of free areas if we consider the manner in which they have developed *against* paramount reality; the processes by which their eventual phenomenal appearance has been conditioned by a series of compromises with that reality. The state of consciousness which existed before the demarcation of free areas commenced was childhood. And the more deeply we realize that the only true paradise is the paradise lost, the more we must recognize that a communal attempt to create an enclave which replicates this paradise, is even more doomed to failure than that voyage to regain the past on which we all travel alone.

7

Momentary
Slips
through the
Fabric

In our previous pages we constructed a tangled picture of the relationships between man and everyday reality, a picture of the ways in which we attempt to manipulate the symbolic forms in which the world presents itself to us. At times our analysis must have seemed profoundly pessimistic. What we gave with one hand we took away with the other. We allowed that individuals might escape the press of reality, might develop a sense of special identity, by periodic resort to self-awareness, role distance, script evasion, fantasy or free areas. But we then went to great lengths to argue that in many cases such devices were not only regular and determinate aspects of all our lives, but were also profoundly conservative. They helped to nudge away our sense of reality and its routines for a short time, but when we examined such escape routes we found that they hardly constituted alternative worlds. They were instead rather precarious edifices, in many cases constructed out of material offered by the world from which we sought to escape. The more we attempted to rely upon them for relief the more fragile they became. The fantasies which held up the roof began to crumble, gusts of self-consciousness began to threaten the flimsy walls, whilst down the road the armies of co-option and commercialization drew nearer. Our way out of society was a cul-de-sac, it gave us the illusion that we were moving elsewhere but eventually provided us with little more than a frail and short-lived absence from reality, rather than a successful escape from its timetables and conventions.

There are times, however, when we look out at the world and suddenly find that the familiar perspectives through which we perceived it, the cognitive themes through which we apprehended it, have slipped away. We sense that we are seeing something for the first time. At such moments we have no scripts at hand into which we can immediately locate the experience, we have no ability to stand aside from the phenomenon, preserving our independence from it by a show of self-consciousness. Neither at such moments are we able to relegate the occurrence to the world of fantasy, for it appears to be located as much in the world as in our heads. We will call these incidents *momentary slips through the fabric*, or *reality slips*. There are other names like fits, satori experiences, trances, revelations, flashes, visions, but none of these words are useful as a generic term for each already implies some interpretation of the meaning of the experience. The phrase 'reality slips' preserves the possibility that such moments are meaningless, that they are not natural candidates for any particular psychological, philosophical or religious interpretation. Such slips are not, or course, everyday matters, although, as we shall argue, they may well be becoming more commonplace within our present culture. They do, however, clearly act as preludes to escape attempts and therefore demand some consideration.

We will borrow a phrase from William James to describe reality slips – they are 'unaccountable invasive alterations of consciousness',[1] moments in our life when we are suddenly overwhelmed by some force or spirit (whether internal or external) which leads to a re-evaluation of the nature of the world, society, or ourselves. Such moments may occur at very different times in our life, at very different places, and with very different effects. They may be partly expected, completely unpredictable, encouraged or assisted by the receiver, or occur with absolute arbitrariness.

We may take two contrasting examples. A friend of ours described a holiday in North Wales. He was staying in a small cottage on the outskirts of a village. The cottage was approached by a long slate path which passed between two carefully trimmed cypress trees. In front of one of these trees was a large piece of triangular slate which had been placed upright in the ground so as to resemble a tombstone. One night our friend returned from an evening walk, pushed open the gate, and began to walk down the path. Suddenly he became very aware of the outline of the cypress trees and the slate 'tombstone' in front of him. His eyes moved from one to the other, he was seized by a sudden sense that this conjunction was somehow odd and bizarre; he found himself unable to move any further along the path, transfixed by the geometrical relationships of the objects. He reported a strange sense of his whole being slipping away from him for a moment. In a second, though, the world returned, the objects resumed their familiar place in the setting and he was able to proceed down the path. In this case our friend offered no explanation of what occurred, he found it totally unexpected. He had not prepared for it in any way, he was not drunk or drugged, and had no history of involvement with ideologies or belief systems which placed a premium upon such experiences.

By contrast, we cite the case of John Lilly, an eminent scientist who, having become dissatisfied with the nature of his traditional research work, turned instead to an investigation of the properties of LSD.[2] His first experiments simply involved injecting the drug and tape-recording his experiences, but later he decided to combine the taking of LSD with a series of sensory-deprivation experiments he had been working on. For these experiments Lilly placed himself in a tank of seawater in such a way that he could float at the surface with mouth and nose and eyes out of the water. The tank was placed in a completely darkened room and Lilly then proceeded to lie in it after swallowing 300 micrograms of acid. In this condition, he reported a total change in his sense of reality. His body 'disappeared', but somehow he remained in space. He was overcome with emotion. 'I sat in the space without a body but with all of myself there, centred. I felt fantastically exhilarated with a great sense of awe and wonder.' He recalls that when he returned from this trip that his life had been transformed.

In the Lilly case, we find a man whose previous experiences with 'the tank' and LSD had programmed him to expect the unexpected. Not only was his reality slip expected, it was also assisted by a variety of chemical and technical aids. Again, unlike our friend from North Wales, he was programmed in advance with some framework into which these experiences – however shattering – could be placed.

In between the 'spontaneous' Welsh experience and the 'programmed' Lilly transformation lie many other instances of reality slips. These exhibit varying degrees of expectedness. Many individuals subscribe to a view of the world which is compatible with sudden breaks in reality, with sudden visions of alternative worlds, or of the mysteries which lie behind this one. They may not always recognize this predilection as related to their reality slip, a fact which leads William James to propose a theory of subliminal motivation in his explanation of such matters. He talks of the 'subconscious incubation of motives deposited by a growing experience' which eventually reach bursting point – the moment when the reality slip occurs. However, he does not advance this as a total explanation. 'Candour obliges me to confess that there are occasional bursts into consciousness', or cases where 'it is not easy to demonstrate any prolonged subconscious incubation'.[3]

The experiences which fall in between our two examples may however lack evidence of such subconscious readiness and instead be characterized by the presence of a number of aids such as alcohol, drugs, special environment, fasting, sensory deprivation. There have been many attempts to analyse how such triggers might work, either to put down the experience ('You were just stoned') or to map out the routes to sudden awareness (the night on the bare mountain). To quote Huxley:

... disease, mescalin, emotional shock, aesthetic experience and mystical enlightenment have the power, each in its different way and in varying degrees to inhibit the functions of the normal self and its ordinary brain activity, thus permitting the 'other world' to rise into consciousness.[4]

The exact precursors of the reality-slippage experience are important, not as reductive explanations but for the possible influence they have on the meaning subsequently assigned to the experience. Somewhere between the contrasting extremes of the unscripted cottage-in-Wales experience and the highly programmed acid-in-tank experience lie the more problematic interpretations. Consider Alphonse Ratisbonne's account of the peculiar events that befell him in Rome in 1842:

Coming out of the cafe I met the carriage of Monsieur B. He stopped and invited me in for a drive, but first asked me to wait for a few minutes whilst he attended to some duty at the church of San Andrea delle Fratte. Instead of waiting in the carriage, I entered the church myself to look at it. The church of San Andrea was poor, small and empty; I believe that I found myself there almost alone. No work of art attracted my attention; and I passed my eyes mechanically over its interior without being arrested by any particular thought. I can only remember an entirely black dog which went trotting and turning before me as I mused. In an instant the dog had disappeared, the whole church had vanished, I no longer saw anything ... or more truly I saw, O my God, one thing alone.

Heavens, how can I speak of it? Oh no! Human words cannot attain to expressing the inexpressible ... I did not know where I was: I did not know whether I was Alphonse or another. I only felt myself changed and believed myself another me; I looked for myself in myself and did not find myself.[5]

In this case there were few reasons which might have led us to predict Ratisbonne's experience. Nevertheless, the reality slip occurred in a very special setting – a church – and was subsequently interpreted as a conversion experience. We also learn from William James that Ratisbonne, although previously irreligious himself, had nevertheless had an elder brother who had been converted and become a Catholic priest.

The problem in interpreting such 'unaccountable invasive alterations of consciousness' both in this case and others is that we have to rely upon retrospective reports and these already have written into them some interpretation of the events. In some cases, of course, such an interpretation may involve the dismissal of the event as lacking in meaning, in that case the elaboration of the experience and the feelings associated with it are not recorded. In other cases however the description of the feelings is far more important. And it is here that the 'nature' of the reality slip becomes contaminated by the construction into which the experience is placed. If, for example, we continue to follow Ratisbonne's description we find it increasingly couched in an explicitly religious vocabulary. Although for a moment its author did not seem to know where he was, or indeed who he was, nevertheless, he quickly recognizes the religious significance of what has occurred to him. He has not had a blackout, a perceptual distortion, or a fit. He has been 'converted'. Now the ability to conceptualize such experiences in this way is not universally available. In societies which do not employ the notion of 'conversion' in relation to religious experiences, individuals who experienced similar sensations to Ratisbonne would be faced with a choice between keeping quiet or else attempting to relate the experience to other similar phenomena which are recognized within the society. Conversion does not exist as a conceptual option which may be adopted by anyone who experiences sensations of the type recorded by Ratisbonne. It is rather a specialized way in which some societies and/or religions bring such matters into continuity with other aspects of life. Missionaries who set off in the eighteenth and nineteenth centuries to convert natives to Christianity were, therefore, involved in a double task; they not only had to convert natives, they also had to convert them to the very notion of conversion.

It is interesting that William James, despite being entirely concerned with the special nature of religious experience, is led in his discussion of 'instantaneous' conversions, to adopt a non-specific view of the nature of these events. He accepts that they are not intrinsically religious experiences; they only become so. This means that their origins and phenomenal appearance to the individual, place them alongside other reality slips which have not been substantially conceptualized in religious terms:

> If abstracting altogether from the question of their value for the future spiritual life of the individual, we take them on their psychological side exclusively, *so many peculiarities in them remind us of what we find outside of conversions* that we are tempted to class them along with other automatisms.[6]

It would follow from this that there is little value in attempting to classify 'reality slips' according to their origins. The fact that they have such varying origins as drug use, the cultivation of religious trances, the immersion in mystical pursuits, does not affect their potential for providing the individual with a sense of having obtained an insight into an alternative reality. Whether some of these experiences are more 'real' than others is not the point:[7] the question is how the experience is subsequently interpreted.

The slip will quickly become saturated with meanings derived from its subsequent conceptualization and it is these which affect its escape status, its significance for our identity. So that when we encounter in Ratisbonne's description such phrases as 'I shuddered at the sight of my iniquities', we are already in the presence of an interpretation based upon a view of the experience as religious, a view which is compatible with some aspects of existing paramount reality, and with such existing identities as the 'sinner'.

A contemporary phenomenon provides another example. In one discussion[8] of the 'transformation experience' which many hippies claim as a starting point for their new life, we find common reference to disorientation of time and space, total personal absorption and sudden detachment from normal social roles and routines. But hippies in reporting their experience did not confine themselves to such phenomenal matters; some also claimed that at such moments they sensed the futility of everyday life in a capitalist society. Their subsequent lifestyle which involved the rejection of capitalist values was validated by its prophetic announcement within the transformation experience.

As a final example we may cite one of the numerous attempts to distil the essence of those astonishing moments of insight, cosmic consciousness. Alan Watts, the great popularizer of the Zen version of consciousness expansion, has set out the common features of those moments when men feel that the ordinary world of here and now is I T: the Godhead, the end and meaning of life, ultimate reality. He concedes that there is no really satisfactory name for this type of experience: to call it mystical is to confuse it with visions of other worlds, to call it spiritual or metaphysical is to suggest that it is not also extremely concrete and physical, while the term 'cosmic consciousness' itself has occultist undertones. 'But', Watts concludes, 'from all historical times and cultures we have reports of this same unmistakable sensation emerging, as a rule, quite suddenly and unexpectedly and from no clearly understood cause.'[9]

This would be a good enough definition of our 'momentary slips through the fabric'. But when Watts goes on to specify the nature of this 'sensation' he is already laying down a particular interpretative script. This script declares: the universe is so right as to need no justification, existence is no longer a problem because of the 'itness' of everything, the whole world has become your own body, the immediate *now* appears the goal and fulfilment of all living. But while Watts concedes that such interpretations draw upon a variety of known religions and philosophical descriptions he still believes there is a basic identity to the experience he has 'discovered'. Watts would insist that he was not interpreting reality slips. However this passage from Berenson's *Sketch for a Self-Portrait* does anything but justify Watts' characterization of it as 'one of the simplest and "cleanest" accounts' of the sensation:

> It was a morning in early summer. A silver haze shimmered and trembled over the lime trees. The air was laden with their fragrance. The temperature was like a caress. I remember – I need not recall – that I climbed up a tree stump and felt suddenly immersed in Itness. I did not call it by that name. I had no need for words. It and I were one.

We do not dispute that there are experiences beyond names and words, but the problem is that even in the act of declaring their 'inexpressible' character, in the manner in which we describe their 'undescribability', we already reveal preferences for 'religious', 'mystical' or 'pan-theistic' accounts of the experience.

The Other Side

Such epistemological problems about the way interpretations interfere with the 'purity' of the experience need not deter us, however, from taking an interest in the significance of these meanings for the individual's altered stance towards reality and his revised conceptions of identity. If reality slips open the 'doors of perception', what do people claim to find on the other side?

There is nothing like a homogeneous revelation common to all momentary slips through the fabric, and the revelations are given fundamentally different and even contradictory descriptions. We will take three examples of what people report to have found when the door swings back. These refer to *order*, *self* and *life*, each of which allows for contrasting transformations.

The revelation about order leads to contrasting notions about continuity, connectedness and meaning. On the one hand some reality slippers discern a continuity – material, magical, or logical – which appears to connect all things and events. The social order or the universe itself is seen to be arranged in a pattern, the contours of which have previously eluded us only through ignorance or impatience. But they are there to be found. On the other hand, there is a transforming vision of the world in which all notions of causality, meaning and connection break down. Things happen but regularity is only mechanical: chance, randomness, ambiguity, arbitrariness are all. In this reality slip, we despair of ever trying to find connections: such a quest is illusory.

The first of these options – the discovery of continuity – is central to most religious and mystical beliefs and is a variant on the cosmic-consciousness theme. It would be tedious to spell out the numerous variations on the idea of patterning; in all attempts to distil the essence of the religious experience of the perennial philosophy, such a vision is dominant.

The contrasting vision, that of the breakdown in connections, is perhaps most sharply indicated – in somewhat different ways – in various existential philosophies and in art movements like surrealism. The world of Kafka and Camus is stripped of connections and meaning; the absurd is the essence. Writing about the particular surrealist version of reality, Shattuck conveys nicely what was made of odd chances and coincidences:

Normally we dismiss them, laugh them off, or at most mention them to a friend as a curiosity and then forget them. The tiny epiphany of involuntary memory around which Proust span out the three thousand pages of his novel bears a considerable resemblance to these occurrences. The difference is he did not dismiss it but faced around and entered in like a secret opening in the fabric of ordinary experience. The surrealists went much further. Driven by extreme inquisitiveness and self-imposed daring, they dropped everything else and affirmed those moments as the only true reality, as experience of both the randomness and the hidden order that surrounds us.[10]

Now intellectually, those two visions might be reconcilable at some level: even the absurd might paradoxically reveal a 'hidden order'. But characteristically the sudden revelation of what is behind the door appears sharply, almost tangibly, as one or the other. We either see the grains of sand arranging themselves in some order or else they lie before you in an inchoate and random mass. In either case, our sense of paramount reality is transformed.

The second group of revelations deals with notions about the power of the self. On the one hand there can be a sudden vision of the self as immanent and transcendent. There is nothing that cannot be done, tribulations, obstacles and burdens disappear before your eyes. You are the monarch of your soul, master of all you survey. Some insights later labelled as 'mystical' reproduce this revelation and it has philosophical echoes, existential notions of freedom and Nietzschean ideas of the superman.

The opposite vision is a sensational loss of self. You have merged into the world of objects, your ego disappears, you have doubts about the substantiality of your own existence let alone any power to influence the world as a subject. Remember Ratisbonne's experience, 'I did not know whether I was Alphonse or not . . . I looked for myself in myself and did not find myself.' Or recall Laing's schizoids' sense of ontological insecurity. Or Eliot's description of coming to the bottom of the stairs and 'just for a moment you have the experience of being an object at the mercy of a malevolent staircase'. And the cry of the Muslim, 'Oh God, I am but dough in thy hands.' Again, either of these contrasting visions can be arrived at intellectually, either is capable of being toned down to cope with ambiguity and paradox. But we are interested in the sudden perception which insists that things are one way or the other.

Our final group of revelations are – if this is possible – even more global in their implications, even more obviously subversive of paramount reality. They concern the very nature of the world itself. On the one hand is the possible perception, arrived at very suddenly, that this life is all. No other worlds, realities, lives, cosmologies, forces, are possible. If things are wrong, it is we who have corrupted them. We do not have to look beyond the shape of a flower, the miracle of childbirth to unlock the secret of the universe. No effort is needed to comprehend the perfect simplicity of things. In the Zen version: 'Sitting quietly doing nothing,/Spring comes and the grass grows by itself.' On the other hand there is the sense of the revelation as opening up an enormous mystery: it shows no less than the existence of another reality besides which the world as we know it takes on a mirage like, strangely unreal quality. There is another life and we have missed it. Our eyes now are opened to something: 'the glory of the coming of the Lord', a celestial kingdom which is creating and judging this world, a dark and awesome world of occult forces beyond ordinary comprehension.

Scripting the Momentary Slip

These then are some of the interpretations of what is to be learnt from the reality slip. We started this chapter by talking of what the slips and the revelations they produce might make of us. We must now see what we make of them. How do we slot these extraordinary experiences into our ongoing life scripts?

The simplest and probably most common method was illustrated by our friend in North Wales and by Shattuck's remarks about how most of us deal with strange environmental coincidences: 'We dismiss them, laugh them off, or at most mention them to a friend as a curiosity and then forget them.' To use concepts beloved by sociologists of deviance: we *neutralize* or *normalize* the experience. It is written off or explained away as just one of those things which happen from time to time. It is as if we have internalized society's prohibitions and scepticism about the existence of different realities or mystical insights so deeply, that we banish such possible interpretations from our consciousness before they can poison us.

A more significant form of fitting the reality slippage into our life script is to absorb its message at an intellectual level. We now begin to see the world in terms derived from the revelation and start re-arranging other taken-for-granted aspects of our conceptual machinery to make them consistent with the revelation. It is as if the slippage has short circuited the disciplined and rigorous exercises advocated by the guide books of mindscapers and arrives at precisely the same point. The Zen experience of sartori or instant enlightenment is again the prototypical interpretation, as is the way Proust's monumental search for the secrets of time was opened up: 'One knocks on many doors that open on to nothingness. Against the only one that leads into reality, for which one might seek in vain a hundred years, one bumps by accident and swings back of its own accord.'[11] The experience then transforms your intellectual cognition even though your ways of arriving at it (and telling others of it) is literally beyond words: 'They that speak, do not know/they that know, do not speak.' You may have been changed by your momentary slip – in Huxley's memorable words, 'The man who comes back through the door in the Wall will never be quite the same as the man who went out' – but the knowledge stays in your head. It is an intellectual orientation. However there will be some who try to go beyond this, who seek to embed the experience and its lesson into an ongoing life script or some clear institutional option. The conversion of the cognition into a way of life is our third possibility.

The key word is conversion: in James's classic definition, this is '. . . the process, gradual or sudden, by which a self hitherto divided and consciously wrong, inferior and unhappy, becomes unified and consciously right, superior and happy'.[12] For this to happen, as we stressed earlier, the person must be converted to the idea of conversion: he must not only make sense of the experience, but locate this sense in some meaningful belief system. For the hippie waiting for the mystical insight to happen, for scientists like Lilly floating in his tank, for the religious believer going to Lourdes or up a mountain to experience a vision, this slip into what Holzner calls an 'epistemic community' is a clearly predictable possibility – although this is *not* to say that it is just a matter of 'suggestibility'. In such cases the future convert is placed or places himself in a situation where he is already prepared with the appropriate definitions. In this sense he is already convertible: he conceives of himself as the kind of person to whom conversion *can* or even *will* happen. When the actual reality slippage occurs, it appears to be virtually the only thing that could have happened. It confirms the previous move.

As we admitted earlier, we cannot always be sure which conversions can be classified as of this kind and which are 'pure' sudden slips which are only retrospectively seen as confirmations of a current belief system. In either case however the momentary slip becomes the basis of a life script of greater or lesser density. The religious and mystical versions range from a complete surrender to a new way of life, for example, by entering a monastery or a hermitage, to entry into a sect which stresses the routine nature of revelations, visions and trances. The key point is the subsequent location of this experience into such scripts: people's lives must be actually changed in a direction which is congruent with one or other established conceptual universe of the religious or mystical kind. However, whether the sense of transformation and the discovery of a new reality which accompanied the initial experience can be maintained alongside the new life plan, the new routines and repetitions which are encountered within our changed lives, is doubtful in view of our discussion of such institutions as communes.

There are also conversions into aesthetic as well as religious and mystical scripts. We have cited elsewhere Proust's enormous life work which owed its origin to precisely the 'same' sudden insight which led others into religious directions. Zaehner comments, '... though he had an intimate knowledge of Catholic theology and Catholic practice, it never occurred to him to explain his own experience as an apprehension of God.'[13]

The specific route that Proust charted – the voyage into the past – is not the only aesthetic response to reality slippage. The great visionary poets and artists have gone in very different directions. Rimbaud, for example, like Blake, advocated the artist training himself to see visions: 'A drawing room at the bottom of the lake, mosques instead of factories ... the poet makes himself a visionary by a long, immense and reasoned *derangement* of all the senses.' But whether through the deliberate exercise of asceticism or hedonism, whether sitting in a cork-lined room or taking drugs, the aesthetic enterprise somehow tries to capitalize on the momentary slip. It preserves it intact, or activates the potential for its reappearance.

There are more mundane ways in which one's life may be reorganized as a consequence of a reality slip. This is not to say that the original experience is somehow less intense or vivid than it is for those who later follow religious or mystical paths. The slip which leads to both religious and 'lay' conversions may be occasioned by a tab of acid, a sudden vision in a church, or something as routine as the conjunction of some cypress trees and a piece of slate. Even in the absence of voices, visions and mystical messages, a radical escape hatch may open.

Benbow, the lawyer in Faulkner's *Sanctuary*, has taken to the road after suddenly leaving his wife. When asked why he did this, he replies, 'Because she ate shrimps.' He goes on to explain how every Friday, for the ten years in which he'd been married, he'd carried a dripping, smelly box of shrimps home to his wife:

> All the way home it drips, until after a while I follow myself to the station and stand aside and watch Horace Benbow take the box off the train and start home with it, changing hands at every hundred steps and I follow him thinking, Here lies Horace Benbow in a fading series of small stinking spots on a Mississippi sidewalk.[14]

The point at which Benbow could stand aside and watch himself is critical. For the paradox about the momentary slip is that although it happens without self-consciousness – and indeed might even be described in terms of ego-loss rather than heightened self-awareness – it must at some point be consciously interpreted. Either it is something which just happens – a praeternatural experience beyond human explanation – or else confirmation of the existence of other forms of knowledge. Lilly, for example, talks about his ability before his experience to imagine the existence of other universes and spaces, without actually knowing them:

> Before the trip, I didn't believe in these universes or spaces, but I defined them as existing. During the LSD trip in the tank I then took on these beliefs as true. After the trip, I then disengaged and looked at what happened as a set of experiences, a set of consequences of the belief.[15]

We have tried most of the escapes described in this book. As creatures of habit, self-consciousness, script evasion and fantasy, as promiscuous travellers along most institutionalized escape routes and dwellers in most free areas we can say that we've been there before. But with momentary slips through the fabric, we have to confess that we are in Lilly's pre-experimental stage. We have no reason at all to deny the existence of such experiences and every reason to suspect that they will have to be slotted into a categorial shelf where they are beyond reach of the monitors from paramount reality. And whereas other routes are being closed off or rendered safe, there is a real sense in which the routes to reality slips are being opened up. This age, more than any other age is the 'age of conversion'. External aids such as psychedelic drugs, sensory deprivation and the various meditation and consciousness-expansion techniques we were so sceptical about in Chapter 5 are becoming more accessible and acceptable. Such aids to enhanced perception, whatever their limitations as ways of life, can be used to edge us closer to the momentary slip. At the same time, the type of psychology explicit in the consciousness-expansion movement – seen, for example, in the popularity of the Castaneda phenomenon – is very much directed to opening the doors. This is the difference between on the one hand psychologies of the *model* or *theory* type (man is like this, he thinks and acts according to these laws) and psychologies of the *map* type.[16] Maps are pragmatic, designed to help us find our way; they say, 'Try this procedure and the following experiences will occur.' Oriental psychology and esoteric systems such as those of Gurdjieff are very much of the map variety and their current popularity will doubtless open new doors.

But – as we've consistently argued – this potential is double-edged. Maps, manuals and ways of transformation are perhaps becoming too explicit in laying down what to expect. It is fine for the doorways of perception to be pointed to and even opened up by guides and teachers, but if we are greeted only by a knowing smile on the other side, the journey might not have been worth it.

8

Over
the
Wall

The reality slips referred to in the previous chapter can hardly be described as forms of resistance to everyday life – although the routes that lead to and from them might very well be. Leaving some men poised at that strange point where they seem to have momentarily fallen through the fabric, we must return briefly to their more prosaic fellows who have been digging and tunnelling away at paramount reality.

We sketched the obstacles some of these attempts encountered, obstacles which often diverted the path almost right back to its starting point. But this does not make them failures. Often they will be employed with a perfect knowledge of their limitations, and their abrupt collapse will in no way prove disconcerting. Even the most short-lived precarious solutions will help to edge us through the day, bring us down to the breakfast table on a Monday morning with a sense that we are somehow a little above or beyond the daily round of being. We have shown that we are still alive enough to struggle. We have not – like the E-Wing prisoners feared would happen to them – given in or given up.

But there are those to whom such temporary relief or sense of victory is not enough. Their commitment to each escape route, or to the general ideology of escape is much more intense. At the same time they realize that a simple exploitation of each device – fantasy, self-consciousness, free areas – is precarious because it is precisely at these points that reinvolvement with paramount reality is threatened. So some of them solve this dilemma by frantically switching escape routes, abandoning each one as soon as cracks appear and immediately investing massively in another. These frenetic individuals are to be found in all sections of society, racing from bedroom to bedroom, ingesting one heinous drug after another, tearing off on exotic holidays and adventures, mounting massive campaigns of artistic appreciation, throwing themselves into transcendental meditation, signing up for the latest cult therapy. And all the while distancing themselves from paramount reality by commenting upon their own emancipation from care and concern, and the pathetic quality of those who, employing less adequate amounts of self-consciousness, remain locked into a routine appreciation of mundane life.

The more evangelical wing of the commune movement might well want to convince these individuals that they could find a quiet resting point in the commune. There, after all, these manic searches should be over, the categories are mixed in a single, all embracing enclave. But such individuals are too hedonistic, too individualistic to sacrifice individual identity work to the communal good, to share responsibilities, to pool resources. They prefer to flit around, more or less invisibly, belonging nowhere, investing temporarily in one route after the other, refusing commitment or engagement with any ideology.

But some of these individuals go too far – and deliberately try to go too far. They open themselves to massive censure and punishment, venturing well into the realm of the deviant. These are men who make massive, extreme and spectacular attempts to go over the wall, to set up life in a territory which enjoys some sort of autonomous existence, and to fight off all those forces which would recapture them. Unlike most of the escapers we have described so far, they do not work at the edges or under the surface. They are often highly visible: open to the searchlights and guns on the turrets.

Where are these people going? To exploit yet further our prison metaphor: when you go over the wall or through the tunnel you might simply 'want out' but you also have some conception of the destination you are aiming for: back home or the open road. Escapes from paramount reality are more difficult to classify in terms of destination as they depend so much on which mode of consciousness has informed them. But it is possible to conceive of three master destinations: away, inside and above.

Going away is the simplest to conceive as it fits the prison metaphor most literally. The notion is that somewhere there, outside the walls, a viable life is possible. By transporting yourself or alternatively clearing away the clutter which is messing up your life, you can move unhindered and free. Taking risks, shedding material and psychological baggage, you move towards a new land and a new life. Scott Fitzgerald, after speculating about his friends who had tried (and failed) at such attempts, provides a fine description of the going-away style, one which might serve for all extreme escapes:

> This led me to the idea that the ones who had survived had made some sort of clean break. This is a big word and is no parallel to a jail-break when one is probably headed for a new jail or will be forced back to the old one. The famous 'escape' or 'run away from it all' is an excursion in a trap even if the trap includes the South Seas, which are only for those who want to paint them or sail them. A clean break is something you cannot come back from; that is irretrievable because it makes the past cease to exist.[1]

For some, though, such a 'break' is inconceivable, for the problem lies entirely in the head, in consciousness itself. They know in advance that going away will only lead to a new jail or back to the old one. Their destination is *inside*;

in Doris Lessing's simple paraphrase of oriental wisdom, 'There is never anywhere to go but in.' The self, mind, ego or whatever it is that makes sense of the world must be put on the line and changed rather than the physical and social contours of the world itself.

A final destination is *above*. The prison is neither of the mind nor of the social world but resides in such very notions as escape, flight, refuge or change. Man is greater than the arrangements of the world and he is more powerful than his psychological constituents. Will is all and if man can only realize this, a true transcendence or rising above the rules of the world is possible. 'I am all and shall become all' is the message of the superman. In the face of total moral relativity, the self is immanent, freedom to act is absolute.

These are the three master destinations to which extreme escapers aspire. But how exactly do they find the way along these routes? The answer is unexpected. For when we draw close to these extreme escapers, we find that they have crawled through the very same tunnels, walked across the same free areas, employed the same modes of consciousness as those other men and women who have appeared in our chapters up till now. But instead of residing briefly within such spaces, living temporarily by such styles, and then crawling back under the wire into paramount reality, they have attempted to turn these little territories into empires. Ignoring the fragility of the building and its penetration by elements from paramount reality, they proceed to declare that this narrow enclosure is in fact the whole of the world, and promptly set about transforming it into just that. There is nowhere else to go, this is home – the struggle is over. Paramount reality is evaded.

Hobbies which previously were confined to the attic in the evening now begin to expand into all rooms of the house and take over the hours of work, holidays which were previously contained within the constraints of the package-tour brochure take on such an exaggerated form that they become more significant than the rest of life;

sex-making, artistic appreciation, gambling, participation in mass culture, step out of the enclaves into the centre of life. There is not now some art in one's life or some sex at odd times, instead life *is* art, it *is* sex. And whereas self-consciousness might previously have been employed to offer a little token resistance, it may now become a central preoccupation, the self is pursued down the alleyways of consciousness, as is the self behind the self and the self behind that self. Fantasy is no longer used as a prop to daily living, an occasional source of mental nutrition. It runs riot. We do not stop our fantasies and re-enter the world, we let them bound away, taking us where they will. And if there are any scripts available, they are played with such manic intensity that lines, props and stage directions are no longer recognizable. Indeed these are the players who improvise with such style and originality, that their acting out becomes public knowledge. *They are the ones who create the scripts*. To name anyone as behaving 'like' them is enough to understand the action.

GOING AWAY

1. The Enclave Becomes Life

Sitting at a kitchen table, night after night, sometimes for ten hours in a row, is a man throwing a pair of dice. He is surrounded by books, charts, maps, diaries, records, all covering one subject: baseball. The dice determine the play in the Universal Baseball Association: every ball thrown, every stroke played, the attributes (age, appearance, character) of every player, every record broken, the whole financing and management of the league, is built into the game. Its creator, proprietor, organizer, master and slave is J. Henry Waugh: all the emotions, ecstasies and tragedies of the game are of his own making.[2]

Henry is the ultimate hobbyist. Fantasy has taken over. No one else can penetrate this world. (A friend who comes to play the game messes it up through not understanding the totality of the obsession and is roughly excluded.) It invades the rest of Henry's life: his relationships (with his friend, his boss, the local hooker) are completely determined by what happens in the game. His job, always interfering with the League's activities, is eventually abandoned because it interferes with the hobby. There is very little distancing, monitoring, self-consciousness: to Henry, the notion that this is 'only a game' or 'only a hobby' is absurd. The game is life itself.

Now Henry is a fictional character, a homunculus of his own creator, Robert Coover, and it is not difficult to find other fictional examples of this extreme escape. There is John Fowles's Collector – meticulously collecting women as if they were butterflies for a collection, the hero of Malzberg's *Screen* (described in Chapter 4), a movie fanatic who totally enters the world of the screen characters he watches.

In real life, these men are usually described as eccentrics or obsessives. Their activities are invaluable to television producers and newspaper editors who are in search of 'novelty' items for the end of their news programmes, or for 'Believe it or not' type columns on their inside pages. There is no shortage of individuals who have transformed their hobby into a way of life. Those who at one time simply collected Red Indian artefacts, have now become 'Red Indians', complete with mocassins, bows and arrows, headdresses and horses. Model-train enthusiasts have constructed a complete railway system which runs day and night throughout the year to agreed timetables. The only respite occurs when the hobbyists keep their engines in the sheds because of an 'industrial dispute'. Another individual has enlarged upon his hobby of record collecting by transforming himself into a domestic disc jockey. The house is entirely wired for sound and he spends his days sitting behind a glass screen playing and announcing his favourite music. The only intervals come at mealtimes when his wife summons him by tapping on the glass screen, whereupon he announces to the 'listeners' that there will now be a short commercial break.

In other houses, sex steps out of the enclaves

and becomes an obsessive feature. The walls are covered with masturbatory aids, machines and gadgets to aid sexual performance are assiduously collected, rooms are decorated in the style of brothels, pornographic movie shows replace the television, whips and uniforms and esoteric underwear are obsessively assembled. We rarely have direct information on such expansions of the hobby into a way of life, but the commercial exploitation of the artefacts which are necessary to its construction in such journals as *Mayfair*, *Exchange and Mart*, and *Collectors' World* would lead us to think that it was a far more common feature than might be gathered from the occasional references to it in the media.

2. Life As Art

'The simplest surrealist act consists in going revolver in hand, into the street and firing as much as possible at random into the crowd.' So a phrase from the Second Surrealist Manifesto, one of the more extreme statements from the aesthetic movement which took seriously the proposition that life should replicate art. The art form was to be based on randomness, chaos and chance but was never just on the level of aesthetic experiments with automatic writing, dreams, somnambulism, or making collages out of random objects. A revolution in everyday life was proposed: 'Social constraint has had its day,' began that famous Second Manifesto and who better to demonstrate this than the artists themselves? The art of firing randomly into the crowd embodied the two principles of outrage and randomness: both guided by the celebration of dream and fantasy and the attack on responsibility and reason.

The early surrealist acts of outrage were highly self conscious: Tanguy capturing spiders which he ate alive to terrify the neighbourhood; Dali giving lectures at the Sorbonne with his bare right foot soaking in a pan of milk. And these had already been preceded by the outrages, amusements and provocations of Dada, which provided the basis for all later attempts for scripting an insult to ordinary notions of how paramount reality should be ordered. Here is a hostile account of a show of Max Ernst's collages:

> With characteristic bad taste, the Dadas have now resorted to terrorism . . . Andre Breton chewed upon matches, Ribemont-Dessaignes kept screaming, 'It's raining on a skull' . . . On the doorstep, Rigaut counted aloud the automobiles and the pearls of the lady visitors . . .[3]

Surrealist attempts to undermine paramount reality by eroding the art–life distinction were no less extreme. Take the highly self-conscious acts exploiting objective chance, which for Breton constituted the 'problem of problems'; the relationship between necessity and freedom. 'To attain a life entirely made up of such coincidences would be to attain surreality', and so these artists actually tried to induce coincidences. Soupault walked around the streets asking people at random where he lived, proposed that everybody switch drinks in the cafés he entered, opened his umbrella on sunny days. Not that all acts were to be so trivial and childish, for above all, surrealism warned against moderation and took their own extreme positions to the logical conclusion. In Aragon's marvellous prose:

> Kill yourself or don't. But don't drag your slugs of agony all over the world, your anticipated carrion, don't leave the revolver butt hanging out of your pocket any longer, irresistibly tempting a good kick in the arse. *Don't insult the true suicide by this perpetual panting*.[4]

The surrealist enterprise is invariably judged to have failed, limited as it was to a group of intellectuals between the wars, and hardly influencing the life of everyman. As a mass movement it was a failure: it remained a small group of people struggling in the most articulate way to use their art to produce a revolution of everyday life. Their persistence and the fact that they actually experimented with their ideas, led them to a full awareness of all the tensions of paramount reality we have considered: they monitored themselves, yet celebrated spontaneity;

they distanced themselves from their role as artists, yet constituted a highly self-conscious art movement; they devised new scripts which then became routinized by their followers into very predictable ones; they exploited fantasy to its extremes, yet always juggled with the contradiction between the ideas that 'life lies here' and 'life lies elsewhere'; they created a free area, yet it was constantly battered by the forces of conventional society. But to the extent that they resisted these forces and resolutely stuck to their chosen escape route, they must be seen to have – at moments at least – evaded paramount reality. In their time they leapt over too many walls to be easily dismissed: they always remained just ahead of their pursuers. The surrealist enterprise consisted of transforming art into life, life into art. Duchamp's passage along this escape route was so single-mindedly extreme that his major artistic statement was not to create anything for thirty-five years.

An alternative to the revolution in everyday life advocated by the surrealists, is provided by those escapers who abandon any search for the reality below the reality, and instead commit themselves massively to the most apparently superficial, epiphenomenal features of contemporary culture. These are the individuals who elect to live entirely in the world of spectacle, who regard showbusiness, Hollywood, Broadway, stardom, not as circumscribed enclaves in which they might occasionally reside and from which they would routinely return to the worlds of home, children and private life, but rather as the true 'reality', the only appropriate sites for identity work.

The word 'superficial' has no meaning for these escapers, unless as a characterization of non showbusiness life. The world of the cinema, with its emphasis upon beauty, sexuality, adventure and experience is to be lived and not observed. Andy Warhol and his followers provide the most developed example in contemporary times, although the original world of Hollywood to which they – and such other 'beautiful people' as the fictional character Myra Breckenbridge – refer, undoubtedly displayed similar characteristics. For Warhol and his superstars, life *is* a film whether the cameras are switched on or not. And films *are* life, even if that means that we will be given movies in which people do little more than sleep or move around the room. Everyone is a star, and a star all the time. The star's sexual life or appetites for drugs are not just features of their lives, but features of their films and public appearances. In this world no one ever leaves the set. The spectacle is reality; the make-up and properties of the movie studio are appropriate aids to identity construction in every part of one's life. No one familiar with any of the Warhol creations – for example *Viva* or his 'own' biography – can be at all sure who, at any one time, is actor or audience, consumer or producer. The cost of such commitment to this world is high; several of Warhol's stars have lost their sanity, their life, or both, as a result of embarking upon this extreme route away from paramount reality.

The notion of the movie as a separate 'life-world' also appears in the activities of Ken Kesey and the Pranksters. High on LSD, sitting astride their multi-coloured bus, Kesey and his followers drove around America taking a movie of everything they saw, disrupting the suburban world with their weird fantasies, clothes and behaviour. They had to make their own movie or they would become swallowed up in someone else's; and their movie was going to be bigger and broader than anyone else's. But there was still a further step – the move to Edge City – to the place where the movies end and the 'flow' begins. That was where one might find not just versions of reality but reality itself. Not that Edge City had any definite location – to define it was to lose it. One just headed towards it.[5]

3. Trips to the Edge

Two men are driving at top speed across the desert in a large red convertible. They are apparently on their way to a motor race near Las Vegas. One is a newspaper reporter, the other is identified as his attorney.

In the trunk of the car there are two bags of grass, seventy-five pellets of mescaline, five sheets of acid, a salt shaker full of cocaine, bottles of various drugs, tequila, rum, beer, raw ether and amyls. Within a space of three days, these drugs together with much else, will be consumed as part of a frenzied orgy of continual movement that makes most landscapers look as if they are doing little more than shuffle to the kitchen to get a can of beer out of the fridge. Among other incredible events, the attorney will lie in a bath holding a hunting knife, his mind completely blown on large quantities of LSD; they will run up unpaid hotel bills at the rate of somewhere between $29 and $36 an hour; almost completely vandalize their hotel room; abduct a young girl from a plane and fill her head with acid; attend – as 'drug-addled fraud fugitives' – a National District Attorney's Drugs Conference and drive down the main Las Vegas street vomiting out of the car, screaming obscenities and making offers to sell heroin to car loads of policemen attending the Drugs Conference.

The trip, of course, is *Fear and Loathing in Las Vegas* and to Hunter Thompson it was not only some sort of outrageous testament to the American Dream of unlimited opportunity, but also a literal reading of the classic holiday message for those jaded with its more institutionalized versions. This is his 'socio-psychic factor':

> Every now and then when your life gets complicated and the weasels start closing in, the only real cure is to load up on heinous chemicals and then drive like a bastard from Hollywood to Las Vagas. To relax, as it were, in the womb of the desert sun. Just roll the roof back and screw it on, grease the face with white tanning butter and move out with the music at top volume, and at least a pint of ether.[6]

This is no mere drive to the Lake District with a picnic hamper. Excesses and outrages of all sorts must be built into the trip in order to transcend the limitations of ordinary landscaping, to construct a realm so far away from home that literally and metaphorically you are beyond reach. The calculation must be a fine one. Any moment the police might catch you, the drugs will destroy you, sheer physical fatigue will overcome you. But the awareness of a 'giddy, quavering sort of high that means the crash is coming' is part of the high, '. . . the moment of truth, that fine and fateful line between control and disaster'. For such escapes, you must take risks and you build in ways of coping when things go wrong: 'Buy the ticket, take the ride . . . and if it occasionally gets a little heavier than what you had in mind, well . . . maybe chalk it off to forced *consciousness expansion*.'[7]

Of course, Hunter Thompson's trip was temporary and was preceded by an episodic realization, 'Every now and then when your life gets complicated . . .' The extremity lay in the risks of the trip and not the conception of its length or ultimate destination. In other more complete escapes of the going-away type there is the final and awful realization that unless a permanent escape is made you will be in the prison for the rest of your life. Escape scripts of this type run right through our culture: the classic 'on the road' trip of the early beats, updated in Kesey's exploits and given another twist in the road movies like *Easy Rider* and *Midnight Cowboy*; the romantic-vagrant and urban-nomad themes; the sudden break in the leaving home tradition; the foreign-legion and merchant-navy mythology; Mr Polly's quest for freedom; the Gauguin trip to the South Seas; the Beatles's song about the girl leaving home . . .

So well documented are the manifestoes and guidebooks of these escape attempts that they take on a symbolic allegorical quality. They appear as pilgrimages, spiritual quests for freedom – as in the contemporary counter-culture's elevation of the Hesse quest for spiritual enlightenment through the itinerant trip to the East.

These breaks stress *relief*, *risk* and *movement*. The sense of relief is obtained from shedding precious possessions, selves, identities, commitments and routine – and travelling light into the new territory. The attempt – in the extreme versions that interest us here – is always to go for a 'clean break' of the sort Scott Fitzgerald meant:

leave everything behind, travel light. The awareness of risks is also critical: we can get caught and returned to the prison or even killed if things go wrong. Simmel's 'adventurer' embodies this sense of risking all:

> When the outcome of our activity is made doubtful by the intermingling of unrecognizable elements of fate, we usually limit our commitment of force, hold open lines of retreat and take each step only as if testing the ground. In the adventure, we proceed in the directly opposite fashion: it is just on the hovering chance, on fate, on the more-or-less that we risk all, burn our bridges, and step into the mist, as if the road will lead us on, no matter what.[8]

Finally, there is the sense of continual movement. Although there is some long-distance goal, the escaper is often on the run for its own rewards: sheer physical movement gives a potent illusion of freedom. He is always fleeing from, looking for, passing through. He cannot but be highly self-conscious of his enterprise, but tries to suspend this and live out the fantasy of being beyond reach of society. He knows that every free area will eventually be contaminated, but feels that as long as he keeps moving, he will be immunized from these forces. In his heart he is pessimistic, but he keeps on hoping.

4. Life as Chance

The constellation of beliefs around luck, fate, chance and risk is a way of linking fantasy to action. A bit of our paramount reality can be laid on the line, put at risk. This can happen in ordinary life – taking a chance on a job, a romance, an adventure – or in a specially set-aside free area, such as gambling. But sometimes this submission to unpredictability can take very much more extreme forms than taking a chance on a new job or buying a ticket in a lottery.

We have already discussed a stylized version of such an extreme escape in the world of the surrealists. The way they gave themselves over to somnambulism, involuntarism, automatic writing and hallucination, the way they deliberately exploited chance, randomness and co-incidence, were designed to inject chaos and disorder into the accepted world of routine. But when Breton wrote that 'only imagination makes me aware of the possible and that is enough to lift a little the terrible restriction', it was clear that his 'terrible restriction' was not just that of routine but of a stable integrated self. The stress on auto-matism implied also an acceptance of irresponsibility: an escape from the control of reason and the imperatives of moral order by denying any control over one's actions. The logical and extreme conclusion of this position is that of *The Dice Man*, someone indeed who went over the walls in so definitive a way that very few can follow his route.[9]

Luke Rhinehart is a successful, happily married psychiatrist who begins to realize, around his thirty-second birthday, the utter boredom and despair in his life. Nothing helps. Not existentialism, not Zen and certainly not psychiatry itself which makes of his fantasies to kill himself, assassinate or rape others, things merely to be accepted: 'Understand yourself, accept yourself, but do not be yourself.' This, he realizes, is 'a conservative doctrine, guaranteed to help the patient to avoid violent, passionate and unusual acts and to permit him a prolonged, respectable life of moderate misery'. Rhinehart has exhausted all free areas.

Bored with what he is, aware that his escapist fantasies would all lead him into further prisons, he slowly realizes that the real burden is that of the stable, integrated self. The implications of this realization do not fully strike him until one night he whimsically decided to roll the dice. If one number comes up he will rape his best-friend-and-colleague's wife. The dice gives the command and from then on dice life and dice therapy truly begin. 'Excited and proud, I stood for a moment on my own personal Rubicon. And then I stepped across. I established in my mind at that moment and for all time, the never to be questioned principle that what the dice dictates, I will perform.'[10] The story then becomes a manic chronicle of a life in which every whim, every fantasy, every inconsistency is

selected by the 'decision' of the dice. A seemingly silly
fantasy, but beneath it is Rhinehart's deadly serious
argument (for all great escapers are serious) that the principle of a stable, consistent, integrated self – which lies at
the heart of secular and religious beliefs – is no more than
an ideology and is certainly no guarantee of personal happiness and liberation.

For the Dice Man's quest is not just an extreme
exploration of the fantasy route. In an even more important
sense it is an extreme resolution of the problem of self-
consciousness. For those that move from the primitive
unmonitored self, to maximum self-consciousness, the
struggle is to find an optimal level of self-awareness. But
the Dice Man achieves the impossible: a total abandonment of any sense of self. At first the dice decided things
which didn't really matter: job problems, leisure choices,
sexual preferences. They did find him new places and new
roles, but, 'During these first months of dice living I never
consciously decided to let the dice take over my whole life
or to aim at becoming an organism whose every act was
determined by the dice.' He was frightened of going
further and in fact the more he tried to destroy his ego
through the dice, the more it grew. The new Dice-Man
ego took over from the old identities: psychoanalyst,
writer, good-looking male, loving husband.

Eventually – after insights derived from such
experiments as corrupting his young son into the ways of
the dice – Rhinehart becomes more fully aware that the
development of any sense of self – of being someone – is a
disaster, an evolutionary error. Men must eliminate this
error, liberate themselves from the sense of self, from all
boundaries, patterns, consistencies, habits. 'Like the
turtle's shell, the sense of self serves as a shield against
stimulation and as a burden which limits mobility into
possibly dangerous areas.'

It is to these dangerous areas that the Dice
Man starts moving in his evolution towards the totally
random man. His residual self changes while exercises
such as Habit-Breaking Week and the successful

conversion of his patients into Dice Living totally changes other people's expectations of him. His marriage and career are ruined. Eventually, in a meeting which considers his expulsion from the Psychoanalytical Association, he presents a full-blown defence of the Dice-Man philosophy and then escapes totally from his previous selves – ending up as rapist, murderer and revolutionary. 'The ability of major selves to overthrow the Die declines, disappears. The personality is destroyed. The man is free.' This freedom – according to Dice Therapy – is a permanent slip from the problems of paramount reality: selfhood, habit, routine. The convert

... feels liberated when he realises that his possible problems can be solved, but are not his to worry about any longer: they've been shifted to the square shoulders of the dice. He becomes ecstatic. He experiences the transfer of control from an illusory self to the dice as a conversion or as salvation.

We have spent some time describing this escape route. Although many of the other leaps over the wall we consider in this chapter are as extreme, none is as self-consciously connected to the problems of paramount reality or identity that lie at the heart of our concerns.

GOING INSIDE

1. The Ancient Way

In the first few months of our teaching in Durham prison, we met a prisoner called Jeff, a small nervous man who politely attended all the discussions without saying much. He appeared to absorb all the talk about outsiders, anarchism and the unfairness of the system: he asked for points of clarification, but never expressed his own attitudes. The other men saw him as a loner and spoke somewhat disparagingly about his fantasy world and his refusal to show any active resistance to prison life. Jeff was eventually transferred to another prison and soon some of the class began to receive letters from him hinting at a religious conversion and talking of visions in his cell. All this was widely interpreted as a sign that Jeff had finally caved in, that prison had driven him mad.

At about this time one of us received an unexpected letter from him which suggested that he had not altogether been 'driven mad' by forces beyond his control. He wrote: 'I have decided to live inside my head.'

The point he had arrived at, in the microcosm of the prison world, was the beginning of that most ancient of routes: the world cannot be changed, only your perception and experience of it. He might indeed – as the other prisoners disparagingly concluded – have given in to fantasy, but this was no mere cumulative swamping by the fantasies we discussed earlier. For the travellers along the road inside do not live by the soap-opera fantasies of mass culture. They have visions of another world. The decision to go inside is not just a manipulation of cognitive processes in order to make time pass or get a course of action moving smoothly along. These travellers are asserting the ontological superiority of the inner vision and devoting their entire lives to searching for and then maintaining this vision with whatever sacrament – symbolic or chemical – draws attention away from the material, linear world. The ultimate purpose is to arrive at a destination which is not 'out there' – as it is for those who go away – but inside. The prison is the prison of the mind.

It would be presumptuous for us to attempt to distil the essence of the belief system which sustains this way of life. In the great Oriental religions, the esoteric psychological systems, in the tradition of Eastern mysticism, in contemporary psychedelic philosophies, the message is the same. Whether or not the contemporary renditions of Eastern faiths are 'correct', or whether the psychedelic or human potential versions replicate the message faithfully, all these phenomena fall into the 'going inside' category. In this respect at least, the great texts of Buddhism, Taoism, Hinduism and Sufi are indeed saying the 'same' as the more banal versions found in Timothy

Leary or Castaneda. 'Dropping out' is to cease playing the social game, to cultivate authenticity and detachment, give up bogus involvements, ambitions and symbolic rewards in order to pursue the development of inner wisdom. 'Turning on' is the method of achieving this: the sudden awareness of internal states, heightened consciousness, all the experiences we discussed as momentary slips through the fabric. And 'tuning in' is the sequel to all this: the shift in values and responses which leads you to be more permanently receptive to a new mode of consciousness.

Who are these people? Any list would be self-evident: a catalogue of the mystics, saints, gurus, holy men, visionaries and seers who have charted and followed this path. It must be clear, though, that inclusion in this list is reserved for the extremes. These are people who are life-long travellers, who sacrifice all in order to make the momentary slip permanent, who strive to be continually in a state of ecstasy.

2. The Voyage of Madness

Clearly the path inside is a dangerous one. It can look like a retreat into a fantasy world, a world in which we voyage so far from paramount reality that we go over an edge. And in our society, one of the edges is that of sanity. It is precisely the parallels between mysticism and certain states of mind labelled as schizophrenia which have been exploited by some currents in contemporary psychiatry. Again in the present context it doesn't matter whether or not schizophrenia and mysticism are comparable, but only that they *can* be compared as examples of voyages inside. Laing, in charting the psychotic experience in this way, is providing a culturally available script for the going-inside style. We cannot dispute that the way is extreme nor – from what we know of those like Artaud and many nameless other 'cases' – can we doubt that it has been followed. Here is Laing on the nature of this route:

> Can we not see that this voyage is not what we need to be cured of, but that it is itself a natural way of healing our own

appalling state of alienation called normality? In other times
people intentionally embarked upon this voyage. Or if they
found themselves embarked, willy-nilly, they gave thanks, as
for a special grace.[11]

We hardly need words like 'grace' to be convinced that
Laing's schizophrenics are going along the same route as
the mystics. He is quite clear that the ultimate source of
knowledge is to be obtained by exploring inner space and
that the end is deeper than the ego: an existential rebirth.
And the psychotic apprehension of this alien fantasy
world, far from being pathological, is close to those revered
states which mystics aspire to and which they can attain
only with discipline and training. The voyage is in and
back, through and beyond to the original Alpha and Omega
of experience and reality. For Laing the split between
inner and outer world is resolved in the same way by the
mystic and the schizoid. And, finally, self-consciousness,
the ever vigilant demon who haunted all our everyday
escape attempts is exorcized: the point is reached where
we float without an ego, without any sense of the
boundaries between self and other, inner and outer.

3. Into the Tank

Madness and mysticism are not the only ways
inside. They have themselves provided hints for those in-
trepid travellers who have taken all sorts of risks in order
to explore their own mental states and thus provide the key
for others to open the doors of perception. We are not
talking of the occasional user of psychedelic drugs, nor the
dabbler with those techniques of consciousness expansion
we were so dismissive about earlier – but those who dedicate their whole lives to exploring the inner worlds which
have occasionally been revealed to others in momentary
slips.

Consider John Lilly, to whom we have already
referred. He was an eminent scientist, who had established
a reputation in the fields of biophysics, neurophysiology,
electronics and neuroanatomy, besides being a qualified

psychoanalyst. Reaching the end of the road of conventional science, he abandons the safety of the laboratory – but not the logic of the experimental method – in order to explore the contours of altered states of consciousness. There is nothing particularly extreme about this if the exploration is confined to studying others. But Lilly not only studied himself – with ruthless rigour – but exposed himself to extraordinary dangers in so doing. He experimented with prolonged states of solitude, with sensory deprivation and LSD (all combined in the experiment we described in Chapter 7 where he floated in a tank, having taken a large amount of acid), hypnosis and submission to a guru. After one drug experience he made a suicide attempt and some index to the dangers he was exposed to is provided by his reflections after a particularly arduous series of exercises:

> During the Pampas, I went through several 'physical death–rebirth' experiences. I pushed myself into regions of exertion beyond what I thought were my limits. I literally risked what I conceived of as over exertion with 'heart failure' as the expected result. This 'heart failure' did not occur. I found that I had gone through a barrier of fear in the body and into a new high-energy space of physical functioning . . To go up, I had to push through that which held me down – fear of bodily death . . .[12]

We cite the case of Lilly not, of course, just because he used extreme techniques but because he serves as a model for all those who return from their voyages convinced of the significance (and indeed existence – which most of us might question) of higher states of consciousness.

GOING ABOVE

1. The Great Beast

Aleister Crowley, the 'Great Beast', the 'wickedest man in the world', the man who 'endeavoured to become a God and ended something less than human, having in the course of seventy-two years driven more men and women to drink, insanity or death than most incarnate devils' is perhaps the most flamboyant traveller we could find along this escape route. A chapter in his autobiographical novel *Diary of a Drug Fiend* is entitled 'Over the Top' and indeed in everything he thought and did, Crowley went right over the top.

His ideas, for the moment, concern us less than his life. They derived from an extraordinary mixture of Buddhism and Hinduism, the Tantra and Black Magic, Eastern mysticism and the Kabbalah, the occult and paganism. His master identity was Beast 666: an incarnation of the Beast from Revelation and the key to his position in the complex magical order he founded and which he thought would eventually supercede Christianity. Its core belief was his famous motto: 'Do what thou wilt shall be the whole of the law' – a simple statement (borrowed from Rabelais and Blake) embodying the belief in the eternal as the ultimate unity, in which all opposites, including good and evil would be reconciled. How better to escape the contradictions and demands of paramount reality than to believe 'I am living in eternity, and temporal things have become tedious and stupid symbols'? Particularly stupid and tedious to Crowley were attempts to distinguish any morality: 'There is no good. Evil is good. Blessed be the Principle of Evil.'

This principle and the perpetually invoked 'Do what thou wilt' led Crowley into every excess:

Our High Magick is most high if on its snow-wrapped crater-cone we stand, in air too virginal to have known dust of plains or smoke of cities, air to intoxicate us laughing mad so that we fling our limbs abroad and scream: 'Love is the Law, Love under will.'

What this meant was a life-time of total, and highly self-conscious, dedication to creating and maintaining an enclave for himself well beyond the reach of conventional society. In this territory he practised 'Sexual Magick' – sexual perversions of every sort; used most available drugs including opium, cocaine, heroin and mescaline; invoked most imaginable magical forces and rituals; converted (or corrupted – depending on one's perspective) a whole body of disciples and adepts; and generally explored every possibility, short of murder (a path followed by a later inheritor of his ideas, Charles Manson), which was excessive and depraved.

Crowley was painfully aware that his sense of power needed a rich dramatic script and stage on which to sustain it. In his time he was Scottish nobleman, magician, drug addict, gargantuan seducer (picking up 'scarlet women' at will), poet, confidence trickster, traitor, high priest and pornographer. Although conventionally dismissed as a charlatan and fraud, there is little doubt of his personal commitment: his performance was sustained for too long a period and his monitoring of it was too intense. Through half a century of magical ceremonies, writings, frantic attempts to raise money, mistresses, public events and scandals, he persisted with the logic of his position, however absurd (for example, his practice of kissing women he first met with the 'serpent's kiss' – biting their arms with his two sharpened canine teeth, or his occasional practice of defecating on carpets, explaining that his ordure was sacred like the Dalai Lama's). No amount of ridicule and persecution deterred him; his escape route towards making himself a God was protected in the way his biographer Symonds indicates:

> The progress he made in this direction was due in part to the fact that he was not afraid of madness; he pressed on into realms that would daunt all but the most courageous or the most foolhardy. From the point of view of the occult sciences, his merit lies in the system of guards (safeguards against obsession) which he devised for protecting the traveller on these secret and dangerous planes.[13]

We are not at all interested in the merit of Crowley's ideas for the occult sciences. More fascinating to us is the system of psychological guards he devised to keep him going. Fraudulent, absurd or psychopathic as his life was, he managed to construct it beyond the reaches of society and to avoid the many 'secret and dangerous planes' we have discussed. This was not without cost and it was not without anguish and depression. His last words were reported as, 'I am perplexed.'

2. There is No Good, There is No Evil

> Both read Nietzsche and absorbed the gospel of the superman. But if it is asked exactly why they committed murder, the only valid answer is because they *chose* to. They were free, they were intelligent, they were rich. Life offered them no sense of resistance, of goals worth striving for, so they set up an imaginary goal and played a game; then the game turned to reality.[14]

Thus Colin Wilson, on Leopold and Loeb, the famous child murderers of the twenties.

Only a minute proportion of murders can be discussed in anything like these terms, only a minute proportion who entertain a 'going above' belief system ever act in so appallingly extreme a way. But there is something in this unusual conjunction of beliefs and action which indicates what happens when extreme consciousness of self combines with 'momentary slip' revelations about the omnipotence of the self and the insignificance of the social world. This transcendent-belief system – an elaborated version of Colin Wilson's 'Outsider' mentality – stresses the total superiority of the individual, a complementary inferiority and weakness in everyone else (the mass, the victims), a permanent status as being beyond all judgements and criticism, a conscious amorality and a sense of being before his time. There is literally no script to accommodate the fantasy and so he has to make his own. Pure will has now to be combined with the definitive act, the legitimating gesture that inaugurates an entirely new drama. 'His next problem is to find an *act*, a definite act that will give him power over his doubts and self questionings.'[15] And the act must be extreme and irreversible.

Murder is such an act and there are at least two types of ideological murder which fit the extremes of our

going above category. The first is the existential murder –
fictionalized in Camus's Outsider, Dostoyevsky's Raskolnikov – and found in real life in such cases as Leopold and
Loeb. Murder occurs after freedom is seen as terror: it is
not just being allowed to do what you like, but intensity of
will: 'Do what thou wilt shall be the whole of the law.' If
we do not claim our freedom, there is the void and these
scripts often describe the act of murder as an escape from
routine, boredom, triviality. Only a few murders might
fall in this category: others occur at moments of passion,
are shaped by economic motives, might be matters of blind
compulsion. But the murders in *The Possessed*, in *Crime
and Punishment* and in the real life examplars of this type
were crimes of freedom, rather than compulsion.

There is a second category of ideological
murder which fits the 'going above' destination, one where
the superman belief system is more explicitly articulated.
The most notorious exemplar in recent years is Charles
Manson.[16] However derivative and unclear our information might be about the case, there seems little doubt that
his gruesome murders were preceded by some sort of
enlightenment experience (a reality slip?) and exposure to
a series of philosophies (which Sanders terms his 'sleazo
inputs') which transported him into an eternal now where
time was transcended and the earthly opposites of good
and evil, life and death were seen to be either non-existent
or identical. As Zaehner correctly argues, it would be facile
to dismiss Manson as mad: there was little doubt that he
knew what he was doing, that he had a fully constructed
cosmology and that with a logical mind he acted on his
belief.

Manson shared with Crowley and other mystics
a belief in the transcendence of time and space (and therefore of death) and the disappearance of the ego or self:

The end and goal of both Hinduism and Buddhism
is to pass into a form of existence in which time and space and
all the opposites that bedevil human existence are totally transcended and in which one is literally dead to the world but alive
in a timeless eternity. This ritual death Charlie had already

experienced, and, as a result of the experience, he had taught his disciples that they must kill themselves in this way in order to kill others and be free from remorse.[17]

Manson and his Family would not relegate evil to some outer region; they found their own escape route through embracing and indulging in evil to its furthermost extremity. His superman ideology (at times he presented himself as Jesus Christ), his relationship to his followers, his attitude to the masses, his immersion in the culture of violence, his claim to have found full freedom and his total lack of any remorse must all qualify him for an extreme position in the 'going above' gallery.

We cannot go much further than transcending life and death themselves, either by killing or being killed: 'There is no good, there is no evil ... You can't kill kill ... If you're willing to be killed, you should be willing to kill.' Such statements coming from a man convicted of nine brutal murders and probably responsible for many more must be seen as making real, if highly specific philosophical sense. Manson the social outcast (a nameless illegitimate child, petty thief, hardened prisoner) collected a band of disciples, retreated into the desert, and then with sex, power and psychedelic drugs moulded his followers according to his will and then descended on the unholy city to terrorize its spoiled hip inhabitants. This was indeed a working out of the full horror script of American culture.

In talking about 'going above' as an elaboration or exaggeration of self-consciousness we are not making the patently absurd claim that it is just this or that extreme self-consciousness that will eventually lead to murder. The point is that at a certain junction of psychological and cultural forces, the relationship between identity and society becomes no longer negotiable in everyday forms. The accommodation, compromises, reinvestments we have described are no longer viable and the choice is made literally to remove the self from society, to refuse – at the point of terror, at least – to acknowledge the existence of a social self which is embedded in roles, statuses, career timetables. (One obvious extreme escape which we do not consider in this text is suicide. In a sense this is a form of 'going away' – the trip beyond Edge City – but other types of suicide may fit the 'going above' category. The killing of oneself, like the killing of others, becomes a declaration that personal identity transcends every societal inhibition: individual autonomy is absolute).

We have talked about some strange and terrible trips in this chapter. They reflect the preoccupation with extremes that we carried with us when we started this book. And although we have suggested that these extreme phenomena in some senses are extensions of everyday escape routes from paramount reality, we don't want to repeat the error we discussed in our preface of trying to force action into homogeneous categories such as 'deviance'. These extremes are amenable to an analysis which uses concepts such as self-consciousness, fantasy, scripts, free areas, but this is not to reduce them to the mundane and the ordinary – if indeed anyone would hazard doing this with Crowley, Lilly, the Dice Man, Manson...

Whatever we say about these trips, we have to award them the grudging status of special, unique, extreme. There is an obvious sense, though, in which they are failures. In the same way as their impetus is dramatic, so is their end. These travellers find themselves culturally co-opted, or – more dramatically – their biographies catch up with them: they are physically burned out or else finally caught by the forces of social control. 'Going inside' is safest – leaving aside the risk of psychosis – and is thereby more amenable to co-option into accepted life styles. Those who go away may burn themselves out, dying slow deaths through alcohol, drugs or the hazards of continual movement. (Holmes records his feelings at his friend Kerouac's funeral: '... a lonely disappointed man, who had been down all the roads – the drugs, the screws, the fantasies, the highs, the hopes – and knew in his own ravaged nerves what was left at "the end of the night".'[18] And 'going above' cannot but end with massive social sanctions, the prison cell or the scaffold.

In the end, paramount reality triumphs over its most determined enemies. Left behind though are the signs and sites of its few defeats – markers for future protagonists.

9

A Case of
Mistaken
Identity

This book has described a world of scurrying human beings. Periodically or permanently dissatisfied with the picture of everyday reality which occupies their consciousness, they busily search for ways of ignoring, distorting or subverting that reality. At times they merely stand still and shift their mode of consciousness, at others they abandon aspects of their present regime, home, job, leisure pursuits and turn to substitutes, in the hope of finding autonomy and shaking off the sense of routine and regularity. Sometimes they turn inwards towards their fantasies and imaginings for comfort, at others they look outwards for consolation, carving free self-expressive enclaves out of the heart of reality. And then there are some who use their adaptation not as a means by which life may be occasionally resisted or identity marginally re-assembled but as an entire domain of freedom – an all-embracing alternative reality. All these manoeuvres are precarious; they are likely to be undermined at any moment by the re-assertion of the claims of paramount reality. All involve some risks, ranging from ostracism by a few friends and acquaintances to the wholesale hostility of the mass of society.

The dissatisfactions which prompt these escape attempts are numerous. In some cases we picture ourselves as ridden by torments, consumed by a terrible sense of our own alienation, bowed down by the dreadful boredom of contemporary existence. In our previous chapter we described some who saw their human predicament in just such terms. But for others the dissatisfaction is less dramatically expressed and less intensively experienced. For these people it is the intermittent appearance of predictability, routine, monotony, repetition and boredom, which feeds their desire to find some relief beside or beyond everyday life.

We have not, however, considered whether the dissatisfactions which prompt escape attempts are only intermittent ones or informed by some continuing ideology of escape. We might have given the impression that we see everybody who tries any sort of escape as subscribing to a similar world view. This is obviously not so. Any of the less extreme routes we described may be taken by people with quite different pictures of the world and with only a very crude idea that their actions are informed by anything like a coherent ideology. People react in different ways to the impositions of paramount reality, and we will suggest three master metaphors, commonly employed in everyday language, which describe these varieties of accommodation.

There are times, for example, when most men feel *at home* in the world, when they have a comfortable acceptance of the arrangements and conventions of everyday life, a sense that the world was indeed made for people like them and that it could not be otherwise without producing considerable discomfort. This is not a glib way of describing a particular set of people who lack a sense of social relativism, but rather a characterization of those aspects of all our lives which produce the feeling that 'this is where I live'. When this attitude is uppermost then reality is embraced, routines are dignified as rituals, conventions are religiously observed, scripts performed with pleasure and satisfaction. Even those who usually declare themselves least 'at home' in society have interludes when things feel right. It is indeed customary in our society to mock those who have revolutionary intentions by pointing to the aspects of their lives in which they display signs of being at home, a non-critical acceptance of customary arrangements. No particular behaviour is indicative of this attitude to reality; any activity will do. We might feel as at home with the world, marching with a banner through the streets of London, as sitting in slippers watching the late-night television.

To be 'at home' with reality is to experience it as non-problematic, to fit ourselves uncomplainingly to its timetables and schedules, its systems of reward and punishment, not because of any compulsion, but because this is 'the way to do it', the 'way to get by without fuss or trouble'. What might be 'escape routes' for others – the holiday, the hobby, the night out – are not seen in escapist terms at all. These free areas are just woven into the tapestry of social life. They might give us room for doing a bit of identity work, but they are not launching pads for establishing a sense of separateness from society.

However, the very ability which allows us to say 'this – not anywhere else – is where life really is', makes it unlikely that many of us can keep such a metaphor going through every twist of our life plan. A sense of comfort is not always there. On the contrary, we might experience the world as a highly oppressive and restrictive presence. This is the metaphor of the world as *burden*: we speak of things 'getting too much', of our work or family 'getting on top of us', we see our lives as loads which we somehow have to get rid of. Again, there is no one set of activities which fits this metaphor: we might feel quite un-oppressed and easy going about work, yet experience a sexual relationship as a terrible burden. For some of us, at some times, only some parts of our lives feel like a burden; for others, at all times, all parts are burdensome. Like Tommy Wilhelm, the hero of Bellow's *Seize the Day*:

The spirit, the peculiar burden of his existence lay upon him like an accretion, a load, a hump. In any moment of quiet when sheer fatigue prevented him from struggling, he was apt to find this mysterious weight, this growth or collection of nameless things which it was the business of his life to carry about. That must be what a man is for.[1]

What is a transitory feeling for most people is converted here into a total statement about the human condition – 'That must be what a man is for.' If the business of life is to carry a burden, we look for somewhere to put it down, somewhere to rest, to find refuge.

But what of those times when there seems nowhere to go – when there is a sense not just of strangeness or oppression but when everything we see around us is transformed into walls, gates and moats. This is our third metaphor (the one this book has tended to be cast into), life as a *prison*. We are locked into a prison created either by ourselves or by others, by routine or by self-consciousness. We are trapped and want out. Again the idea of escaping can be something which simply occurs to most people every now and then and might be limited to restricted parts of their life – or else it can be converted into a master metaphor about paramount reality. For an example of such conversion we use Aldous Huxley's classic statement about what the Doors of Perception were leading from:

Most men and women lead lives, at the worst so painful, at the best so monotonous, poor, and limited, that the urge to escape, the longing to transcend themselves if only for a few moments, is and always has been one of the principal appetites of the soul.[2]

For Huxley, the prison was that of the self – to him unhappiness and self-consciousness were in some way connected – for others, the prison is behavioural and environmental rather than subjective. In either case, though, the life plan becomes conceived in terms of the same guiding metaphor.

Constructing Meta-Grumbles

Most dissatisfactions with everyday life take paramount reality for granted. Often we will complain that we have not enough money, insufficient chance of promotion; we may feel unhappy because of our failure to find a loving partner, or be a successful father. But although these concerns may prompt broader dissatisfactions with life, none of them may be enough to set us in search for an 'escape'. They are grumbles about the way aspects of the life plan are going rather than signs that we wish to escape the demands of that plan. In contrast the sort of broader dissatisfactions which are expressed in the shape of such metaphors as 'life as a burden' or 'life as a prison' undermine the life plan itself, involving at least some tentative questioning of why we should work in the first place, some cynicism about the nature of human relations in the world, some feeling that there is something absurd about us being a father to children. In bewilderingly short periods we can move from a petty dissatisfaction (how the paunch is starting to bulge) to a general sense of personal inadequacy, to a cosmic reflection about what on earth we are doing being worried about appearances when there is no real meaning in life. Or else the sequence is reversed: we wake up as it were with the metaphor and it then starts to poison every trivial turn of the daily round. A personal problem about sexual relationships or domestic routine may as readily lead us towards a feeling that life is a burden or a prison, as any after-dinner reading of Sartre or Kierkegaard.

Whatever dissatisfaction comes first, general or specific, the type of identity work which has to be done to repossess the self (who I am) from the objects which have seized it (what I do) cannot be done within the life plan. The dissatisfactions are prompted by a flaw that lies elsewhere. They are in effect grumbles about the basis of our other grumbles – to use Maslow's phrase – 'meta-grumbles'.

Our ability to have such meta-grumbles cannot

be taken for granted; this is not simply an individual option which can be exercised by members of any historical or contemporary society. The emergence over the last century, for example, of the idea of the romantic outsider – somebody who can be a member of society but simultaneously take a stance against that society – has lent credibility to ideas of rebellion, escape, liberation. The sheer possibility – not available to primitive man – of totally relativizing his life, seeing it as one among many, puts a premium on self-consciousness, makes a mode of mental management such as unreflective accommodation not simply untenable but something almost to be stigmatized. Meta-grumbles are only possible in societies which combine a glorification of the unique self with a high sense of relativity about the arrangements of life.

Thus, meta-grumbles about work become possible only when 'work' is defined as a distinctive segment of life, one which may be contrasted with others which are characterized as 'non-work'. In some traditional societies work is not an activity which is temporally, spatially, or conceptually separated from other parts of our existence, it is an aspect of living rather than a distinctive form of life. In such societies it would make little sense to demand that work become more like leisure, or to observe with cynicism that leisure was becoming more like work. If the two areas do not exist as differentiated forms, then neither may be employed to draw attention to the inadequacies of the other. For us, however, the recognition of the distinction between work and non-work is a recurrent feature of the life plan, a possible source of meta-grumbles.

It is the very bounded nature of the life-world of work that enables us to express dissatisfaction not just about the concrete problems which occur at work but about the whole nature of work itself. So work may appear to us not as a natural activity but perhaps as an immovable object to which we must periodically attend, a giant slag heap at which we must shovel away for the greater part of our lives. It stands out there as a world to which we periodically subscribe, but in which we do not really live.

The degree to which we feel at home in our other life-worlds varies. Whereas work may appear as an alien activity in which we reluctantly abandon ourselves to regularities and routines, our domestic lives may appear more natural private areas, domains which are to be lived in, rather than carefully kept at a distance. We may sense the existence of a dichotomy between these private and public spheres.[3] In the public sphere the individual controls his participation for fear of being caught up in alien and meaningless routines while in the private sphere he 'attempts to construct and maintain a "home world"' which will serve as a meaningful centre of his life in society'. But the home world is equally prey to the sense of relativity, and can equally promote escape attempts. Our endeavours to establish it as the one meaningful life-world will be threatened by the intrusion of other worlds. Friends may demand to know why we are married; they will point contentedly to their own arrangements and declare our commitment to monogamy to be absurd. 'Too much like hard work,' they may comment, successfully undermining the meaningfulness of our private domain, by comparing it to the alien public one. Our children may mock domestic privacy, regarding it not as evidence of a meaningful existence, but rather as a claustrophobic indication of the narrowness of our lives. And we are bombarded with rhetoric condemning the bourgeois family as the last dying institution of capitalism. For our own part, we may seek partners outside marriage, expanding our 'private lives' into a dozen minor life-worlds, visiting our mistress in her flat on Tuesdays, calling in at the local massage parlour to be jerked off on Thursdays and spending Saturday evenings crying over old times with two divorced drunks in the local pub. Which of these is then our real private world?

It is our experience of the plurality of social worlds, then, that relativizes each one of them and in turn sets the stage for meta-grumbles. All this in contrast with life in traditional societies where

... whether with his family or at work or engaged in political processes or participating in festivity and ceremonial, the individual was always in the same 'world'. Unless he physically left his own society, he rarely, if ever, would have the feeling that a particular social situation took him out of this common life-world.[4]

But the plurality of life-worlds does not only provide the necessary conditions for the emergence of a sense of relativity and therefore the possibility of meta-grumbles – it also determines the types of *goals* which will be sought as a solution to those particular grumbles. What exactly is being sought by all the escapers we've described in these pages? Up till now we've concentrated on the grumbles themselves – the sense of boredom, routine and repetition, which set men off in search of an alternative reality. But what are the beckoning signs which help to promote the claims of the escape zones, and the new identities which are for sale in them? What are the advertisements in the window of the escape-attempts supermarket?

True Self

Largest of all is the invitation to step inside and find your *true self*. No other concept so dominates the literature of despair and pessimism in our society; no other prize is so frequently promised in the guides and handbooks to alternative reality. The link between this goal and the pluralization of our life worlds is evident. We see our existence as made up of different life-worlds, various phenomenal universes within which we display separate modes of consciousness. Our very lack of full commitment to any or all of these worlds produces within us the sense of some entity which stands back from reality, an entity which is presented within all of them but which is fully realized in none – a sense of true self. Paradoxically we gain this sense of self from our awareness of its imperfect realization in the worlds to which we subscribe:

Throughout the modern era, the quest of the individual is for his self, for a fixed and unambiguous point of reference. He needs such a fixed point more and more urgently in view of the unprecedented expansion of theoretical and practical perspectives and the complication of life, and the related fact that he can no longer find it anywhere outside himself.[5]

In everyday life, this sense of self seems doomed to remain a partial construction. It is never fully articulated in any one of our life-worlds, for our sense of relativity ensures that we give less than full personal commitment to each one of them. Our sense of self flits about our everyday lives, it is a resource which we may summon when we are described as creatures of routine, when we are declared to be no more than what we do. It is an inner point of reference which helps us to defend ourselves against paramount reality, but when we come to look for it as a distinctive entity, a guarantee of our independence and individuality, it is peculiarly illusory. It is almost as if our true self has been stolen from us and we are left with only traces, echoes, memories. The intimations of self that we have do not cohere; they hang about our lives but do not seem to constitute it.

The escape-attempts salesmen offer us a place where these intimations may be woven together into an entity. They offer an end to relativity, a promise of some absolute element in our lives. The slogans declare that the true self may only be constituted in special enclaves or right outside the pluralized life-worlds which make up paramount reality. These are the new sites upon which self may be mounted. Their salesmen are certainly not shy about advertising the quality of their products:

The underground church, the freak community, the zodiac, existential psychology, encounter groups and the free university are pioneer efforts in offering new sources of self and should be understood as such. Repression of these experiments means repression of self and is a greater tragedy than over-population, environmental pollution, and war itself.[6]

Sadly, however, the prospects for obtaining this sense of a true self by resort to these new 'sources' are liable to be undermined by the various corrupting influences to which we have continually referred. Once there is anything less than full commitment to the new 'source' (and this disengagement may be readily induced by our sense of the commercialization, or the programmed nature of the enterprise), then we are back upon the wheel of relativity. Our new search for a real self may then have done little more than add another self-conception to the stock derived from our supposedly 'unreal' involvement in work, marriage, bureaucracy, leisure. We have added an encounter group, commune, or free university, identity to our collection, but we have not dissolved our old repertoire of roles, or fused them into some new entity.

Meaning

Linked with the search for true self goes the hunt for *meaning*. Again it is the pluralization of life-worlds which simultaneously creates the sense of meaninglessness and prompts the search for a corrective. None of the life-worlds in themselves provide a sense of the meaning of life – what overall sense of meaning may we obtain from the factory floor, the office desk or the breakfast table? – and neither do they integrate with each other to provide any overall sense of the nature or purpose of life. Life-worlds co-exist, but do not cohere. The principles and beliefs which seem appropriate at work seem irrelevant in bed at home, the motives and values that we cite as significant in our moments of leisure seem incompatible with those which are displayed in our political and religious lives. 'The *multiworld existence* of modern man requires frequent gear-shifting.'[7] As he moves from one small world into the next, he is faced with at least marginally different expectations, requiring different role performances, in concert with different sets of people. The small life-worlds of modern man belong to different 'jurisdictions' and different realms of meaning. We lack a single symbolic vocabulary which binds together the elements of our different life-worlds, a vocabulary which would allow us to evaluate across the range of our activities, which would give moral priority to this or that part of our lives. This was not always a problem.

Through most of empirically available human history, religion has played a vital role in providing the over-arching canopy of symbols for the meaningful integration of society. The various meanings, values and beliefs operative in society were ultimately 'held together' in a comprehensive interpretation of reality that related human life to the cosmos as a whole.[8]

It was religion that gave overall meaning and enabled us to feel at home in society. But now religion itself has become one more life-world, a segmented aspect of existence. It occurs at certain times, on certain days and in certain places. Religious programmes line up alongside programmes on hobbies, holidays, sport and politics. They are expected to keep within their boundaries and those who periodically strike religious attitudes are called upon to recognize the distinction between such postures and those which are appropriate to their involvement in other life-worlds.

The escape-attempts supermarket advertises meaning alongside true self. By reference, for example, to the type of experience that we described as momentary slips through the fabric, man is persuaded that he may dramatically grasp the way in which all aspects of his existence are integrated. Everything will 'fall into place' – the incongruities, paradoxes and contradictions will shake themselves down into a pattern. Marriage, work, sex, death will be comprehensible in terms of a single formula. We must stand back from life to find its meaning.

There are many vocabularies of symbols which set out to drive a thread of sense through our pluralized life-worlds. Each concentrates upon certain features to the exclusion of others declaring that only these features are significant, only they provide a line of meaning through the apparent absurdity of our disparate existence. Meaning they declare lies in nature, within the wisdom of our own bodies, within a higher consciousness, within the nature of economic relationships, within the love that we feel for other people. But each vocabulary of symbols enjoys only a precarious and often momentary transcendence over the worlds it seeks to encompass. For as each new vocabulary is announced, so is it scrutinized for particular elements which may happily be accommodated within our existing life-worlds. Instead of transforming our world, the new symbol system is dragged into it and mutilated. Phrases from the vocabulary of dialectical materialism decorate the posters in our bedroom, sentences from the vocabulary of mysticism are woven into the rock songs on the juke box, concepts from the vocabulary of pantheism are held up for our titillation in cigarette advertisements. Instead of integrating all worlds, the new vocabularies find themselves sucked down into the grammars of everyday life. Meaning proves as illusory as true self.

Progress

The third beckoning sign promises higher forms of happiness through progress and novelty. This is a familiar promise. Each of the careers which go to make up our life plan carry within them promises of advances – more pay and status at work, a growing contentment with our marriage, an increasing sense of satisfaction from our children, an improving ability at leisure pursuits. But these promises of advance may do little to beat off the sense of standing still. We observe the hollow nature of the advances which are obtained by other men, and having seen this, our own desire for development along similar lines becomes less passionate. Work does not become any better, our marriage does not provide more fulfilment, our children do not provide increased satisfaction. The development begins to appear only as a movement through time, not a transition to a happier state. No sooner has an anticipated future become the present, than it loses its attractions: this incurable imperfection of temporality was seen by Proust as a 'soul error'.

Yet, despite our hidden awareness of how elusive progress is, we still maintain the idea that happiness lies ahead of us, that if only we could shift paramount reality in this way or that, then we could climb just one step nearer to nirvana. If the progress to happiness along recognized career paths appears uncertain then new roads to happiness must be sought. The escape routes are ready and waiting. The promise of novelty through escalation lies all around us. We can move from holidays at home, to holidays in Europe, America and Africa. We can put aside alcohol and marijuana and move on to LSD, to cocaine, to heroin. We can progress from pornographic magazines to strip shows, to blue movies, to live exhibitions, move our hobby from the attic into the whole house, leave behind the pools coupons and the betting shop and turn to the racetrack and the casino. Repetition must be avoided, novelty embraced. Only if we experience life as progress, as everchanging, we can be sure that we are on the path to personal satisfaction. But again the promise of novelty is confounded by our sense of *déjà-vu*, by the feeling that no matter how much we change settings and roles and properties, that still we become assailed by certain recurrent features of the scene which belie our attempts to maintain its novel status. Scripts catch up with us. Novelty is elusive.

Inside and Outside

Some men may on occasions resolve their dissatisfactions, their meta-grumbles, within the course of everyday life; that indeed was the significance of our chapter on the escape functions of different modes of mental management. And similarly some men may claim that they uncover a sense of true self, of meaning and of novelty in one or in all of their many life-worlds. But underlying most of the escape routes that we have described is the notion that salvation may only properly be obtained by somehow placing ourselves *outside* society. We have a recurrent sense in our lives that society is only partly made for us, that there is a gap between the invitations which it issues and our own aspirations.

We simultaneously seek to place ourselves *within* that society in order to enjoy the traditional benefits that it provides, but at the same time resist it in order to declare that we are something more than what we do within it.

This paradoxical insider–outsider status which men appear to seek can be traced most obviously to the historical emergence of a sense of individuality. For historically, individuality emerges as a stance which is taken against society. In the eighteenth century this stance was struck against traditional institutions. Men were to be liberated from these institutions so that their *common* individuality might appear – their equality. In the nineteenth century, however, the stance was not against historical institutions but rather against one's contemporaries. One differentiated oneself against other members of the social group. In Simmel's terms, 'Eighteenth-century liberalism put the individual on his feet, in the nineteenth, he was allowed to go as far as they would carry him.' The new sense of individuality was a sense of uniqueness derived from concentrating upon the innumerable points of unlikeness which pertain between oneself and one's fellow men.

So extreme has this individuality become that the notion of 'doing your own thing' – at one time the most reprehensively anti-social of all ideals – can now become elevated into a positive ethical principle. The selfishness embodied in this principle is selfishness about the self. Society – social institutions, objects, relationships – has taken away our self and we have every right to repossess it. The ethos of possessive individualism ('bourgeois individuality', as it is sometimes called) has for many of us taken the place of possessive materialism: the collective and individual escapes we have described are really expeditions of repossession for those to whom the self is all that really matters.

The development of individuality as an attribute to be held apart from society, is related directly to the pluralization of our life-worlds:

Life in a wider circle and interaction with it develop, in and of themselves, more consciousness of personality than arises in a narrower circle; this is so above all because it is precisely through the *alteration* of sensations, thoughts and activities that personality documents itself.[9]

But this differentiation of the individual as a result of his membership of different life-worlds is liable to have the paradoxical effect we described in discussing the quest for true self. Being now a creature unlike any others as a result of his partial commitment to a variety of different worlds, he now searches for a still point at which his acquired uniqueness may constitute an object for reflection.

Contemporary individuality is regarded as something wrested from the innumerable contacts that we make in our everyday life. It is a property which is gradually constructed by our concentration upon the differences between ourselves and other people and by an awareness of holding back from commitment to particular interactions and activities. We are members of the social world but construct our individuality out of every intimation that we may gather about the ways in which we are less than full members.

The nature of our dissatisfactions with the world and the goals which we seek in order to rout such dissatisfactions are determined by this contemporary conception of individuality. Routine and repetition become major enemies for 'the more uniformly and unwaveringly life progresses, and less the extremes of sensate experience depart from an average level, the less strongly does the sense of personality arise'.[10] True self, meaning and progress become goals because the attainment of each one of them would reflect our individual transcendence over the meaningless, repetitive, soulless nature of the many life-worlds we inhabit. By our diligent use of escape routes we seek to construct in our minds that which does not appear to us in the world. We attempt to create free areas in which our individuality having been wrested from society, may now enjoy a certain immunity.

The ability of society to co-opt, infiltrate, and

subvert those very areas which we had hoped to hold sacred for the attainment of meaning, progress and self has increased throughout this century. No sooner has a new road to the true self been encountered than it is boxed and packaged for sale in the escape-attempts supermarket, no sooner has a new vocabulary of meaning been articulated, than it is raided for concepts and slogans by calendar makers and record producers, no sooner have we begun acting in an entirely novel way than we see coming over the horizon a mass of others mimicking our every action.

Never before has life offered so many opportunities for us to articulate our freshly-won individuality; but paradoxically, the acceptance of any or all of these opportunities may merely serve to re-introduce the sense of meaninglessness, routine and repetition against which we initially established our sense of individuality. In these circumstances, some may decide that only extreme escape attempts will work. Only the most outrageous, violent. surreal endeavours will resist co-option.

It is not, we think, far fetched to imply such causal connections between the paradoxes of individualism and the growth of certain extreme forms of crime and deviance. The ethos of possessive individualism extols the value of individual identity but the market economy of advanced capitalism cannot deliver the goods to everyone. The struggle for identity can become even more fierce than the struggle for material goods because each victory is short-lived and leaves one stranded, co-opted by the spectacle of commodities. Only the immensely powerful, gifted or resourceful can keep going; the less lose out in the Darwinian struggle for identity and in a real sense their needs are frustrated. These are Maslow's meta-needs: when the needs for food, security, material well-being are satisfied, sexual 'needs' take over and are succeeded by needs for self-esteem and social acceptance and finally for a sense of ourselves as unique individuals.

An increasing number of individuals find themselves with such meta-needs frustrated and they become the outsider criminals, the in-betweeners of our society.[11]

They are too intelligent and have absorbed too much of the ideology of individualism to accept themselves as useless non-entities, destined to be buried in dreary jobs and numbing domesticity – but they are unable to assert themselves through any socially acceptable type of identity work. Like Raskolnikov, like Barbusse's hero, like all the anonymous underground men who are the heroes of the existential literature of dread, they have no special genius, no special talents, perhaps not much imagination.

It is from this pool of people, perhaps, that the so-called meaningless murderers of this century are drawn. While the older motives of greed and sexual passion still dominate, there are an increasing number of outsider murders, symbolic magical acts which attempt to short-circuit the cultural solutions to individualism. These are what Colin Wilson calls resentment murders: a rage against society which expresses itself in the gratuitous action of cruelty. People like Manson and Brady, but perhaps above all the lone sniper who mounts a tower to shoot at random (remember the pure surrealist act) are the symbols of our times. These bring to life Dostoyevsky's fictional murderers; what Raskolnikov and Stavrogin suffered from was boredom. Dostoyevsky grasped the possibility of a crime arising not from compulsion but emptiness and he anticipated also the connection between boredom – the stagnation of wasted days, bleakness and frenzied self-loathing – and the problem of individuality. In his prison memoirs, *House of the Dead*, he explained an unpredictable act of violence: '. . . perhaps the sole reason for this sudden explosion from a man from whom we might least expect it is an anguished, fevered expression of his own individuality'. We can only speculate that the combination of a further diffusion of the ideology of possessive individualism with the growing institutionalization of escape routes will become intolerable for more people.[12] The escapes will have to become more extreme.

In the meantime. . .

A Comic Solution

We can hardly conclude our guided tour of escape attempts by recommending the adoption of such extreme solutions. The flashes of light that they produce are too quickly extinguished by the shades of the asylum ward, the prison cell, the execution shed. As an alternative we will construct a comic scenario which is based upon the less extreme escape attempts we have described in these pages, a scenario which, nevertheless, takes seriously our comments upon routine, repetition, fantasy and free areas, but which would not place its users totally outside society. This model involves the calculated disruption, extension and even the abolition of many of the forms of living, the categories of experience, that we have described in these pages. We are not, of course, presenting it as a literal model for living, but rather as a reminder of the structured features of paramount reality. At the same time, it will also bring together into one collective comic strip many of the discrete ways of coping with the problems of identity and reality which have punctuated our discussion.

The fictional hero of this comic strip first addresses himself to the problems of routine. What can be done here? Fortunately, there is already a model of action waiting for him. Luke Rhinehart's National Habit-Breaking Week is available for elaboration. So, true to its stage directions, he rises in the morning, drinks a cup of Ovaltine, eats a hearty meal of steak pie and chips, and then climbs out through the bedroom window before setting off to work on roller skates by a previously un-reconnoitred route. Throughout the day, silliness is actively embraced in the cause of fighting routine. Accusations of 'childishness' are particularly welcomed as indicators of success as is the indignation shown by colleagues about such sacrilegious attacks on taken-for-granted routines.

But habit breaking by itself will not be enough. The conventional modes of mental management for particular routines must be regarded as cavalierly as the routines themselves. So where routine commitment occurs, then our subverter demonstrates self-consciousness. Discovering unreflective colleagues at the wash-basin he comments at great length upon the relativity of hygiene habits in the modern world. Encountering other colleagues busily engaged in distancing themselves from their work, he expresses total commitment to the task at hand and declares that his real goal in life is to succeed as an invoice clerk. It is only behind his desk that he is fully committed. If his partner in love-making expresses the slightest self-consciousness about the activity, he refuses to introspect, won't play at escalating meta-awareness and behaves as though being reflective was totally out of place in such a situation by showing unmonitored commitment to the task in hand. He makes love as non-committedly as he shaves. The quest for novelty and progress must, of course, be totally abandoned. He never expects life to improve, happiness to increase, nor relationships to develop. He embraces any repetition, delighting in the way that life approximates the dominant societal scripts, revelling in the way television programmes and advertisements reproduce features of his life. Instead of distancing himself from successive falling-in-love scripts, for example, he actively commits himself over and over again to the same behaviour; instead of beating off the feeling of *déjà-vu* as relationships degenerate, he is ecstatic at the reappearance of the familiar. Going round and round in circles is his greatest pleasure.

And when a fantasy overtakes his mind he immediately seeks out others with whom to discuss it. He persistently tells those around him of his bizarre imaginings and insists they do the same, whether the setting be a board meeting or a job interview. The inner world for him is to be as public as the outer. Neither will he allow his fantasies to be mere accompaniments to his life, stoppers, starters and maintainers. They are obsessively pursued for their own sake; special times are set aside for their positive cultivation. Over coffee, he regularly describes his current masturbatory fantasies.

Any enclaving of free areas is resisted. He treats work as a hobby and his hobby as work, regularly enthusing about his achievements at the office but complaining bitterly about the necessity to get home and work away at his model-making. Holidays are either eschewed or taken at inappropriate times of the year in boarding houses in Luton and Wolverhampton. When he goes hiking, he walks from Didcot to Slough along main roads, his motoring excursions involve the continuous circuiting of Birmingham's Inner Ring Road. Through such devices a state of total boredom is periodically and deliberately induced.

His age varies. He skips and jumps to the sounds of the Rolling Stones on the transistor at work and settles down at home to Vera Lynn long-players. At work he dresses in torn Levis and hippie beads, but at home he is attired in a formal evening suit with scarlet cummerbund. He has many names; he is Douglas to his wife, Luigi to his mistress, but Vince to colleagues at work and 'Stud' to acquaintances in the bar.

The word 'really' does not exist in his vocabulary. He is never 'really in love', 'really happy' or 'really depressed'. Each life-world is kept strictly separate – each is as important as the other. There is no carry over, no discussion of one in any other, no translation of emotion from context to context. He has no interest in putting anything together; his delight is to rip things apart. Instead of explanations and coherence he favours differentiation and dissonance. Not one identity but many, not one system of meaning for all aspects of life, but one for every aspect.

To aid all this he employs drugs and dice. Dice are rolled to decide between alternatives, to disrupt the sequence of activities, to give the lie to notions of biographical determination, to ensure unpredictability in identity, age and behaviour. Drugs are used to induce inappropriate moods and emotions – severe depression during love-making, transcendental hallucinations of oceanic bliss during invoice counting.

Our comic hero resembles many types of real

people in his reckless determination to escape from aspects of paramount reality, in his refusal to search for novelty, progress and meaning, in his happy acceptance of multiple selfhood within pluralized life-worlds. At times he appears as a child. That is appropriate in someone who makes fantasies explicit, who regards each aspect of life as equal in importance, who lacks a single conception of identity. At other times he reminds us of a madman. Again, this is appropriate in someone who fails to match moods to situations, who revels in disjunctions and dissociations, who regards reality as illusory. And when we examine other parts of his behaviour, his belief in randomness, in eccentric holidaymaking, in categorial mixing, we are reminded of the wilder antics of some of the surrealists. It could hardly be otherwise. For, like them, he is involved in an assault upon the taken-for-granted aspects of everyday life. It is in these that he sees the basis of oppression, the genesis of contemporary dissatisfactions.

But for all his temperamental and behavioural affinities, he can hardly stand as a model for other men who might feel trapped by the lack of coherence between their ideals of meaning and identity, and the nature of everyday life. Anyone, other than a child or a madman, who adopted even a small proportion of his devices for disrupting paramount reality, for disattending life-plans, would quickly face the type of social ostracism that befell our extreme escapers. And were the numbers of such men to increase so that their deviation became less evident, and their ostracism, less inevitable, then we would have merely produced a new paramount reality, a new set of regularities, a new package of enclaves, each with its appropriate emotional colouring, and accompanying style of mental management.

Nevertheless, some minor victory might have been won. Such reorientations in our approach to life would at least force the abandonment of the illusory goals of real identity, true progress, overall meaning and genuine novelty. They would have produced a pluralized consciousness which matched our necessary experience of the world. We might then be less prey to the feeling that life was a burden or a prison. We would feel at home in a world of contradiction, ambiguity, monotony and repetition. No longer beguiled by the promises of self-realization in the world as presently constituted, we might then more clearly see that the fundamental poverty of human life was endemic to contemporary reality and was irresoluble with the instruments provided by that reality.

Revolution?

Hidden somewhere in the sociological and political texts we considered before we wrote this book are the beginnings of a liberatory theory for the conscious transformation of everyday life in contemporary capitalist society. There are many reasons for us having resolutely avoided theories, rhetoric and manifestoes of this type: a predeliction for the concrete rather than the abstract, a greater ease in talking about individuals than societies, a desire to classify and describe rather than produce yet another overarching theory, a determination to avoid the endless exegesis of this or that variety of marxism. But, above all, because we respect the everyday struggles which these theories contemptuously ignore by reference to the false consciousness of the masses. But at this point we must at least acknowledge those theories which see such everyday struggles as doomed not because of problems of 'mistaken identity', but because they are not part of that revolution of consciousness which Marx contemplated.

These theories emerge from the writings of Reich, Marcuse, the Surrealists, the International Situationists: all those attempts to reconstitute marxism as a critique of everyday life. They begin by seeing that the struggle against economic and political exploitation must be accompanied by a simultaneous movement to transform consciousness. People are trapped by reification: as long as there is a perception of the world which takes the institutional determinants of exploitation and oppression as given and natural, no complete alternative reality can be imagined. Classical marxism failed to comprehend these subjective barriers to revolutionary change, a failure made more apparent by the quiescence of organized working-class politics and the spectacular movements of cultural reconstruction (the eupsychias of the counter-cultural and identity liberation groups).

It was Freud's original enterprise of liberation through self-consciousness which gave Marcuse, Reich, the Frankfurt school – and in a different way the surrealists – the connection to Marx's aim of social liberation through total consciousness about society and history. Reich, for example, aimed at a movement to incorporate sexual politics into conventional revolutionary politics, to combine an attack on authoritarian family structure and sexual morality with an assault on the economic system. Marcuse went beyond Reich's simple Sex-Pol movement and showed how an increase in sexual freedom alone had no revolutionary implications and could be integrated into commerce, entertainment, advertising and political propaganda.

How viable are such attempts at the revolutionary reconstruction of everyday life? Their first problem is that they all make identity assumptions of the 'true self' variety, particularly by postulating the existence of 'real' needs which have somehow become hidden or repressed under capitalism. Clearly, something extraordinary is required to bring such non-repressive needs to consciousness and to liberate new desires. This literature talks of the need to develop and refine the human psyche:

A qualitative change must occur in the character of human needs extending to the very depths of the biological infrastructure of the personality and demanding the transformation of the existing forms and contents of human life into qualitatively new ways of living.[13]

But how are such radical transformations to occur? The slogans are many: through a 'critical revolutionary science', a 'multi-dimensional revolutionary project', a new 'cultural praxis', a 'practice capable of facilitating the individuals self-transformation'. We are back in the supermarket of self: packaged in all the revolutionary jargon and the obligatory references, is the same promise that lay behind our other escapes: 'the emergence of the embryonic social self lying buried underneath the defences . . . which the individual has had to develop to survive in an atomized society'.[14] And all this is to be achieved through the new small group experiences: affinity groups, communes, consciousness-raising groups. These will become micro-political bases for the formation of the new revolutionary culture and consciousness. Even the most committed advocates of this revolution though are aware of its limitations. Brown has stated these in terms, if not language, very similar to our own:

> In the face of the quasi-imperialist logic by which the bureaucratic system of controlled consumption has extended itself – not only spatially through the unification of the world market, but also through the colonization of every sphere of daily life – the attempt to transform the new affinity groups into 'liberated enclaves' or counter societies . . . that seek a partial or localized transcendence of alienation and reification are as easily contained or consumed by the larger social order as are attempts at individual escape.[15]

Precisely. But in the face of such critiques, it must surely be an act of faith to remain optimistic about the chances of a cultural revolution. It might be right to assert that the revolution must 'actualize itself through a new praxis aimed not at the *evasion* of everyday life, but at its *transformation*' – but how on earth can this be done? For the 'masses' not even the 'liberated enclave' of the commune is a possibility and they will surely not draw much consolation about the poverty, alienation and boredom of their everyday life from being told that it needs a new praxis for its transformation. They've heard that one before – and they are as unlikely to be impressed by it as they were by slogans from that other revolution.

Two Endings

And so we end this book with a nihilism and pessimism more profound than the mild scepticism with which we regarded the individual escape routes of our earlier chapters. What hope is there of escape? The slogan of getting it together advanced by communes and the cultural revolution is illusory; the extreme exponents of the individual outsider's escape end up destroyed and defeated; an escape scenario based even on our very own ideas about fantasy, mental management and free areas just looks ridiculous and is quite untenable for most of us; the most revolutionary theories about everyday life offer everything except a way of dealing with everyday life now – and anyway all these escapes are based on a series of ontological errors about our real needs. Nothing in reality can help us cope with it.

This sort of conclusion – and we have been trying for many years to find the right ending for this book – points inexorably back to the fundamental pessimism of the sociological tradition. Destiny is social destiny, there is no reality other than that to be found within the density of social life. This is the same pessimism as Freud's: the desire to escape the self is part of the sickness. There is nowhere to go, either in society or in the mind.

And yet . . .

Our book can also end in a quite different way: as a homage to the self, a celebration of the struggle to rise above social destiny. None of our scepticism or pessimism should hide our continual amazement and delight at how people keep up this struggle, how they keep trying to dislodge the self from society – not in spectacular ways but in the infinite number of ordinary and short-lived ways we have recorded. A celebratory ending like this would be Russian or American rather than European or English. In the traditional European novel, society is the whole arena in which life is worked out. In the Russian tradition and the great American novels, there is a sense of a human spirit which can take on a whole society in the name of individuality, freedom, identity, integrity, independence, authenticity. There is always confrontation: 'There the human spirit is a tremendous palpable reality capable of scattering and distancing any claims that the material world is the ultimate reality.'[16]

Such confrontation and restlessness is not simply an incidental feature of the contemporary American novel (one of the most highly developed forms of self-consciousness that interests us) but is, as Tanner persuasively argues, its central obsession. His survey of American fiction of the last two decades[17] reveals time and time again the same themes we have encountered from our sociological vantage point. There is the abiding dream that the unpatterned, unconditioned life *is* possible – but the nightmare that life is, after all, patterned. And in the world of Burroughs's *Soft Machine* and Heller's *Catch 22*, the patterns are far more complex and horrible than the simple social scripts of our Chapter 3. The heroes of such different novelists as Bellow, Updike, Burroughs, Barth, Vonnegut, Heller, Roth and Mailer find themselves trapped in a paramount reality, seen as a series of manifestly false scripts, movies and fictions. Yet the desire to step out of this into some kind of free space is checked by a dread of what might happen in such a formless world, a world without the safety of social conventions:

... the dread of utter formlessness, of being a soft, vulnerable, endlessly manipulable blob, of not being a distinct self. The nightmare of non-identity, of no-form, is a recurrent one. On the other hand, any one adopted armature which will contain and give shape and definition to the jelly or clay is at the same time felt to be an imprisoning deathly constriction ...[18]

Tanner describes how Hawthorne – a novelist from a much earlier period – interpreted a true story of a man called Wakefield who one day, apparently for no reason, made a sudden escape attempt. He walked out of his house, leaving his wife with no explanations, and lived hidden in the next street for twenty years. Then one day he came back to his original house as if he'd only been away a few hours. This was Hawthorne's moral:

Amid the seeming confusion of our material world, individuals are so nicely adjusted to a system, and systems to one another and to a whole, that by stepping aside for a moment, a man exposes himself to a fearful risk of losing his place for ever. Like Wakefield, he may become, as it were, the Outcast of the Universe.

The more recent heroes of American fiction – like the heroes of our book – are only too aware of this risk. The feeling that society is an arbitrary system – in Updike's words a 'compromised environment' – out of which one might simply try to escape is always followed by the realization that 'by stepping aside for a moment' there might be the void. The enclaves, free areas, escape tunnels might disintegrate into jellies – yet the identity left behind is a prison. So these heroes oscillate between total inertia and mindless role-playing. They attempt disentanglement but then are caught in new commitments and struggle to re-enter the world. They sometimes find openings, hidden apertures in the social fabric; more often they resort to inner space, to fantasy. But they do believe – and here we share the optimistic theme Tanner detects – that somewhere between inertia and commitment lies a space of personal freedom. We are back to the way these heroes celebrate a sense of movement:

Like Conrad's Axel Heyst, they aim to be 'invulnerable because elusive'. The dance on the periphery may not be leading anywhere, but at least it celebrates a refusal to sleep, a resistance to arrest; a mode of motion turns out to be a way, perhaps the only way, of life.[19]

An ending which confirms these fictional possibilities is one we find more consoling than our nihilistic one – even though it might rest on a mistaken sense of identity. We would prefer to see the self as a construct which only becomes alive by being wary, elusive, mobile, keeping some distance from social reality. 'I escape, therefore I am,' is ultimately the only ontological message we can manage. An ideology of bourgeois individualism this certainly is and it would be absurd to claim that we are not prone to it ourselves or that it should not be subjected to the same relentless relativism to which we have exposed other ideologies. Such bourgeois individualism – the obstinate clinging on to the idea of a separate self – is decadent and reactionary; its radicalism is expressive rather than instrumental, the limitations of any cultural rather than structural politics.

The search for identity which we have described is an impulse to deny time, to ignore the sweep of history. It must be limited as an ideology because the facticity of the external world cannot be denied. We are not just born into some free floating balloon of identity – but into a specific time and place. To base a resistance plan against everyday life on the invulnerability of the individual self must fail because of the ways that self is located in time and history and rooted to specific sets of social relationships.

Such an ideology is not only politically limited: it is also no guarantee of any existential consolation. We have described rather than transcended the ruinous pre-occupations of a society which celebrates the value of the unique individual identity, a self-consciousness which our society has developed almost to the point of the pathological.

But it is the only world we seem to know.

Notes
and
References

Chapter 1: Open Prison

1. Saul Bellow, 'Deep Readers of the World, Beware!', *New York Times Book Review*, 15 February 1959.
2. Stanley Cohen and Laurie Taylor, *Psychological Survival*, Penguin, 1972.
3. Philip Larkin, 'Reference Back', *The Whitsun Weddings*, Faber, 1964.
4. Peter L. Berger, Brigitte Berger, and Hansfried Kellner, *The Homeless Mind*, Penguin, 1974, pp. 69–70.
5. Peter L. Berger and Thomas Luckmann, *The Social Construction of Reality*, Penguin, 1972, p. 35.
6. ibid., p. 39.
7. Theodore Roszak, *Where the Wasteland Ends*, Faber, 1973, p. 101.
8. Erving Goffman, *Asylums*, Anchor Books, New York, 1961, p. 320 [Penguin, 1968, p. 280].

Chapter 2: The Mental Management of Routine

1. Quoted in Richard Mills, *Young Outsiders*, Routledge & Kegan Paul, 1973, p. 10.

2. Bertrand Russell, *Portraits from Memory and Other Essays*, Allen & Unwin, 1956, pp. 198–202.

3. Winston White, *Beyond Conformity*, Free Press, Glencoe, 1961, pp. 154–5.

4. William James, *Principles of Psychology*, Macmillan, 1890.

5. It is of course Goffman's classic analysis of role distance which shows most clearly how the individual's attempts to distance himself from his role (I am not what I do) might indicate actual attachment to the role. Erving Goffman, 'Role Distance' in *Encounters: Two Studies in the Sociology of Interaction*, Penguin, 1972.

6. Georg Simmel, 'The Transcendent Character of Life' in *On Individuality and Social Forms*, University Press, Chicago, 1971, p. 335.

7. Goffman, op. cit., p. 120.

8. Simmel, op. cit., p. 364.

9. Gregory Bateson, 'Style, Grace and Information in Primitive Art' in *Steps to an Ecology of Mind*, Paladin, 1973, pp. 101–2.

Chapter 3: The Nightmare of Repetition

1. Sigmund Freud, *Beyond the Pleasure Principle*, Hogarth Press, 1950, p. 114.

2. Norman O. Brown, *Life Against Death*, Sphere, 1968, p. 88.

3. Doris Lessing, *A Proper Marriage*, Panther, 1966, p. 90.

4. John Gagnon and William Simon, *Sexual Conduct: The Social Sources of Human Sexuality*, Hutchinson, 1974, p. 19.

5. Eric Berne, *Games People Play* Deutsch, 1966 [Penguin 1968].

6. Gagnon and Simon op. cit., p. 19.

7. Anthony Powell, *A Buyer's Market*, Fontana 1967 pp. 167–8.

8. Kenneth Burke, *A Grammar of Motives* World Publishing Co. Cleveland. Ohio. 1962.

9. Elizabeth Burns, *Theatricality*, Longman, 1972, p. 11.

10. For a particular critique of the notion of 'spontaneity' in sex, see Gagnon and Simon. op. cit., Ch. 1.

Chapter 4: The Inner Theatre of the Mind

1. John Irwin, *The Felon*, Prentice-Hall, New Jersey, 1970. Ch. 4.
2. Jerome L. Singer, *Daydreaming: An Introduction to the Experimental Study of Inner Experience*, Random House, New York, 1966, p. 4.
3. ibid, p. 21.
4. Luke Rhinehart, *The Dice Man*, Panther, 1972, pp. 194–7.
5. Robert Freed Bales, *Personality and Interpersonal Behaviour*, Holt, Rinehart & Winston, New York, 1973, Ch. 7.
6. Singer, op. cit., p. 187.
7. Gore Vidal, 'On Pornography' in *Sex, Death and Money*, Bantam, New York, 1968, p. 1.
8. Peter L. Berger and Thomas Luckman, *The Social Construction of Reality*, p. 39.
9. Georg Simmel, 'The Adventure' in *On Individuality and Social Forms*, p. 189.
10. John Gagnon and William Simon, *Sexual Conduct: The Social Sources of Human Sexuality*, Hutchinson, 1974, Ch. 9.
11. Herbert A. Otto, *Fantasy Encounter Games*, Nash Publishing Corporation, New York, 1972.
12. Barry Malzberg, *Screen*, Olympia Press, 1970, p. 96.

Chapter 5: Free Areas, Escape Routes and Identity Sites

1. We need hardly expand on Goffman's marvellous characterization of the use of gambling for identity and character work. See Erving Goffman, *Where the Action is*, Allen Lane The Penguin Press, 1969.
2. Georg Simmel, 'The Adventure' in *On Individuality and Social Forms*, p. 191.
3. John Gagnon and William Simon, *Sexual Conduct: The Social Sources of Human Sexuality*, Ch. 2.
4. Peter L. Berger, Brigitte Berger and Hansfried Kellner, *The Homeless Mind*, p. 181.
5. Gagnon and Simon, loc. cit.
6. Dean MacCannell, 'Staged Authenticity: Arrangements of Social Space in Tourist Settings', *American Journal of Sociology*, Vol. 79, No. 3, 1973, p. 602.
7. ibid., p. 596.

8. 'A Bit of What You Fancy Does You Good' was the title of Carol Wright's article in *High Life*, August 1973.

9. MacCannell, op. cit., p. 601.

10. ibid., p. 602.

11. We are indebted to David Bouchier for his unpublished sociological observations as courier and expedition leader on such holidays.

12. Simmel, op. cit., p. 188.

13. Guy Debord, *Society as Spectacle*, Paris, Buchet, Chastel, 1967.

14. James MacBean, in *Sight and Sound*, Summer 1971.

15. Pauline Kael, *I Lost It at the Movies*, Cape, 1966. See also Parker Tyler, *Magic and Myth of the Movies*, Secker & Warburg, 1971, for a fine defence of self-conscious re-investment.

16. Quoted in Hans Richter, *Dada: Art and Anti-Art*, Thames & Hudson, 1965.

17. Bruce L. Maliver, 'Encounter Groups Up Against the Wall', *New York Times Magazine*, 3 January 1971.

18. Eleanor Criswell, 'Overcoming Our Metagrumbles' in *The Great Escape*, Bantam, New York, 1974, p. 9.

19. Alan Watts, *Psychotherapy East and West*, Mentor, New York, 1973, p. 15.

20. ibid., p. 14.

Chapter 6: Getting it Together

1. Norman O. Brown, *Life Against Death*, Sphere, 1968, p. 33.

2. Erik Erikson, *Childhood and Society*, Penguin, 1965, p. 14.

3. Brown, op. cit., p. 35.

4. Raoul Vaneigem, 'Banalites de Base', *International Situationiste*, No. 7, Paris, 1962.

5. Richard Neville, *Play Power*, Jonathan Cape, 1970, p. 258.

6. ibid., p. 263.

7. Peter L. Berger, Brigitte Berger and Hansfried Kellner, *The Homeless Mind*, pp. 193–4.

8. Andrew Rigby, *Alternative Realities*, Routledge & Kegan Paul, 1974, p. 305.

9. For the analysis in this paragraph, we are indebted to Philip Abrams's and Andrew McCulloch's unpublished research on communes in Britain.

10. As described in Rosabeth Moss Kanter, *Commitment and Community, Communes and Utopias in Sociological*

Perspective, Harvard University Press, Cambridge, Massachusetts, 1972, pp. 18–31.

Chapter 7: Momentary Slips Through the Fabric

1. William James, *Varieties of Religious Experience*, Fontana, 1960, p. 236.
2. John C. Lilly, *The Centre of the Cyclone: An Autobiography of Inner Space*, Paladin, 1972.
3. James, op. cit., p. 237.
4. Aldous Huxley, quoted in Sybille Bedford, *Aldous Huxley: A Biography*, Chatto & Windus, 1974, Volume 2, p. 117.
5. Quoted by James, op. cit. pp. 226–7.
6. James, op. cit., p. 237 (our emphasis).
7. It *is* the point in debates such as the classic one between Zaehner and Huxley about whether praeternatural experience produced by drugs such as L S D or mescalin is the 'same' as specifically religious experience. Zaehner's case is that while drugs might indeed modify consciousness and even produce literally ecstatic states (in which the ego has the impression it escapes from itself and stands outside itself) these effects are religious surrogates, profane forms of mysticism. See R. L. Zaehner, *Mysticism: Sacred and Profane*, Oxford University Press, 1961.
8. Richard Mills, *Young Outsiders*, Routledge & Kegan Paul, 1973, Ch. 3.
9. Alan Watts, *'This Is It' and Other Essays on Zen and Spiritual Experience*, Collier, New York, 1960, p. 17.
10. Roger Shattuck, preface to Maurice Nadeau, *The History of Surrealism*, Penguin, 1973, pp. 20–21.
11. Quoted in André Maurois, *The Quest for Proust*, Penguin, 1962, p. 127.
12. James, op. cit., p. 194.
13. Zaehner, op. cit., p. 50.
14. William Faulkner, *Sanctuary*, Signet, New York, 1954, p. 13.
15. Lilly, op. cit., p. 58.
16. This difference is discussed, for example, in Ralph Melzner, *Maps of Consciousness*, Collier Macmillan, 1971.

Chapter 8: Over the Wall

1. F. Scott Fitzgerald, *The Crack-Up*, Penguin, 1965, p. 53.
2. Robert Coover, *The Universal Baseball Association*, Signet, New York, 1969.
3. Quoted in Maurice Nadeau, *The History of Surrealism*, Penguin, 1973, p. 67.
4. Louis Aragon, *Traité du style*, Nouvelle Revue Française, Paris, 1928.
5. See Tom Wolfe, *The Electric Kool-Aid Acid Test*, Bantam, New York, 1969; and also Tony Tanner's discussion of Edge City in *City of Words: American Fiction 1950–70*, Cape, 1971.
6. Hunter S. Thompson, *Fear and Loathing in Las Vegas*, Paladin, 1973, p. 19.
7. ibid., p. 85.
8. Georg Simmel, 'The Adventurer' in *On Individuality and Social Forms*, p. 194.
9. Luke Rhinehart, *The Dice Man*.
10. ibid., p. 59.
11. R. D. Laing, 'A Ten Day Voyage' in *Politics of Experience*, Penguin, 1967, p. 136.
12. John Lilly, *Journey to the Centre of the Cyclone*, Paladin, 1973, p. 162.
13. John Symonds, *The Great Beast*, MacDonald, 1971, p. 10.
14. Colin Wilson, *A Casebook of Murder*, Mayflower, 1969, p. 201.
15. Colin Wilson, *The Outsider*, Gollancz, 1956. p. 156.
16. Our main sources about the Manson case are Ed Sanders, *The Family*, Rupert Hart-Davis, 1972; R. C. Zaehner, *Our Savage God*, Collins, 1974; and Victor Bugliosi, *The Manson Murders*, Bodley Head, 1974.
17. Zaehner, op. cit., p. 60.
18. John Clellon Holmes, 'Gone In October', *Playboy*, February 1973, p. 162.

Chapter 9: A Case of Mistaken Identity

1. Saul Bellow, *Seize the Day*, Penguin, 1966, p. 44.
2. Aldous Huxley, *The Doors of Perception*, Penguin, 1959.
3. Peter L. Berger, Brigitte Berger and Hansfried Kellner, *The Homeless Mind*, Ch. 1.

4. ibid., p. 64.

5. Georg Simmel, 'Freedom and the Individual' in *On Individuality and Social Forms*, p. 223.

6. T. R. Young, *New Sources of Self*, New York, Pergamon, 1972, p. ix.

7. Benita Luckmann, 'The Small Life-Worlds of Modern Man', *Social Research*, Vol. 37, No. 4, 1970, pp. 580–96.

8. Berger *et al.*, op. cit., p. 75.

9. Simmel, 'Group Expansion and the Development of Individuality', op. cit., p. 294.

10. ibid., p. 291.

11. This argument draws heavily on Colin Wilson's preoccupation with existential murder. See his original *The Outsider*, Gollancz, 1958, and the later 'Murder trilogy', *An Encyclopaedia of Murder*, Pan, 1964; *A Casebook of Murder*, Leslie Frewin, 1969, and *Order of Assassins*, Rupert Hart-Davis, 1972.

12. Our understanding of this type of institutionalization is close to Marcuse's well-known formulation about 'repressive tolerance'. See especially, Herbert Marcuse, *Eros and Civilization*, Beacon Press, Boston, Massachusetts, 1955.

13. Bruce Brown, *Marx, Freud and the Critique of Everyday Life: Toward a Permanent Cultural Revolution*, Monthly Review Press, New York, 1973, p. 176.

14. ibid., p. 180.

15. ibid., p. 182.

16. We derive this particular distinction from Tony Tanner's discussion of the Russian nature of Bellow's novels: Tony Tanner, *Saul Bellow*, Oliver & Boyd, Edinburgh, 1965

17. Tony Tanner, *City of Words: American Fiction 1950–70*, Cape, 1971.

18. ibid., pp. 18–19.

19. ibid., p. 84. It is beyond our scope to discuss Tanner's description of how the *writer* finds his own realm of freedom in the 'City of Words' itself, by the creation, for example, of 'lexical playfields' in which these tensions can be worked through.

MORE ABOUT PENGUINS
AND PELICANS

Penguinews, which appears every month, contains details of all the new books issued by Penguins as they are published. From time to time it is supplemented by *Penguins in Print*, which is our complete list of almost 5,000 titles.

A specimen copy of *Penguinews* will be sent to you free on request. Please write to Dept EP, Penguin Books Ltd, Harmondsworth, Middlesex, for your copy.

In the U.S.A.: For a complete list of books available from Penguins in the United States write to Dept CS, Penguin Books, 625 Madison Avenue, New York, New York 10022.

In Canada: For a complete list of books available from Penguins in Canada write to Penguin Books Canada Ltd, 2801 John Street, Markham, Ontario L3R 1B4.